THE STATE IN EURASIA

LOCAL AND GLOBAL ARENAS

Anita Sengupta
Suchandana Chatterjee

Maulana Abul Kalam Azad Institute of Asian Studies
Kolkata

in association with

KNOWLEDGE WORLD

KW Publishers Pvt Ltd
New Delhi

2011 FPBA BEST PUBLISHERS AWARD (ENGLISH)

The Maulana Abul Kalam Azad Institute of Asian Studies was set up at the joint initiative of the Government of India, Department of culture, Ministry of Human Resource Development and the Government of West Bengal. Registered as a Society under the West Bengal Registration of Societies' Act of 1961, with Prof. Nurul Hasan, the then Governor of West Bengal, as the President of the Society on the 4th of January 1993. It is funded by the Department of culture, Government of India. Presently, His Excellency, Governor of West Bengal, is the President of the Society. An acre of land in Bidhannagar (Salt Lake City), Kolkata, was allotted to the Institute by the Government of West Bengal for building the Institutes campus.

The Maulana Abul Kalam Azad Institute of Asian Studies is a centre for research and learning with focus a on social cultural, economic and political/administrative developments in Asia from the middle of the 19th Century onwards with special emphasis on their links with India, and (b) on the life and works of Maulana Abul Kalam Azad.

ISBN 978-93-81904-47-3

KNOWLEDGE WORLD

Published in India by

Kalpana Shukla
KW Publishers Pvt Ltd
4676/21, First Floor, Ansari Road, Daryaganj, New Delhi 110002
Phone: +91.11.23263498/43528107
Email: knowledgeworld@vsnl.net • www.kwpub.com

Printed and Bound in India

Contents

for a wider international audience. The emerging state projected itself, not as a brand new state but also as an assertive political player. Similarly, the articles examine how the rhetoric that accompanies this reassertion is both a celebration of the state and a statement for the international community. It underlines how the 'art of politics' pursued through old style diplomacy has shifted to encompass the new art of brand building and reputation management.

The volume focuses on the performative role of the five Central Asian states in the arena of politics, diplomacy, culture, historical memory, rhetoric, and their interaction within the Eurasian space. It reflects on ways in which the state interacts with the historical, social, and cultural aspects of society and how discourses in these fields dovetail with or diverge from the political discourse. In the Eurasian case, part of the performance has been dramatic—Independence Day celebrations, for instance, whose carefully staged displays are meant to impress the foreigner and but are also symbolic representations of authority and legitimacy of the state. However, a large part of the performance has been through the continuous portrayal of images—Manas in Kyrgyzstan or Amir Timur in Uzbekistan that has not only called for ethnic unity but supported the style of functioning of the respective governments. Relations between formal institutions and informal structures, emerging conceptions of democracy in the background of both the Tulip Revolution as well as events in western Kazakhstan, the nature of bilateral and multilateral alignments and accommodation between regional and international actors, and the role of the state in the arena of culture are some of the aspects through which the performative role of the state has been examined in the volume. The volume shows how the state acts as an agent of influence and control not just on performative traditions and its norms but also in the creation of a single community as the basis for the nation.

This volume has been compiled out of presentations made at the international seminar '*The State in Eurasia: Performance in Local and Global Arenas*' organised by the Maulana Abul Kalam Azad Institute of Asian Studies in March 2012. At a seminar organised in Kolkata, India, the discussions began with a special panel, which examined the role of the Indian state in Central Asia. Most discussions on India's relations with the Central Asian Republics stress on the enormous soft power that India enjoys in the region. Unfortunately and contrary to the entire dialogue on the significance of 'soft power', this winning of 'hearts and minds' in the words of Joseph Nye has not really translated to advantage for India, in the Central Asian region, in the last twenty years. A possible answer could be that India saw no advantage in converting this 'soft power' to hard power. The escalation obviously has to come from the state concerned. Nye also suggests that converting 'soft power' requires well-designed strategies and skillful leadership. The ability to shape the preferences of others, to be 'attractive' for emulation needs to be worked on. The discussions were focused on how to reconnect with the region not just through the evocation of a common cultural space but also through strategic designs that focused on linkages in a number of areas.

The discussions in the panel 'India and Central Asia: Twenty Years After' stressed that while there are a number of issues where India has found common ground with the region, there also remain certain challenges that would have to be overcome. The most important is perhaps the fact that the trade level between India and the Central Asian states is below potential. This is aggravated by the fact that connectivity, both air and land needs to be developed. There also remains the need for smart use of limited resources through capacity building programmes in IT, e-network, telemedicine, and education. Over the next decade, the need to step up economic linkages through support to the north-south corridor, encouragement to the private sector to engage with the region, stepping up energy linkages, and developing newer areas of co-operation would have to be taken note of. There is also the need to emphasise common security concerns in Afghanistan and engage in dialogues through multilateral forums like the SCO, which are in the process of reinventing themselves. The necessity to explore the growing economic space in Eurasia, that is likely to be revitalised with the beginning of the Presidential term of Putin, was also emphasised. Increasing people-to-people contact through the cultural centres in three of the Central Asian states remains a priority. Along with this, sharing her experience of building civic institutions and extending support for the large numbers of medical tourists, who visit India, are some of the other areas where India could benefit the region.

Among policy prescriptions for the coming decade implementation of agreements was stressed as important along with an emphasis on a viable land route. A meaningful economic presence along with the development of the aviation sector would also go a long way towards furthering the relation. It was also stressed that as far as the region was concerned India should emphasise extension of non-reciprocal benefits, a policy pursued by India towards small states in its immediate neighbourhood. Given the geostrategic location of the states, this would extend India's strategic depth. In any case, it is critical for us to carefully look at China's neighbourhood now, which extends into the Central Asian region. There was also discussion on who would be a reliable partner in the region. With the prospect of a Eurasian Union, gathering strength the obvious choice seemed to be Russia. In any case, there was agreement on the fact that the projection of India as a serious geopolitical player in the region is the requirement of the day.

In keeping with this discussion, the volume begins by looking into the changing image of India in Eurasia since 1991. This is not a subject greatly dealt with by scholars within India, or within the broader arena of Eurasian studies. Despite spontaneous impulses about engaging with an India presence (whether through expeditions, or through exhibitions) in Russia, these initiatives have not shown any consistent trend. However, one does notice, the existence of a continuum in the Eurasia-South Asia region, where interest in past links have been revived and reconstituted to portray connectivity. The continuity in the linkages is characterised, for instance, by the Jadid inheritance among the Tatars of the Middle Volga and the dissemination of Jadid literature in the Central Asia-South Asia-West Asian region in the 19th and 20th century—which is being keenly studied in the post-Soviet period by the oriental academies of Central Asia. There is also a preoccupation with India's Buddhist legacy among the Buddhist population in Russia. Similarly, a host of cultural initiatives highlights the Indian presence in the Transcaucasus. In his article, Hari Vasudevan argues that the transformations in the Indo-Russian relationship over the last two decades can only be explained in terms of mutual image construction. He underlines that aspects of this image have to be evoked within a broader context that takes note not just of the visual or the verbal but also those centred in political and economic discourse, and sometimes, on personalities or groups of personalities. Vasudevan presents an evaluation of image formation of India in Russia today, against a background of perspectives on the past. Recent developments in India's strategy of engagement with Tajikistan have been traced by Ajay Patnaik in this volume. Patnaik underlines that through greater economic involvement in Central Asia, India would be able to forge closer integration with Central Asian states like Tajikistan, as well as northern Afghanistan, that would be of advantage to both states.

While the significance of the global arena and the complex connectivity and interdependence of globalised spaces cannot be reduced, the reality of local experience remains equally important. This demands an understanding of a variety of perspectives that takes note of the formal and informal ties between communities and the larger polities within which they exist. Here, 'everyday' experiences that are contingent on the cultural permeability of borders and the experience of people, assume importance. The next set of papers underline how historical consciousness and nation building are interlinked processes in the post-Soviet scenario. Ravshan Madjidovich Abdullaev looks into the process of evolution of public and historical consciousness in contemporary Uzbekistan. He underlines the fact that that in periods of transition an in-depth reconsideration of the most significant pages of national history has its value and illustrates it in his article in some depth. This connection is further reinforced in the considerable attachment to indigenous forces and patterns that are entwined with the image of the 'baatyr' (hero) or the epic 'Manas'. These reflect social security mechanisms within the nomadic setup of the Kyrgyz, which also sometimes reinforces national identity, as in the case of the mountain Kyrgyz of the Tianshan region. Taking the specific case-studies of baatyrs in the Chui region, Ilhan Sahin draws our attention to the nature of social networking in the region revolving round the activities

Contributors

H.S. Vasudevan, Professor, Department of History, University of Calcutta, Kolkata, India.

Ajay Kumar Patnaik, Professor, School of International Studies, Jawaharlal Nehru University, New Delhi, India.

Ablet Kamalov, Leading Research Associate, Institute of Oriental Studies named after R. Suleimenov, Almaty, Kazakhstan.

Ravshan Madjidovich Abdullaev, Director of the Institute of History Academy of Sciences, Tashkent, Uzbekistan.

Ilhan Sahin, Professor, Kyrgyz-Turkish Manas University, Faculty of Letters, Bishkek, Kyrgyzstan.

Yunus Emre Gürbüz, Lecturer, Department of History, Kyrgyzstan-Turkey Manas University, Bishkek, Kyrgyzstan.

Pınar Akcali, Associate Professor, Middle East Technical University, Department of Political Science and Public Administration, Ankara, Turkey.

R. G. Gidadhubli, Professor and Former Director, Centre for Central Eurasian Studies, University of Mumbai, Mumbai, India.

Mukesh Kumar Mishra, Central Asian Studies Division, School of International Studies, Jawaharlal Nehru University, New Delhi, India.

Mirzhoid Rakhimov, Head of Contemporary History and International Relations Department of the Institute of History of the Academy of Sciences, Tashkent, Uzbekistan.

Lopamudra Bandyopadhyay, Fellow, Global India Foundation, Kolkata, India.

Angira Sen Sarma, Research Fellow, Indian Council of World Affairs (ICWA), New Delhi, India.

P.L. Dash, Professor of International Relations, ICCR India Chair, University of World Economy and Diplomacy, Tashkent, Uzbekistan,

Debidatta Aurobinda Mahapatra, Assistant Professor, Centre for South and Central Asian Studies, Central University of Punjab, India.

Sharad K. Soni, Assistant Professor, Central Asian Studies Division, School of International Studies, Jawaharlal Nehru University, New Delhi, India.

Rashmi Doraiswamy, Professor, Academy of International Studies, Jamia Millia Islamia, New Delhi, India.

Dilorom Karomat, Fellow, Maulala Abul Kalam Azad Institute of Asian Studies, Kolkata, India.

Introduction

It has been twenty years since the emergence of the post-Soviet states, and over the course of the last two decades, there has been a significant reflection on the direction the politics of the region has assumed. The transformation from being a part of the 'Soviet' to 'independent integration' within the global system has been an ongoing process with multifarious manifestations. These have involved both attempts at reconnecting with the past as well as movement towards new definitions of identity. In all of this, the state has played an important part—in the forging of new nations out of disparate identities, in the making of national languages, and the reinterpretation of historic events or portrayal of personalities. However, in an increasingly globalised world, nation-state building is no longer an activity confined to the domestic arena. The situating of the state within the global space and its 'image' in the international community becomes in many ways as crucial as the projection of homogeneity within the state. Nation building and nationalist rhetoric, therefore, is intended, as much for the international public as the domestic audience whether it is the projection of Kazakhstan as the 'Heart of Eurasia', Kyrgyzstan as the 'Island of Democracy' or Turkmenistan as a 'Neutral State'. Though not as well articulated the image that the Uzbek state presented was that of an 'ancient state at the crossroads of civilisation', while the Tajik state projected its Iranian heritage. In the course of the immediate past, certain events like a second change of regime in Kyrgyzstan followed by the Osh incidents, the Kazakh presidency of the OSCE, post-Niyazov developments in Turkmenistan, post Andijan events in Uzbekistan, and effects of the Afghan situation on Tajikistan have required a closer look at the shifting domestic and international 'image' that the state portrays in Central Asia, as reflected by the role that it plays in the local and global arenas.

It is not surprising, therefore, that most states, cities, ministries, and government agencies now boost their own logos and 'mission statements' in order to reposition themselves in a fluid globalising world. As Peter van Ham argues, this change implies more than merely window-dressing. The relationship between politics and cultural symbols/'images' represents multiple possibilities. This relationship became particularly relevant for states that emerged in the wake of the disintegration of the Soviet Union in Central Asia. These were essentially states that had not seen the development of an independent movement prior to the implosion at the centre, and where an 'externally imposed collapse led to internally invented signs of certainty'. Their emergence raised questions about the legitimacy of the state/nation not just from within the state but also from the global arena. How the 'new' states legitimised their existence as separate entities and redefined themselves in a new form, both internally and externally, therefore, assumes importance. In the course of this redefinition, competing images were articulated and new discourses were generated.

The volume looks into the shaping of post Soviet Central Asia where the projection of aspects like a common ancestry and history played a significant part in creating the image of an ancient state with a homogeneous people. Here, the performative role of the state in the face of the reality of a multiplicity of histories and identities in the region is evident. In fact, in a number of cases, it resulted in rhetoric or policy that took note of this multifarious heritage and recognised its significance in the wake of a homogenising global tendency. However, imperatives of state building within the global arena is also evident in the irony of a state that proclaims its existence as an ancient state, retrieves its ancient identity yet speaks of its promises and potentialities in the language of the newborn. Therefore, one finds in this stage of transition juxtaposition of a cultural rediscovery of the past and a projection of the state as a developmental state. The volume highlights the fact that while parts of the nationalist discourse was intended for a domestic audience, part of it was aimed at the international arena with the aim of capturing global attention. Public diplomacy and the creation and promotion of 'national' images were attempts to raise the prestige of the country and primarily aimed at the international business community and the global political leadership. The articles in the volume examine the rhetoric that accompanied the process of defining the 'new' state both for its own members as well as and role of the baatyr in the Soviet and post-Soviet periods. Emre Gürbüz discusses the celebrations centering Manas and its heroes, and how the 'hero-centric' narratives have been legitimised by the independent state of Kyrgyzstan. In 1995, Manas was the theme of nation-wide celebrations, in the course of which memorials were built and the 'seven commandments' of Manas were introduced in school text books as the foundation of Kyrgyz culture. Gürbüz underlines how in 2010 and 2011, after the revolutionary upsurge in the country, Manas was portrayed as a source of inspiration and a savior in times of crisis, both at the official and the popular level. Gürbüz goes on to analyse the revival of the mythical hero with examples from state activities and peoples' thoughts.

Ablet Kamalov's article looks into the experiences of a community whose cultural linkages extend beyond the political borders of their present locale, by analysing Uyghur history writing in post-Soviet Kazakhstan and focusing on discussions of the principle trends in local historiography. He argues that this is determined by changing political priorities of the new nation-state, on the one hand, and, its relations with neighbouring China ruling over the Uyghur homeland—Eastern Turkistan, on the other. Marginalisation of Uyghurs studies, which had been developed in the Soviet times, resulted in the growth of popular nationalist histories of the Uyghurs. Uyghur nationalist narratives in post-Soviet Kazakhstan is shaped by intensified nation building process and search for national identity of the titular nation of the country. Being a transborder ethnic group, the Uyghurs express loyalty to the Uyghur nation and the country of residence, which is reflected in attempts to address general Uyghur history, contesting the Chinese version of the Uyghurs as people without independent history, as well as local histories in the Kazakh neighbourhood.

Transition in the Central Asian region was accompanied by expectations about democracy. The articles that follow debates the search for democracy as the region made its transition from a socialist economy to a market economy. While there is still some expectation about indigenous forces, there are dominant fears and concerns about a fledgling democracy. Inter-ethnic divisions between the Kyrgyz and the Uzbeks, for instance, have created difficult situations for the country's elite and the prospects of parliamentary democracy are being questioned at different levels by governance. Pinar Akcali traces political developments in Kyrgyzstan in the post Akaev era, and indicates the unstable character of coalition politics in Kyrgyzstan since the ouster of President Bakiyev. However, she argues that a number of positive steps towards democratisation have been taken in Kyrgyzstan, and these seem to be hopeful indicators of Kyrgyzstan regaining its ground as the 'island of democracy'. In her article, she looks into aspects like the recent constitutional changes that have been adopted because of two decades of experimentation with democracy, which seems to effectively curb executive power in the state. R.G. Gidadhubli gauges the various levels of regional tension in Central Asia that have accounted for political instability in Kyrgyzstan. Mukesh Mishra makes a detailed study of the constitutional process as the guideline of evolution of democracy in Kazakhstan in the aftermath of Soviet disintegration, where he focuses on the reforms in the country's political structures. He argues that while there remain certain challenges, the state has a strong basis on which it could move forward and highlights them in the course of the article.

The discussion on the process of nation building and image construction that the region has been engaged in since 1991 was also reflected through its foreign policy. Mirzhoid Rakhimov discusses aspects of Uzbek foreign policy. He argues that Uzbekistan's relation with leading countries and regional and international organisations has not been without problems, and has passed through several transformations due to a number of factors. Lopamudra Bandyopadhyay attempts a comparison of Turkemistan's foreign policy in the Niyazov and post Niyazov eras, in an attempt to understand the shift in the course of policy making with regard to foreign affairs. She argues for a better understanding of Turkmenistan's foreign policy taking into consideration the geopolitical importance of the country. Angira Sen Sarma looks into the changing dynamics of Turkmenistan's foreign policy in the post Niyazov era. In the course of the article, she examines Turkmenistan's changing equations with the three major players in the region—Russia, the US, and China. She argues that in the past few years Turkmenistan has expanded its ties with foreign partners, especially in terms of diversification of its energy markets. She also argues in favour of expansion of opportunities available for India today to revitalise her relations with Turkmenistan. The 'positive neutrality' policy followed by Turkmenistan under Niyazov had kept the country insulated from the outside world. Turkmenistan's engagement with other countries was limited during Niyazov's time. With Niyazov's death, there were expectations that Turkmenistan will witness change in foreign policy approach. However, the developments in the past few years indicate that the country will continue to engage with the outside world in a limited way. Economic considerations will continue to be the main driver of its relationship with foreign countries. Although Turkmenistan under Berdimuhamedov is interacting relatively more with the outside world, Sen Sarma argues there is no substantial change in its policies.

A range of ideas about shifting identities and forces have been dealt with in the course of case studies of Kazakh borderlands, which otherwise tend to remain unrepresented in the entire gamut of ideas about elitist groupings and power-play in energy-rich Kazakhstan. This is an aspect that has been dealt with by P.L. Dash who points to the local elite maneuvering in west Kazakhstan's Mangistau district and Zhanaozen, which became the pivot of labour unrest on the eve of second decade of independence-day celebrations in Kazakhstan. Dash takes a close look at the incidents to analyse the causes of discontent, and posits it in the context of transformations within the region. Debidatta Mahapatra is concerned about the links between forces of extremism, terrorism, and migration, and state responses to the emerging scenario, which he identifies as crucial and discusses in length in his article. Sharad Soni reflects on Kazakh-Mongol relations, which is seldom treated beyond the framework of nomadic identity. Based on recent field surveys in Bayan Olgi province of Mongolia, Soni underlines Mongolia's 'multi-pillared' approach, which is coterminous with the multi-vectored foreign policy approach of Kazakhstan. There seems to be a convergence of foreign policy approaches of Kazakhstan and Mongolia in the aftermath of 1991, and Soni argues that Kazakhstan's Eurasian vision has structured its relations with Mongolia.

The role of the state in cultural aspects of transition has been dealt in the two final articles. Rashmi Doraiswamy looks at changes in Central Asian cinema in the last two decades. She focuses on Kazakhstan where continued state sponsorship has resulted in a flourishing industry. She analyses two post-Soviet films from Kazakhstan—*Nomad* and *Mustafa Chokai*—in detail to understand cultural discourses on the nation, and highlight how discourses in the cultural field dovetail with or diverge from political discourses and are intended to imagine a Kazakh identity. Dilorom Karomat writes about state initiatives and activities of Fond Forum in the cultural sphere in Uzbekistan. She argues that the events organised by the state and the Fond Forum came as opportunities for cultural interactions at all levels, and became a crucial factor in societal development.

Prior to the formation of nation-states, the state was never seen as crucial for the determination of the identity of communities. It was at best seen as a guarantor of an arrangement under which all communities existed. This was transformed in an era of 'nations and nationalism' when it was asserted that identities were to be largely defined by the nation state. In fact, in a number of cases the state not only defined the boundary within which identity was to be circumscribed, but also the basis for the definition. The rationality on which this basis was determined defined the principal characteristic of groups and subsequently assumed a significance of its own. As nations were constructed within the boundaries of the state, the projection of a numerical majority defined in terms of rationally delimited criteria became crucial. In this projection, the state came to play an increasingly significant part not just in defining the 'nation-state' but also in legitimising it within the international arena. It is this performative role of the state in the Eurasian space that been the focus of this volume.

1. Post Soviet Indo-Russian Relations and the Image of India in Post Soviet Russia

Hari Vasudevan

I

It has become a near orthodoxy in the twenty years following Soviet disintegration that the tenor of Indo-Russian relations has been a pale shadow of the intimacy of the Indo-Soviet friendship. The Druzhba that Surjit Mansingh termed 'not quite an alliance' has not only failed to find new force in the two decades that followed the end of the USSR, but within half that time, its vivacity and vigor diminished to a point where the relationship lacked distinction and luster. Possible explanations are easy to find in whispers at South Block or in the debating circles of the Institute for International Relations and the International Economy off Leninskii Prospekt in Moscow. However, they drift into the vagaries of personality and chance and seldom provide that far reaching clarifying insight that is genuinely instructive.

Figures such as Andrei Kozyrev and G. Kunadze of the Ministry of External Affairs of the Russian Federation have been fall guys for what took place—the Westernisers who broke with Soviet friendship and evolved the pander to Washington and London that are said to have characterised the early years of the Yeltsin Presidency. But that this 'phase' in Russian foreign policy (firmly denied by Kozyrev in his memoirs) lasted for merely two (albeit crucial) years, is ignored in such arguments.

A firm conviction, meanwhile, has been expressed by India's 'old Russia hands' that the new Russia wished to distance itself from the Soviet legacy and policy moved to work away from stress on old commitments such as the one to India. This has been an important over-arching explanation, and draws in a range of actors in the changing scenario of post-1991 and the cultural mood of its social and political elites. But the perspective requires more subtle nuances integrated. For, as I have pointed out elsewhere, when dealing with the economic relationship, changes in the discourse on needs and requirements might alter, but they could also find common ground.[1] Again, by the same logic as that applied to India, Iraq and Syria should have been abandoned, and the lack of any tendencies in this direction is an indication of limitations to the proposition.

To revert, finally, to arguments that trade fell away, and that this crucially changed the character of the relationship, there is evidence to suggest reorientation and continuity rather than fall in trade from 1992 if the territories of the Russian Federation of the USSR are considered independent of the Former Soviet Union. There is also evidence to indicate greater force in the economic relationship than is customary, given the enterprise of India's private sector. It may also be stressed, that changes in trade patterns had begun during the Gulf War when the three way 'swap deals' between Iraq, India and the USSR came to an end. Hence, the malaise that affected the relationship must find other factors by way of explanation that are more long term than those that relate to the disintegration of the state or the policies and character of the Russian Federation.

Apologists for the Indo-Russian relationship—mainly to be found in the SIS of the JNU in Delhi and the ranks of the Institute of Oriental Studies in Moscow—have pointed to a troubled time of economic disruption in Russia during the privatisation and inflation of the Yeltsin reforms. They have also pointed to compulsions innate in the logic of post-Soviet dismemberment that required introversion in Russian foreign policy and a focus on the 'near abroad' (i.e. the countries of the former Soviet Union). The implications of the reading are that the apparently low level of India-Russia interactions came of disorientation and material weakness. They have also pointed to clear evidence that this did not prevent bonhomie between India and Russia, citing Russian steadfastness in supplying India with cryogenic rockets despite the US opposition, continuous take-off of aircraft from Russia by India in the mid 1990s, a steady stream of high level summits and the ebullience of Evgenii Primakov's approach to India both as Minister of External Affairs and as Prime Minister. In the 2000s, the list expanded to include President Putin's inclusion of India in the list of investors in Sakhalin oil, the commitment to raise trading levels announced in 2006, and the easily worked out commitment by Russia to supply nuclear energy plant to India in the aftermath of the Indo-US nuclear deal.

This does not make room for the clear indication that firm coordination of policy in crucial areas such as Central Asia was not sought. Nor does it explain why industry that was still prey to the controls of the state ignored links with Indian economic actors, whether statist, para-statal or private. It fails to draw in changes in Indian perspectives. Indian policy makers, led by Montek Singh Ahluwallia in the domain of economics and finance, and Brajesh Mishra and Shiv Shankar Menon in the realm of foreign policy, have systematically made a bipartisan commitment to a new relationship with the US that has become the cornerstone of India's international relations, fervent denials notwithstanding.

A bottom line that may be universally accepted in the circumstances—and better left as a pro-tem verdict on the subject—is that Indo-Russian relations has not been the same as Indo-Soviet relations. The world had changed and the countries with it. Computations of the balance sheet to arrive at positive or negative balance is, as in all such cases, a matter of the calculator, the figures and the assumptions of the person undertaking the calculation.

II

What has been remarkable in the ping pong of the discussion of Indo-Russian relations, though, is that all the assessments have been based on rapid scissors and paste work from the press and the internet, supplemented by learned interviews with learned/unlearned statesmen and policy makers—often mixed with excellent but unexplored insight. There has been, for instance, no analysis of the economic relationship of the level that was conducted by Nirmal Chandra or Padma Desai for the

Indo-Soviet relationship. There has certainly been no examination of the social context, or the impact of the changes that have taken place because of disintegration.

It is within this context, I would argue, among the subjects that require attention, is the subject of mutual image construction as it has evolved in the last two decades. In circumstances, especially in Russia where image-building has radically altered since 1991 and the social apparatus for negotiation and engagement with image construction is weak, this is a subject that cannot be ignored. In many ways, some of the issues mentioned above—the chinks in the Indo-Russian relationship—are the upshot of nature of communication and conception at a social level. They are linked to national and personal projections in the other country and must be treated and analysed as such. To do so is not easy, but it is the intention of this lecture to take a short step forward. Working out of a historical perspective, this article presents an evaluation of image formation of India in Russia today against a background of perspectives on the past.

The discussion does not limit itself to the strictly visual or verbal. This has been done in the case of the current subject, by R.H. Stacy in his focus on literary metaphor in pre-revolutionary Russia,[2] or writing on the painter, Vasilii Vereshchagin's, India series.[3] However, it has been clear that these aspects of 'image' have taken shape in a broader context to obtain and evoke elaboration and authority. The implications of the sociological literature on the subject, some deeply philosophical, have pointed to this. Images are often phenomena that are centred in political and economic discourse, and sometimes pivot on personalities or groups of personalities that draw on such discourse. The image of India in Russia and vice versa has been composed of all of this over time. It has also been made up, as in the past, by the technological parameters generated by time and circumstance. Today's circumstances are a particular diversion along a path well trodden, but constituted now by distinct factors.

III

The foundations of this subject have been the focus of earlier scholarship. Over two decades ago, during the heyday of Perestroika in the USSR, in a major statement on the image of India in Russia in the past, G. Bongardt Levin and A.A. Vigasin[4] traced sources of the imaging of India in Russia from the middle ages onwards. Drawing attention to the importance of texts such as the Alexandrine Romance in the early second millennium CE, they showed how these Byzantine collections of stories of India during Alexander the Great's campaign to the Indus spawned illustrations and descriptions. They further showed the importance within a limited sphere of the 15th century traveller, Afanasii Nikitin and others—somewhat later—in the 18th century, such as Raphael Danibegashvili and Gerasim Lebedev.

Vigasin's later writing showed the complex nature of this image formation—pointing to the contribution made by Indian traders, who not only supplemented Russian links and connections with Iran, Central Asia and India, but also provided inputs into pictures that members of Russian society were keen to form of India. This is clear from the Indologist's remarkable essay on the Astrakhan merchant, Raghunath, his fellow merchant and relative Narotam, who stayed in St. Petersburg in 1733 at the palace of Prince Cherkasskii—heir to the Kabard explorer and cartographer of the Caspian and Central Asia—appealing before the Senate against judicial decisions taken against him in the matter of the succession to Raghunath's property. They provided information about Indian languages to the 18th century official G. Ya. Ker, and this led to larger conversations.[5]

The late 18th and 19th century further developed the points of contact and communication, through Russian translations of ancient Indian classics and a firm awareness of the British Empire in India. The visits of Saltykov and Vasilii Vereshchagin provided important images in Russia of India. As P. Shastitko and Tatiana Zagorodnikova have shown more recently, it was further supplemented by images provided by Helena Blavatskii, Tsarevich Nicholas, Nicholas Roerich, and those coming to Russia by chance from India—Maharajah Dilip Singh, the adventurer Balaji, the musician Inayat Khan, and so on.What remains uncertain is the range and importance of such image formation.

Certainly before the early 19th century, a degree of rigor and sophistication was wanting, and the images and notions were the concern of a limited elite in Russia—though communities existed (the Tatars for instance) where this was less so. Cartography in India, while existent, was not well developed and certainly was not widely known. Impressions were linked to specific individuals and experiences. A substantial difference can be noted from the late 18th century at this level, and travel became easier and information more accessible in the mid-19th century. In Russia at the same time, the social life of such imaging acquired a greater force with alterations in the use of the print media. The images formed during this time and after have had a degree of importance overall in the period that has followed, even if they have been reformulated off and on.

In political circumstances where what the British officer Connolly called the 'Great Game' was unfolding during the mid-19th century, the geography and security arrangements for British India had a specific value. But it is uncertain how far Indian conditions attracted public attention and left an impression on the Russian society. Information concerning individual events connected with India has been noted. When Vasilii Vereshchagin exhibited his oils of India done in the 1870s—oils that covered an area from Rajasthan to Delhi and the Himalayas,[6] his exhibition received attention according to the statistics. But the circumstances leave an unclear picture. In 1880, Vereshchagin presented his India series—along with his Balkans series. The exhibition took place at the Bezobrazov house on the Fontanka in St. Petersburg. The footfall was over 3,00,000; and when he repeated the show at the Society for the Encouragement of Art in 1882 the footfall came to 32,000.[7] The meaning of these figures remains an enigma, though. Was the footfall a testimony to Russian nationalism concerning the Balkan wars or Russian curiosity concerning the east? Why did Vereshchagin present the series in tandem? The only conclusion to be drawn is that the exhibition was placed before a large number in the public and finds echoes in Vereshchagin's Central Asia series and Palestine series. Whether in passing or directly, they focused attention on 'oriental' locales. This certainly was the feature of Imperial Russian public life.

That this, as well as the reviews in the 'thick journals' of the time of histories and other literature on India, developed a taste for things eastern is beyond dispute – as was to be demonstrated in other instances (such as the other 'events' and occurrences mentioned above). True, the Russians were primarily fixed on their own history—and mobilised the whole gamut of social and human sciences to pursue it. Equally, private enterprise, such as that represented at the Moscow exhibition of 1888, had almost nothing from 'oriental' spaces of the Empire.

In Russia, 'images' in the strict sense, at the time of the Revolution, were formed, with a degree of modern technical sophistication, at three levels. Sound was mass produced and circulated in country bars as well as the homes of the rich.[8] But this tended to be almost wholly Russian songs. The magic lantern had been in existence since the end of the 19th century and focused, where used, on Russian locales, but could run to use of photographic material on China and Central Asia, but not India.[9] Film was exclusively Russia focused, with some work on the border provinces of the Empire—though with nothing that is known about India. These areas supplemented the highly advanced print media—all of which (journals, newspapers, novels, essays), though, included India material, normally culled from British sources.

Such images supplemented high and low theatre and folk practice—some of which included song on military campaigns. The theatre certainly included Indian themes (as in the case of the showing of Shakuntala on the eve of the Revolution). That 'oriental' taste figured among the Russian public and were the product not only of official concern, but private curiosity, and local enterprise, cannot be doubted. Equally, though, it must be stressed that these were tastes focused on China, Central Asia and Persia—countries and regions in various ways under Russian influence.

What took shape as an 'image of India' varied in the circumstances. It drew from the local lore of different communities—Muslim and Buddhist especially—which was never generalised in the newspapers and thick journals that made up the core of public perceptions. In the mid-19th century, in St. Petersburg and Moscow, and in the press, the image of an exotic colonised nation stood out. The notion of deep commitments to mysticism and philosophy were the focus of Indologists and publicists.

The modernisation of the country, even in the Presidency towns, was hardly ever touched on. Rebellious sentiments against British rule and regions on the point of insurrection were also to draw attention, though there were no discussions of the implications of such rebellion for the Russian Empire.

IV

It was under the Soviet state that the Planned Economy and the rigors of an all-Union perspective on cultural policy guided by the CPSU, and many pluralist aspects of the manner of image formation in the Russian Empire disappeared. This is not to say that much did not survive in memory, in academic study and in the course of the development of religious practice. But at the time of standardisation through a system of universal education that originated in the 1920s, the printed word came to have great social compass and meaning—and a uniformity was introduced into what was produced and recommended. The range that the state and the Communist Party possessed to direct and regulate culture was reinforced by material aspects of Soviet society—especially the formation of centrally regulated housing around the industrial centres that grew up around the Planned Economy. These blocks of communal flats were structured with mass entertainment inbuilt (mainly 'clubs' and cinema houses). Collectivisation of agriculture achieved some element of regulation in the countryside after its first onset in the troubled years of 1929-32. The private space of the home and the shared apartment was penetrated by radio (before the war) and television (from the 1960s).[10] The state, and through it the Communist Party, had full control over these media, as it did over the major newspapers and journals.

From the 1950s, independent India came to have a unique place in the list of recommended subjects for interest in educational institutions, succeeding a special place that China had occupied in the years immediately following the Communist revolution. India fitted into the ranks of the countries that had special relations with the Soviet state without being a direct part of the Warsaw Pact and the Comecon. Whatever images existed or were sponsored about politics or history in

India, they came to receive greater stress than was the case of many other countries in Asia an Africa. Both in the printed media, the radio and the visual media, programmes on India were given special status from the time of a special mention of the country during the Khruschev years, when K.P.S. Menon was ambassador.

The composition of this image was quite at variance with that which had evolved in public life under the Russian Empire. It was a picture that was built up by a new breed of Indologists who specialised in the Soviet version of Oriental Studies that took shape in the 1920s, which integrated less industrially developed and colonial nations into an overarching framework of patterns of economic and social change, based on Marxist categories. A considerable mobilisation of material took place to provide the foundations of this endeavour. It was undertaken by the All Union Association of Oriental Studies, the Scientific Centre for the study of Colonial and National Problems and other prominent institutions of the 1920s. It did not deal with esoteric literature concerning religion and mysticism—though the Oriental Studies Institutes were permitted to continue with some research on these areas. S. Oldenburg and A. Scherbatskoy led this trend in 'continuity'. But others focused on other issues. The names of Snesarev, Reisner, Diakov, and Antonova presented a new image of India. The character of industrial, commercial, and agricultural change, the main features of local politics, and the character of imperial policy became the focus of attention as Indians were promoted from exotic and mystical medievals to fellow workers in the cause of universal liberation.

The propaganda pamphlets of the early USSR conveyed these impressions. And when India's independence came, in the mid 1950s, following Nehru's visit to the Soviet Union and the Khrushchev-Bulganin visit to India, the aspirations of the national state were projected. In Moscow, a shop with fine products and curios from India attracted attention of the Soviet nomenklatura from the 1960s.

It should be emphasised, however, that the character of cultural policy had a firm Soviet centre to it. The construction of 'nationality', especially after the Stalin years, was more restricted than was the case in the Russian Empire, whatever the nature of a heavy Russian accent on the Empire at that earlier time. The 'construction' excluded the elaboration of the experiences of Soviet 'nationalities' outside the territories of the USSR in the past and ideology and rhetoric foreclosed any positive assessment of alternatives other than the political choices that brought them into the Russian Empire. The interest displayed in broader spaces that were associated with ethnicity, religion and history that were part of the character of cultural self awareness as it manifested itself among different communities during the time of the Empire, was now circumscribed. Only when these could be used to the advantage of the USSR were they encouraged. Hence, Tatar and Buryat nationalism narrowed in range. Armenian and Turkmen nationalism that could be used to effect in Persia, was permitted a different range. Quite distinctly, as a result, India lost a degree of standing in nationality areas that were Muslim or Buddhist. However, the overall focus on this 'friend of the Soviet Union' provided a more enhanced status at an authoritative central government level than had been the case in the past.

Most important, at a broader, non-governmental level, the Hindi feature film came to acquire a special role in Russian public life, where the run of the mill entertainment from Hollywood penetrated in dribs and drabs. After the display of Hindi films at a festival of 1954, the products of Bombay filled a special role in Moscow's life—as they did in Soviet life generally. These ranged from those films in which Raj Kapoor acted ('Awara') to Mithun Chakravarti's output ('Disco Dancer'). They provided a lightness and happiness that the somewhat grim output of Soviet cinema could not compete with. The products of Hollywood of this era were that too soul searching and complex for Soviet audiences looking from a break from a hard life of queues and a production line that was slow to innovate on labour saving technology.[11]

V

The streamlining of culture in the USSR, and the exceptional role given to India in what took shape, quickly transformed in the successor states in the post disintegration period. In the Russian Federation, this was partly linked to the technological revolution that took place in the country, where the visual media were suddenly open to digital modes of which state organisations had no real knowledge. The 'opening' of the country to foreign enterprise and the lifting of curbs on circulation of foreign print, visual and audio material occurred at the time of a major change in such media in the west when the internet and PC and the mobile phone became a source of cultural construction. Opportunities galore were suggested by the new technology. There could be no government choice in the matter of what was seen except in terms of the refusal of permission of various organisations to set up their organisations in Russia and steps to prevent access to material. The complexities and limitations of doing this have been evident in regimes such as those in Central Asia and Myanmar, not to mention the PRC, once computers and internet services are accessible. Curbs in the Russian case became even more difficult given the lack of preparedness of Soviet official institutions to deal with this material and—more important—the lack of certainty about when and how curbs were to be applied at a time when Russian public/official life was proceeding through major changes and 'democratic' values were in the ascendant.

The early years post-1991 witnessed the arrival of visual diskettes in large number—to be followed quickly by VCDs and DVDs, and the generation of this material in Russia. Private enterprise on small and large scale participated in the distribution of the profusion of visual images in the country. In parallel, authorisation was given for the formation of a series of major TV stations that were associated with private business houses. These included the oligarch Gusinskii's NTV. Standard TV became more diversified and imaginative. Regional channels also arrived and with them cable television, which gave access to a variety of locales. In border areas, a series of channels from the newly independent states were also available—catering to a range of tastes and ethnic interests.

The film output of the US and various dubbed versions of European soap operas held pride of place in the entertainment industry of the new Russia. This occurred at the time of further changes in everyday life. Consumption and consumer products became loaded with culture-specific tags. In the USSR, advertising had been rare in any developed form. In Russia, it became the rage in a short time. The profile of consumers was set around a 'Russian' core in the country, even if there was no large scale out-migration of non-Russian group in cities or regions. In numerical terms, non-Russian ethnos with whom Russians had coexisted came to be concentrated in newly independent states other than Russia when disintegration took place. This affected the advertising strategies that new companies, independent of state curbs and directives, devised for the Federation. Material that drew from Eastern European and Western European lifestyles and customs was found appropriate for such strategies.

This was even more so since the bulk of companies that provided advertising learned their lessons from the West. What is left of this first wave is symbolised by Tom Gins, Mikko Lehtinen, Vesa Manninen, and Joachim Back—major producers in the late 2000s of commercials. Equally, although a host of private companies from various countries set up shop in the Federation in the post 1991 years, there was a tendency for US and European companies to lead the pack, working from the advantages bestowed on them by the Freedom Support Act and the various packages originating in EBRD schemes for Russia. Although many withdrew over time, they provided templates in production, packaging, and production that remain prominent.

In the circumstances, India gradually lost status in what may literally be called the public eye. The Hindi film, for instance, which had been a major item of popular consumption, had to compete with other fare that achieved similar ends. Potential viewers normally subscribed to special channels. Indian products found their way into the Russian market, but normally as low cost items with little advertising. It was only in the case of tea that India acted as a ready reference point—with projections of the country around the product. But even here, the competitive edge of Sri Lankan and Kenyan products limited the edge of the image.

In a number of republican locales within the Russian Federation, however, individuals who had failed to make the 'big list' in the case of the USSR, suddenly found attention. Initiatives were also undertaken at a regional level that gave India prominence. In Bashkortostan, the fresh look at distinguished individuals of the past included a positive evaluation of Togan Validov, a major Bashkir nationalist of the revolutionary era who ended his life in Turkey. Significantly, any mention of his life automatically led to India since he had conducted a correspondence with the liberal politician M.A. Ansari. Elsewhere, in Tatarstan, a singular case may also mentioned that has an 'India' flavour that is of interest. Musa Bigi [Musa Bigiev] (1875-1949) found attention in the new literature on the Tatar intelligentsia, and with him accounts of a larger world of Islam that he represented that drew him to India. Bigiev's life was one of those included by the Tatar Republic in its list of biographies recommended for schools and higher institutions of learning.[12]

Bigi went to the Apanaev madrasa in Kazan relatively early in life—completing his early years in a Russian school at Rostov on the Don, and moving on in accordance with the wishes of his mother, Fatima Khanum who wanted to see him a religious Islamic scholar. He was clearly not satisfied by the Kazan's atmosphere, where the Muslim community was dominated by influential traders, living within the confines set for them by official life run by Russian gentry and the Orthodox Church.[13] The changes the educationist and public activist Ismail Bey Gasprinskii was inspiring at this time were yet to take seed against the background of conservative Islamic commitment and Tatar-Bulghar pride. Bigi then spent years between an Islamic education (in Bukhara and Samarkand) and Russian schools until he drifted to Istanbul.

Here, under the influence of the Tatar Akhet Zade he decided on more disciplined study in Egypt and the Hijaz, which led him to India and scholarship that was Hindu and Muslim. He met scholars of different faiths, read the Mahabharata and a range of Hindu literature, learning Sanskrit as he did so. Years of further reading followed, initially in Egypt (three years) and later Syria—from where he returned to Russia in 1904.

Quickly emerging as an activist, Bigi worked with newspapers in St. Petersburg during the revolutionary years (1904-05). Following this up with scholarship on the history of the Koran he took a hand in the administration of a madrasa in Orenburg. Comparative religion attracted him repeatedly. For instance, he pointed to the problem of long fasts for Muslims of northern regions, after a visit to Finland in summer 1910 in his essay 'Fasting during Long Days'. He evolved an eclectic sense of Islam—with a concern with the forgiving nature of God, taking issue with eminent figures of Islam in Tatar country, such as R. Fakhruddin and Z. Kamali. He remained in Russia after the Bolshevik Revolution, and met and discussed issues of Muslim education with Lenin, before setting out to travel and read in 1923, proceeding by way of Berlin and publishing a strident critique of Marxism in his 'ABC of Islam'. This earned him a term in prison on his return. But he was able to get out and left the country by way of Turkestan and Xinjiang—never to return—in 1930.

Bigi spent some time with friends in Bombay before making his way back to his old haunts in West Asia. But his ecumenical sense of faith drew him once again to India and to studies of Sanskrit texts in Banaras as well as to Berlin and a series of journeys in search of complex patterns in Islam. Although years in British prison in Peshawar and a wandering existence were his fate during this time, Bigi's devotion to his spiritual quests was unrelenting—leading him to exhaustion and death in Cairo in 1949.[14]

Important to note, the fresh attention paid to Bigi's life in Tatarstan does not imply that this has been a figure around which there has been a 'gathering' in favour of India. But attention to a range of figures whose catholicity of interest allowed them to think more broadly has permitted local exploration of connections where India figures. This, however, has had to vie with the rise of fundamentalist Islam among Muslims as a whole in the Federation—as a consequence of which attention to India might not always lead to positive perspectives.

Let me draw attention to another local instance of attention to India in the Federation.

In the town of Samara, the projection of an image of India, stretching over a large provincial domain and extending to a larger national space, has been the achievement of a local organisation whose roots lie in innovative aspects of latter day Soviet educational thought that has been given new life in the Federation post-1991.

That image is firmly connected with an initiative of Nikitina and Yuri Rodichev and their Centre of Spiritual Culture. This was a venture set up during late Perestroika, before Soviet disintegration, when institutions were falling apart, goods were in short supply and inflation was picking up. Many felt it important to focus on what held people together and made life worth living—without costing vast sums. Using the technology available, the founders evolved a school, an exhibition space, and, with some Indian help, a publishing house. From this base, they organised travelling exhibitions—which targeted other provincial towns, and went abroad. India figured prominently in their permanent exhibition: the attractions of India as a place of contemplation and the draw it had exercised over Russians such as Nicholas Roerich; and the range of Indian culture more generally. Over time, the Centre became a place for young people to get together, for mothers to leave their children knowing that this would not be an ordinary creche.

The departure was not unusual. Educational initiatives outside the routine of state schooling were jealously guarded under the Soviet state from Party encroachment and disciplinary action. *Komsomolskaya Pravda* was the centre in the 1980s of the journalists who supported out of the ordinary education that projected the most creative aspects of the world. Initially such initiatives were the focus in the so-called 'communard' movement organised by the Communist educationist I.P. Ivanov, who detested the bureaucratic straightjacket of Stalinist education. The tradition was taken up by Richard Sokolov, V. Khiltunen, O. Marionicheva, B. Minaev (the chief editor of the 'free thinking' journal *Ogonek* during perestroika), the Nikitins and V. Iumashev (whose principles finally led him to head Boris Yeltsin's administration).[15] It was into the hands of a group stimulated by this tradition that the reputation of India had passed in Samara.

The modern building and exhibition halls that feature India prominently are the upshot—as are translations of the 'Ain-i-Akbari' in Russia and large Roerich calendars for 2007.

Such records may be supplemented by others. The list would include the regular tourist migration to Goa, the ISKON sponsored visits to

Brindavan and the pilgrimages of Russian Buddhists to Bodh Gaya and Dharamshala. They would also include the special popularity of the work of Amitav Ghosh and Vikram Seth among the rapidly growing readers of English in the Russian Federation.

VI

These elements, distinctive though, have not snowballed into a phenomenon of significance even with the stout support of the Jawaharlal Nehru Cultural Centre of the Indian Embassy in Moscow on occasion. They have remained a piecemeal even if important to groups and regions. The state of affairs contrasts firmly with, say, the image of the US or China or smaller countries such as Britain or France.

Why this is so is an important question. Many possible arguments exist—some of which revert to the issues highlighted during the introductory section of this presentation. To point to the more serious possibilities here, however, is beyond the scope of this article, which is more concerned with drawing out the rough outlines of the anatomy of a phenomenon rather than providing a more general evaluation of its significance.

Notes

1. Hari Vasudevan, *Shadows of Substance. Indo-Russian Trade and Military Technical Cooperation,* (New Delhi: Manohar Publications, 2010).
2. R. H. Stacy, *India in Russian Literature,* (Delhi: Motilal Banarsidas, 1985)
3. Bruk, Yakov, *Vasilii Vereshchagin,* (Moscow: Skanrus, 2004)
4. G. Bongard-Levin and A. Vigasin, *The Image of India,* (Moscow: Progress Publishers, 1984)
5. *Izuchenie,* p. 66 ff.
6. Yakov, *Vasilii Vereshchagin.*
7. *Ocherki Istorii Leningrada* (Nauka 1956) vol. 2, p. 646.
8. See Ivan Bunin's first novel, *The Village,* set in post 1905 Russia, for instances of the gramaphone's use in the most.
9. For some of the range covered by Russian photographs, see Chloe Obolenskii, *The Russian Empire. A Portrait in Photographs,* (London: Jonathan Cape, 1980). To date, there is no evidence that Russian visitors to India photographed at this time, let alone filmed. But the full output of the Consulates in Bombay and Calcutta have not

been examined from this point of view.

10. TV arrived in Soviet Russia before the Second World War, but its large-scale use dates to the 1960s.
11. See Sudha Rajagopalan, *Leave Disco Dancer Alone. Indian Cinema and Soviet Movie going after Stalin* (New Delhi: Yoda Press, 2008). Rajagopalan quotes many instances to demonstrate the popularity of the Hindi film. Typical is the following statement. 'Once I had children, I did not go out much. However, I went once a week to the Indian film club—This time was sacrosanct, non-negotiable. A friend was in love with Mithun...she recently travelled to India, looked for his home and waited outside to meet him. It was only her return ticket home that forced her to abandon her wait.' (p. 30).
12. *Tatarskie Intellektualy. Istoricheskie portrety,* (Kazan: Magarif, 2005).
13. See the fine essay on Kazan province in B.B. Veselovskii, *Istoriia zemstva za sorok let,* St. Petersburg, 1909-11, vol. 4.
14. *Tatarskie Intellektualy* op.cit. pp. 203-212.
15. V.V. Shubin, *Ot 'zastoia' k reformam 1917-85 gg,* (Moscow: Rossspen, 2001).

2. India-Tajikistan relations: Prospects of a regional development framework

Ajay K. Patnaik

Following the disintegration of the Soviet Union, India was quick to accord diplomatic recognition to the independent Central Asian republics in 1992, and soon, opened embassies in these countries. The tremors of Soviet disintegration and the urge to forge bonds with their cultural neighbourhood on a new basis prompted the new states to look towards countries like India. However, most of the international community including India was generally apathetic towards Central Asia. The outbreak of the Tajik civil war soon after independence spread insecurity in the rest of Central Asia. This was the time when India's involvement would have helped the Central Asian states get over the transition pains. However, India's own economic difficulties in the beginning of the 1990s, resulting in sweeping economic reforms and encouragement to the private sector and free market, meant that Central Asia was not a priority for economic engagement. These markets were considered too risky and unattractive for Indian business. Yet, the cultural and historical affinity with the region could not be wished away. The difficulties faced by Central Asia was evoking discomforting emotions in India, even though the policy makers were focusing more on mending ties with the West following the Soviet collapse.

Indian leaders, however, travelled to the region and subsequently, India provided credit lines to purchase Indian goods. These steps were not adequate considering the level of economic dislocation faced by the Central Asian region. While Russia inherited the Soviet debt toward India and managed to recover it over a decade or so by free supply of Indian goods in exchange, Central Asian states had to rely instead on limited

Indian credit to purchase goods from India. During Prime Minister Narasimha Rao's visit to Central Asia in the early 1990s, New Delhi announced a credit line worth US$ 5-10 million to each state. Some would suggest that India could have filled the vacuum at a time when Central Asian states were looking for partners who were in synchrony with their modern and secular ethos. India's involvement in the region fell short of expectations. However, others would argue that India's assistance need to be appreciated given the difficulties the country itself was facing. Yet, there is no denying that India's Westward focus affected its willingness for greater engagement with its 'extended neighbourhood', including Central Asia. This is borne out by the still low level of trade India has with most Central Asian countries even after its economy became stronger. The then Indian National Security Advisor, J.N. Dixit, even lamented on the very limited nature of relations with Central Asia till the early years of this century. Speaking at a seminar organised by the Institute of Defence Studies and Analysis (IDSA) in New Delhi in November 2003, Dixit said, "Though there have been contacts both at the inter-governmental and people-to-people level, the fact of the matter is that due to logistical difficulties and differences regarding political priorities of both sides, India is not giving sufficient attention to Central Asia."[1]

He also suggested, "India has to undertake an attitudinal change towards Central Asia. It must, as it has focused attention on ASEAN countries, perceive the Central Asian countries as an integral part of its neighbourhood. India's policies towards Central Asia should be predicated on the perception that multi-faceted relations are essential for the security and stability of the integrated strategic region extending from the northern limits of the Central Asian republics to the southern extremities of the South Asian region."[2] However, India's approach of minimal involvement in Central Asia had already undergone some change as the geopolitics of the region took a turn to Delhi's disadvantage.

Shifting Focus: Taliban and Pakistan's Search for 'Strategic Depth'

The victory of the Taliban in Afghanistan in the mid-1990s changed the geopolitical situation both in Central Asia and in South Asia. As a result, the security of Central Asia and that of India became closely connected. The post-Soviet states were afraid of any destabilisation coming from Afghanistan, while India was worried about Pakistan's search for 'strategic depth'. As a result, Delhi could not afford to have a condescending attitude towards Central Asia.

Islamabad's foreign policy goal during the anti-Soviet war in Afghanistan gradually veered round to establishing control over the country once the Soviet Union left the Afghan territory. The *mujahedeen* war not only made Pakistan a frontline state but also created opportunity for it to acquire what is called 'strategic depth' vis-a-vis India. For the first time, Pakistan was in a position to control and influence Afghanistan's political future. Beginning with Zia-ul-Haq, this goal became the major geopolitical objective of subsequent Pakistani leadership, backing more and more radical religious elements that spread destabilisation from Kashmir to Kabul and beyond into the Ferghana Valley. However, running after what has so far proved to be a 'mirage' seriously affected Pakistan's image. By the time the US war against Taliban began in Fall 2001, Pakistan's influence in the Central Asian region was at its nadir, except for its contacts with Turkmenistan, the only Central Asian country whose zeal to export its oil and gas to Indian Ocean through Pakistan and a Taliban-led Afghanistan. According to experts like Eqbal Ahmed and Ahmed Rashid, this strategic depth in Afghanistan was a misnomer. To expect that a devastated, isolated and poor country like Afghanistan would provide depth to Pakistan was mistaken thinking, fraught with dangerous consequences for the Pakistani society itself.[3]

From India's point of view, Pakistan's search for depth did not end with the victory of the Taliban in Afghanistan. The focus was also on Central Asia, which, with its oil, natural gas and other resources, could provide greater strategic advantages. Through the Taliban, Islamabad could hope influencing Central Asia future orientations on a strategic and economic level, but also on a religious one. The Ferghana Valley region, where the impact of Islamic orthodoxy has been traditionally stronger than in the rest of Central Asia, became the focus of fundamentalist Islamic forces. Tajikistan, devastated after a long and bloody civil war, was at the receiving end of cross-border terrorism from Afghanistan and assassination attempts were made on Uzbek president's life in 1999. The Ferghana Valley that straddles Uzbekistan, Tajikistan, and Kyrgyzstan, has been a hotbed of militancy sustained by the international terrorist networks. In August 1999 and again in August 2000, militants made abortive attempts to occupy villages in the southern part of Kyrgyzstan. The official aim was to create an Islamic state with territories from the above three republics.

Taliban became host to one of the most radical Islamic groups in Central Asia, the Islamic Movement of Uzbekistan (IMU).[4] The nexus between drug trafficking and terrorism in the golden crescent became a major reason for political and social instability in the region. Afghanistan during the 1990s emerged as the second largest producer of drugs in the world. This gave the Taliban government enormous financial benefits that went to training, arming and funding campaigns of some terrorist groups.[5] After Iran, Central Asia was badly hit by the explosion in Afghan heroin. Tajikistan and Kyrgyzstan developed as important opium routes and became significant drug producers themselves. Heroin addiction increased alarmingly in these countries, as they became part of the heroin export chain.[6]

The common threat of terrorism resulted in a growing convergence of views on the need to cooperate and jointly fight this menace. Realising that Central Asia held the key to the two of its major worries—Pakistan's expanding influence over Afghanistan and beyond, and the threat of a growing belt of fundamentalism and cross-border terrorism—India chose to cooperate closely with the Central Asian states. Its diplomatic anti-Taliban actions was not confined to maintaining an Embassy of Afghanistan in New Delhi representing the Rabbani leadership, ousted by Taliban, or hosting the families of the anti-Taliban leadership. In all diplomatic forums, India condemned the Taliban and played a crucial role in the campaign against international recognition to the Taliban. It also provided financial assistance to the Northern Alliance led by Ahmad Shah Massoud—India reportedly supplied the Northern Alliance with high altitude warfare equipment, worth about US$

8-10 million between 1999 and 2001, and sent defence advisers and helicopter technicians.[7]

The defeat and ouster of Taliban has put on hold Pakistan's hopes of achieving some strategic edge over India. However, given the still unstable situation in Afghanistan, the need for continued co-operation between India and Central Asia is very critical. India feels neither totally secure nor comfortable about the reports of continuing attempts to destabilise Afghanistan, despite the US presence in both Pakistan and Afghanistan. Indian policy makers believe that Islamabad continues the policy of what one former Indian foreign secretary described as 'sustainable terrorism' and the international community has been unable to address India's concerns.[8] To ensure its own security, India needed to focus on greater involvement in the Central Asian region. However, it was only with India's economic success and the installation of a friendly government in Kabul that Indian policies in Central Asia underwent transformation.

Strategic Significance of Tajikistan for India

Tajikistan's significance for India—especially since the time Taliban came to power in Kabul, and even after its ouster—has been seen generally in geopolitical terms by both Indian policy makers and scholars writing on the subject. The geostrategic location of Tajikistan bordering Afghanistan, Pakistan occupied Kashmir (PoK) and China, is said to have serious security implications for India. C. Rajamohan, a noted Indian strategic specialist, even observed that Tajikistan's location makes it 'the fulcrum of regional geopolitics'.[9] Some of the narratives go to the extent of suggesting that Tajikistan can help India counterbalance the Chinese influence, while others underline that Tajikistan is a crucial for India's 'forward policy' in the region. Countering Pakistan's search for 'Strategic Depth' in Afghanistan and fighting terrorism and extremism with Tajik support is part of the same narrative.

Of course, this discursive framework necessarily includes the Ainy airbase, which India is supposed to be using in Tajikistan. Support to Northern Alliance and use of Ainy are symbols of India's assertive policy in the region following the coming to power of the Taliban in Afghanistan in the mid-1990s. Though Taliban is out of power, Ainy allows India to help in Afghanistan's reconstruction efforts, including transporting of men and materials for building roads and other infrastructure in that country. Instead of looking at this Tajik-Russian airbase as a facility used by India for a limited purpose with the concurrence of those two powers, Indian scholars and commentators have created a massive strategic sand castle around Ainy. Ainy is mentioned as the first Indian base outside its territory. Sudha Ramachandran even says, "A base at Ayni allows India rapid response to any emerging threat from the volatile Afghanistan-Pakistan arc, including a terrorist hijacking such as that of Indian Airlines Flight IC814 in December 1999. It also gives New Delhi a limited but significant capability to inject Special Forces into a hostile theater as and when the situation demands. And should the base at Ayni grow in the coming years, it would enhance India's options in the event of military confrontation with Pakistan. India would be able to strike Pakistan's rear from Tajik soil."[10] Another article suggests that the base goes beyond India's concerns vis-a-vis Pakistan and Pakistan-backed religious extremism in the region. Ayni has to do with India's growing interests in Central Asia as well, which includes Central Asian energy as well as increasing involvement in the region's security. Ainy, according to this view, also has to do with India's big-power ambitions.[11]

Another scholar Viktor Dubovinskiy of the Institute of History, Archaeology and Ethnography of Tajik Academy of Sciences, goes even further. In a paper (presented at the international conference on 'Geo-political Dynamics of India-Tajikistan Relations' held on June 29, 2010 in Dushanbe jointly organised by the Indian Council of World Affairs (ICWA) and the Tajik Academy of Sciences), he underlined that in the developing situation in and around Afghanistan, India is called upon to perform the onerous responsibility of 'consolidation of all constructive forces of the southern sub-region of Eurasia in the struggle against political and religious extremism'. He added that in his view, 'India possesses both resources and political will for this purpose and is capable to resist to any calls and risks in the zone of its geopolitical responsibility'.[12] These analytical narratives are neither without relevance nor without basis. Right since the days of Northern Alliance, when it backed the group under the leadership of an ethnic Tajik commander Ahmed Shah Masood, India has looked at Tajikistan as an important country for its Afghan policy. From Farkhor to Ainy, the facilities that India used inside Tajikistan were intended for its Afghan humanitarian efforts.[13] From this perspective, one important landmark was the Indian Prime Minister's visit to Tajikistan in November 2003 when India was offered by the Tajik government to renovate and upgrade the Ainy air base.

Recent Indian interests in Tajikistan are related to uranium and natural gas. According to the Tajik president, the country has 14 per cent of world's uranium reserves and some natural gas fields in the southern part of the country. Following the Indian President's visit in September 2009, it was announced that Indian companies plan to invest US$ 12 million in the development of gas fields located in southern Tajikistan.[14] However, India's activities so far do not indicate that it is going to speed up the implementation of these plans. Another such example is the announcement made during the same visit by the Indian President Pratibha Patil that Indian firms intended to invest US$ 28 million in the construction of a cement plant and the development of gas fields in southern Tajikistan. However, these plans have not been implemented.[15] During that visit, Tajikistan invited India to explore the huge hydropower potential in the country as part of efforts to intensify bilateral economic cooperation and explore new areas of partnership between the two sides. Tajik president invited investment as Tajikistan has about 400 projects that require foreign investment. However, there is no urgency shown so far by the Indian side.[16] At a Tajik-Indian business conference held in Dushanbe on September 08, 2009 (attended by President Patil), President Rahmon made his desire for increased Indian involvement clear, noting that Tajikistan currently uses only 5 per cent of its water energy resources, and that only 20 per cent of the cotton fibre produced in the country is currently processed. He not only encouraged investment in these sectors but also suggested Indian businesses consider investment in the Tajik tourism, hotel management, mineral prospecting, and agricultural goods processing sectors.[17]

Though there are some changes in India's approach due to India's energy security needs and a more active policy has been pursued since the beginning of this century, Central Asia is yet to acquire the level of priority in India's external policy that China accords to this region. The results of the two contrasting approaches are evident. Today, China is the largest trade partner of most Central Asian states. India's trade with the region is comparatively miniscule. Compared to China's more than US$ 28.18 billion and Iran's nearly US$ 1.8 billion trade turnover with Central Asia in 2008, India's trade with the region was only US$ 366.73 million.[18] Tajikistan's trade with India is even abysmally low compared to other Central Asian states despite political and strategic closeness between the two countries. Bilateral trade in 2011 totalled about US$ 32.57 million.[19] Indian investment is not even worth mentioning. Indian companies have invested only US$ 17 million in upgrading a hydropower station near Dushanbe (Varzob-1) and about US$ 5 million in a hotel construction in the Tajik capital.[20]

According to Dag Sourander,[21] India's bilateral relations with Tajikistan are based mostly on India's interest in maintaining the balance of power in the region. India's strategic rivals Pakistan, China, and Iran, have all developed cooperation with Tajikistan after its independence. India has an interest in countering the Taliban and in controlling the influence of the Pakistan-oriented Pashtun population in Afghanistan by supporting other ethnic groups in the north of that country, including the ethnic Tajiks (who are actually more numerous in Afghanistan than in Tajikistan).

With this perspective in which Central Asia's significance is linked to India's geopolitical interests in Afghanistan and is security oriented, India has limited success in its engagement with Central Asia. While China is overwhelming the region with its economic push, India is still looking at the region from a security perspective related to stability in Afghanistan. India has to constantly watch the Sino-Pak and Taliban-Pakistan moves in Afghanistan and seek ways to balance or counter it. India's aid, assistance, and reconstruction efforts are focused on Afghanistan and less on its 'extended neighbourhood', that is, Central Asia, though India links Central Asia to its strategy in Afghanistan. If India had focused on Central Asia and linked it less to its South Asian strategy, there was a possibility that India's growing influence in Central Asia would have complemented its Afghanistan strategy. By focusing on the other way round, India has neither been a strong player in Afghanistan nor in Central Asia. It is a supplementary actor in Afghanistan to the US and NATO powers, and in Central Asia it is likely to have a limited influence compared to other regional players like Russia, China, Iran, and Turkey.

An Alternative Vision Based on Development

According to Alexander Sodiqov, "As New Delhi aspires to play a stronger role in Central Asia, its defense and security ties with Dushanbe should be matched with adequate economic cooperation and financial support for the cash-stripped Tajik government. Without achieving this balance, India will remain only a marginal player in the region."[22] Even in its Afghanistan-focused Central Asia strategy, India is handicapped by its problematic relations with Pakistan and by the US antipathy to Iran. Relations with Iran have soured after India twice voted against Iran at IAEA. While China develops relations with Iran, India is more reluctant to go ahead even with agreed projects. As a result, projects like Iran-Pakistan-India (IPI) pipeline, Chahbahar port, North-South transport corridor etc. are not moving forward at the desired speed. With a target of 12 million tons per year, the two present harbours at Chahbahar have a capacity of only 2.5 million, though India has been financially assisting Iran in upgrading the Chahbahar-Milak road inside Iran and constructing a bridge to Zaranj, from where a road to Diloram in Afghanistan's Nimroz province has already been completed by India. The issue of accelerating the work on the port was raised by the Indian side with their Iranian counterparts during the 16th Indo-Iran Joint Commission held in Delhi on July 08-09, 2010.[23]

India needs to vastly upgrade its economic and cultural engagement in Central Asia, and link it to some of the projects initiated already to create regional linkages. Through greater economic involvement in Central Asia, India can look to forge closer integration of three Central Asian states (Tajikistan, Turkmenistan, and Uzbekistan) with northern and western Afghanistan. Chahbahar route needs to compliment this integration by linking India and Iran with Central Asia through Afghanistan. Chabahar-Milak-Zaranj-Delaram highway will open up the Indian market to Afghan agricultural products and other exports, as well as help combat the illicit drugs production. India will be able to transport its goods, including humanitarian supplies, to Afghanistan and Central Asia.

Tajikistan is of course an underdeveloped country, which by itself does not attract Indian private sector. Tajikistan ranks 112 in terms of human development and is the poorest country in the former Soviet Union. In 2007, about 41 per cent of the population lived below the poverty line of US$ 41 per month and 17 per cent also below the extreme poverty line of US$ 26 per month. Tajik families, and the entire Tajik economy, are hugely dependent on money sent back by Tajik labour migrants in Russia and Kazakhstan.[24] Poverty is fuelling the drugs trade, with some reports estimating that between 30 and 50 per cent of the country's economic activity is linked to narcotics trafficking. HIV rates are rising rapidly due to migrant workers and growing drug use. Child labour is widespread, in particular in the cotton growing regions, and girls in rural areas often stay even without basic education, being forced into early marriage.[25]

However, despite its current economic situation, Tajikistan has some potential that can be attractive for Indian investment. With a high and under invested hydroelectricity capacity, Tajikistan offers opportunity for Indian companies. The country is currently only able to produce a fraction of its assumed annual potential of between 40,000 and 80,000 million kilowatts. Discussion of the hydroelectric issue during Indian President's visit in 2009 was a continuation of a policy first announced by Indian Prime Minister Manmohan Singh during President Rahmon's 2006 visit to New Delhi. Its recurrence indicates a commitment to the development of the moribund Tajik energy sector, which in the understated language of Indian diplomacy has been described as being 'mutually beneficial', says Ben Welch.[26]

Indian engagement with Tajikistan should be backed by a comprehensive strategy that revives Tajikistan's economy and strengthens its development. This can be done if India and Tajikistan along with Iran and Afghanistan can be part of a development complex, pulling together their resources to create industry and infrastructure, including pipelines, ports, and highways. India is now showing a greater willingness to play a stronger economic role in the region. This was underscored by the government's initiative to push Indian companies to bid for iron ore blocks in the rich Hajigak mines in Afghanistan as well as to sponsor the Steel Authority of India proposal to set up a steel plant in that country. Hajigak is a 1.8 billion-ton deposit of high-grade iron ore in the central province of Bamiyan. In November 2011, Afghanistan awarded four of the five blocks at the Hajigak iron ore deposit to a consortium of seven Indian firms led by the state-owned Steel Authority of India with support from India's government [the final block awarded to Canada's Kilo Goldmines Ltd. (KGL)].[27]

According to M. Bhadrakumar, a former Indian diplomat and a known strategic expert, "Hopefully, the Hajigak project will be a 'leap of faith' also for the Indian strategic pundits. It is senseless to pursue politics without economics. This realism has long been in coming in our regional policies—be it toward Sri Lanka, Nepal, or Bangladesh. The 'hands-on' interest shown by the new Foreign Secretary, Ranjan Mathai, in the progress in the bidding process testifies to the new thinking."[28] Chahbahar Port has acquired urgency in view of the potential Indian investment in the mining sector of Afghanistan. Afghanistan's Minister for Mines Wahidullah Shahrani believes that a viable alternative route to the difficult Pakistan one could be a railway line from Hajigak running westwards to Iran, along the Zaranj-Delaram highway that India had built in the mid-2000s, to the Iranian port of Chahbahar. Indian Foreign Secretary Ranjan Mathai is also of the view that evacuation of iron ore from Hajigak will mainly have to be through the Chahbahar port.[29]

However, there is slow progress concerning Chahbahar due to

fluctuating Iran-India relations. As stated earlier, with a target of 12 million tons per year, the two present harbours at Chahbahar have a capacity of only 2.5 million. Similarly, there is also unsatisfactory progress in the Iranian sector of the North-South Transport Corridor. Some progress noticed recently (the beginning of the Iran-Kazakhstan railway project and Construction of the Qazvin-Rasht-Astara in northern Iran in order to complete the north-south corridor) are positive signals.

Possibilities of a Regional Development Complex

Tajikistan has sought to establish greater economic ties with Afghanistan, which have been facilitated by the construction of a bridge across the Panj River in 2007. There are customs and border facilities on both sides, and the capacity to handle about 1,000 vehicles every day. Afghanistan and Tajikistan agreed to create free economic zones on both sides of the bridge, and ease customs and visa regimes to promote trade. The bridge has increased the flow of Tajik goods into Afghanistan and has enhanced commercial opportunities on both sides of the river. In addition, Tajikistan, Afghanistan, and Iran agreed to form the Economic Council of the Persian-Speaking Union in 2008, and work is underway to improve transportation links—road and rail—and thus, trade between the three countries. Afghanistan has also sought to import energy from Tajikistan. The three countries also agreed to set up a joint commission to explore possibilities of transferring 500 KW of energy from Tajikistan to Afghanistan and Iran. Other projects agreed upon include construction of Tajikistan-Afghanistan-Iran highway, a railway linking Tajikistan to Iran via Afghanistan, and power grids that connect Tajikistan to Pakistan and Iran via Afghanistan.[30]

Iran has close linguistic and cultural ties to Tajikistan and displays a strong interest in deepening relations. Iran plays a prominent role in improving Tajik infrastructure; it has contributed funds to the Sangtuda hydroelectric power plant, the third unit of which was opened in November 2008. Another important Iranian-backed infrastructure project in Tajikistan is the construction of the tunnel on the road between Dushanbe and Khujand. The tunnel, built and financed by Iran, should make it possible to keep the road between the capital Dushanbe and the second important city Khujand in the north open also in winter.[31] India's efforts in Afghanistan and Tajikistan need to be complimented by Indo-Iranian relations. There are now strong signs that India is breaking out of the shadows of American strategy on Iran. It has decided to go ahead not only with the energy imports but also with the North-South transport corridor project. The meeting of officials of transport ministries of Iran, India, Russia and other countries in January 2012 in Delhi to move forward the project augurs well for India-Central Asia relations. Iran has shown greater urgency to complete its part of the project. India on its part conveyed Iran its willingness to take charge of the project, including building the missing sections of the railway and road link in Iran. Experts from all the fourteen stake holder countries were again scheduled to meet in Delhi on March 29, 2012.[32]

Conclusion

There have been a number of developments in the recent past, and these have created hopes that India would have a different approach now. India has taken steps that can lead to the creation of a development complex that could link India, Afghanistan, Tajikistan, and Iran. The ultimate goal is to make Central Asia and Afghanistan a region of greater international cooperation and not a theatre of a 'New Great Game'. In the process, India would have stronger economic engagement with a broader region that would also help in Afghanistan's reconstruction and stability. Tajikistan would be a key partner for evolving a regional development complex that can link India with Central Asia through Iran and Afghanistan. While geopolitics will remain relevant, a development model could benefit Tajikistan and Afghanistan. Tajikistan is likely to join the Customs Union (of Russia, Belarus, and Kazakhstan) in the future. It could be useful for India to have smooth accessibility to the region. India is working out a special economic agreement with the

Customs Union. If that materialises, the North-South transport corridor and the Chahbahar routes are going to be very important for India. From this point of view, Tajikistan would be an important bridgehead for India in Eurasia.

Notes

1. J. N. Dixit, "Emerging International Security Environment: Indian Perceptions with Focus on South Asian and Central Asian predicaments", in K. Santhanam and Ramakant Dwivedi (eds.), *India and Central Asia* (New Delhi: Anamaya Publishers, 2004), p. 19.
2. Dixit.
3. E. Ahmed, "A mirage Mis-named Strategic Depth", *Al Ahram Weekly*, Issue no. 392, August 27-September 02, 1998; A. Rashid, "Rise of Militant Islam", interview at the Institute of International Studies, UC Berkeley, March 26, 2002; K. Ahmed (editor of the Lahore-based *The Friday Times*), interview at the Institute of International Studies, UC Berkeley, February 19, 2002, both available at http:// globetrotter. Berkeley.edu/people2
4. A. Rashid, "Uzbek Militants Return to Central Asia for Offensive", *Nation*, January 12, 2001.
5. According to Ramtanu Maitra, in 2000, Afghanistan accounts for about 75 per cent of the world's combined opium production, "Afghan drugs: Gold to the Taliban", *EIR Strategic Studies*, September 08, 2000, p. 60.
6. Maitra.
7. R. Bedi, "India Dabbles in the New 'Great Game'", *Jane's Intelligence Review*, June 2002.
8. Indian Foreign Secretary Kanwal Sibal's press conference on October 04, 2002, republished in *The Hindu*, October 05, 2002.
9. C. Raja Mohan India's `Pamir Knot', *The Hindu*, November 11, 2003
10. Sudha Ramachandran, "India Makes a Soft Landing in Tajikistan", *Asia Times Online*, March 03, 2007 http://www.atimes.com/atimes/South_Asia/IC03Df01.html
11. Uddipan Mukherjee, "Presidential Visit to Tajikistan: India among the Pamirs?", Article, #2972, 22 September 2009, Institute of Peace and Conflict Studies, http:// www.ipcs.org/article_details.php?articleNo=2972
12. Report available on http://www.icwa.in/crtajik.html
13. Until 2002, Dushanbe hosted a medical facility set up by the Indian army to treat injured anti-Taliban resistance fighters at the Farkhor airfield, on Tajikistan's southern border with Afghanistan. India also used the airfield to supply the Northern Alliance with military equipment, munitions and intelligence, and to repair its combat helicopters. *Asia Times Online*, August 12, 2006, www.atimes.com;

Based on a bilateral Defense Agreement in 2001, New Delhi refurbished a Soviet-built airfield at Ainy, 25 km west of Dushanbe. The renovation, which cost India over US$70 million, included upgrading the runway, construction of the traffic control tower, hangars, and administrative buildings. Indian specialists handed over the refurbished facility to the Tajik defense ministry in 2010. *www.khovar.tj*, September 03, 2010.

14. In an annual address to the Tajik parliament in April 2008, President Rahmon said that Tajikistan has 14 per cent of the world's uranium reserves. Later that year, the Tajik parliament allowed foreign companies to extract uranium ore in the country. There have been subsequent reports of Russian and Chinese plans to mine uranium in Tajikistan, Uddipan Mukherjee, op.cit.
15. www.cacianalyst.org, September 16, 2009
16. "Tajikistan invites India to invest in hydro power", *Press Trust of India* (PTI) News Agency, September 08, 2009, http://www.dnaindia.com/world/report_tajikistan-invites-india-to-invest-in-hydro-power_1288456
17. Ben Welch, "President Patil Visits Tajikistan – India in Search of a Forward Policy?" December 23, 2009 issue of the *CACI Analyst*
18. *Direction of Trade Statistics* (DOTS), IMF, 2009.
19. "India-Tajikistan Relations", Web site of Ministry of External Affairs, Government of India, posted in August 2011 http://mea.gov.in/mystart.php?id=50044531
20. www.cacianalyst.org, September 16, 2009.
21 Dag Sourander, *Tajikistan, Country Briefing 2011*, Director General for External Policies of the Union, Policy Department, European Parliament, available on:http://www.europarl.europa.eu/meetdocs/2009_2014/documents/afet/dv/201/201106/20110606_country_briefing_tajikistan_en.pdf
22. Alexander Sodiqov, "India's Relations With Tajikistan: Beyond the Airbase", *Eurasia Daily Monitor*, vol. 8 issue 36, February 22, 2011.
23. Indrani Bagchi, "India Pressures Iran on Key Port", *The Times of India*, July 05, 2010; "India, Iran discusses Strategy in Afghanistan, Chahbahar port", *Daily News and Analysis* (DNA), August 06, 2010. http://www.dnaindia.com/india/report_india-iran-discusses-strategy-in-afghanistan-chabahar-port_1419773; "India Keen to Develop Iran's Chahbahar Port", *Dredging Today.com*, http://www.dredgingtoday.com/2010/07/27/india-keen-to-develop-iran's-chabahar-port/
24. Dag Sourander, *Tajikistan, Country Briefing 2011.*
25. Dag Sourander, *Tajikistan, Country Briefing 2011.*
26. Welch, "President Patil Visits Tajikistan – India in Search of a Forward Policy?"
27. *The Wall Street Journal*, November 30, 2011.
28. M. Bhadrakumar, "Getting the Regional Act Together", *The Hindu*, August 27, 2011.
29. Ajai Shukla from Kabul, *Business Standard*, June 07, 2011.
30. "Tajikistan and Afghanistan", Institute for the Study of War (ISW), Washington DC,

August 26, 2007. http://www.understandingwar.org/tajikistan-and-afghanistan; "Tajikistan/Afghanistan: Road Bridge Opens With Aim Of Strengthening Trade", Nizhny Pyanz, Tajikistan, August 26, 2007, *RFE/RL*

31. Dag Sourander, *Tajikistan, Country Briefing 2011.*
32. Indrani Bagchi, "India to Spend Tentacles into Central Asia via Iran", *The Times of India*, March 13, 2012.

3. Historical Consciousness and Contemporary Historical Research in Uzbekistan

Ravshan Madjidovich Abdullaev

Every ethnic and social community has a range of historical ideas about its origin, most important events in its history, previous public figures, and prominent personalities, the interrelationship of its history with the history of other nations and the entire human community. Historical consciousness, which is formed in the course of studying history, is one of the most important factors in determining the spiritual order and state of a nation. The importance of forming historical consciousness and saving historical memory in modern conditions is very significant—it provides awareness to the human community of the fact that they constitute a single nation associable by common historical fate, tradition, culture, language, and common psychological traits.

The increased need in forming historical consciousness is also caused by transition from one model of society to another which, in particular, the post-Soviet countries are experiencing now. It is accompanied by dramatic processes in the spiritual life of society, thereby, bringing about significant changes in public opinion, including the historical one, and revisions of moral values and behavioural orientations. After the collapse of the Soviet Union, most former Soviet republics including Uzbekistan, witnessed the formation of new political-ideological and cultural context, when society began to clearly show signs of resuscitation of those national and spiritual values, which for decades were either ignored, or deliberately interpreted negatively. Countries that declared their independence were in need of national symbols and priorities aimed at preserving ethnic and cultural identity, and resolving the task of national consolidation. To the national elites of these states, the appeal to the most brilliant, important pages of their national history looked quite natural.

It is a well-known fact that the stable functioning of any social system is largely linked with positive historical memory, which directly or indirectly affects the process of identity formation of various communities and ethnic groups. Pride in the historical past of their own people is among the major constituents of historical consciousness, which determines its national dignity. The loss of these traits leads to the formation of colonial psychology, that is, people start to feel their inferiority, underdevelopment, lack of prospects, as well as senses of frustration, and spiritual discomfort appears.

It is well known that for many years, the Soviet government implemented imperial national policy in Uzbekistan, which was based on the idea of alienation of people from its real, unfalsified history, culture and the transformation of its representatives, in the final reckoning, into those deprived of historical memory—mankurts, persons oblivious of their origin and home. People were persistently instilled with the idea that their historical development, prior to the establishment of the Soviet power allegedly led to a 'social crisis', 'continuous wars', 'ethnic hatred' and could not ensure prosperity and decent life in the future. Only the Bolsheviks—the bearers of the communist ideology, as the new messiahs—were destined by the history itself to 'open eyes' to modern 'pagans', and show them the way to the 'truth' and 'social progress'.

It must be admitted that the Bolsheviks were able to create a new type of an empire, which was obviously different from the classical-type empires of the past times, and the type that was not a mere continuation of the old Tsarist Empire. Abdurakhman Avtorkhanov, a renowned dissident and Sovietologist, in this connection, wrote:

> "The Soviet empire, above all, is an *ideocratic* empire. Therefore, any comparison of it with the old empires is not only erratic, but it is simply misleading: we overestimate the possibility and extent of the old empires and underestimate the potential and the horrific consequences with which the successful implementation of the ideocratic program

of the Soviet empire on a global scale are fraught, not only for the external world, but also for the people of the Soviet Union itself. After all, the Bolsheviks could realize their goal, only sacrificing their own population and bringing into action the genocide of other peoples. The Soviet type of imperialism seeks not merely the conquest of foreign peoples and appropriating their wealth, but it still contemplates the ultimate goal to proselyte the conquered peoples in the new communist faith in order to impose them a communist way of life."[1]

One of the most important elements of the so-called 'communist way of life' and 'communist ideology' in the interpretation of the Bolsheviks was demonstrative distancing from the 'false' national spiritual values that failed to fit into the narrow confines of class ideology. Of course, the filter of this ideology also 'infiltrated' the whole history of the Uzbek people (as well as of other people of the USSR) and above all, those of memorable scenes and pages, which could, in the opinion of the Soviet leadership, 'provoke' the growth of national consciousness and 'intoxicate the masses with the poison of nationalism'. Proclaiming themselves internationalists, the Bolsheviks demanded that the national historians should not 'rake over the dust and ashes' of the past of their people, and should not cultivate 'reactionary' traditions and values. Any attempt at an alternative assessment of significant developments and events of national history, culture, and spiritual life was fraught with the most negative consequences (up to repression). Facts of manifestations and adoption of national identity evoked 'inadequate reaction of the authorities or the press, and desire to 'apply an epithet' of 'nationalists' to all the natives-bearers of national feelings, and the usual reflex—to wag finger or shake fist at those reluctant and being out of step in motion to the merging and dissolution in the unified Soviet people in a single, in a new historical community'.[2]

The establishment of dictatorship of one party and one ideology in the Soviet Union, the suppression of all nonconformist forms, suppressing the slightest attempt to appeal to national pride and national consciousness—slowly but surely led the Soviet country to the innermost crisis, and as the events have shown, to its final dissolution. In this connection, the words of the famous Russian politician, former Minister of Foreign Affairs of the Provisional Government P.N. Milyukov, uttered in exile in the mid-1920s, were:

> "Anti-national policy directed by the national majority against minorities ... was extremely rarely crowned with success. For the most part, it led to exasperation, worsening, and aggravation of relations, to the painful growth of persecuted national feeling, to weakening, and at the first opportunity, even to the disintegration of states allowed themselves to wage such a policy."[3]

Today, after long years of national humiliation, the Uzbeks, alongside with the other nations of the former Soviet Union finally got a historic opportunity—to exercise their right to self-determination and independent living. After the collapse of the Soviet Union and after the first euphoria and ecstatic affection of gaining sovereignty gradually began to subside, the Uzbeks had clearly understood that independence is only the first step to a long-awaited goal, and this is not a panacea for various social and other upheavals lying in wait for the people. It became clear to many people that such a thorny, independent path of development taken by the country would require tremendous efforts from everyone to overcome numerous complexes and stereotypes inherited from the past.

Indeed, a sense of confusion and inadequacy, and lack of faith in capabilities of the nation were typical of a certain segment of society, especially in the early years of independence. During those years, questions such as 'why we need independence', 'what does it give us', and the likes were often heard in Uzbekistan. People who asked those questions were educated in the ideals of the communist doctrine. Real socioeconomic difficulties facing the country immediately after the collapse of the Soviet Union, even stimulated more pessimistic feelings, and increased the number of those nostalgic for the old Soviet-era of general 'leveling' and relative social stability.

It is known that the phenomenon related to idealisation of history in the mass historical consciousness is especially noticeable when a cardinal change occurs in social development and social directives and views, attitudes and opinions, and practices of the recent past undergo re-evaluation. At this moment, the historical science and its researchers have an important task—to hinder 'germination of seeds of strife', of social and ethnic conflicts. In the present conditions, it is extremely important, according to a well-known Kazakh scientist-orientalist, Meruert Abuseitov, to identify those points of contact between peoples and cultures, such moments of relationships between them, which would lead to the rapprochement of different groups of mankind, to generalisation of varied and often contradictory experience.[4]

After the collapse of the Soviet Union, in many former Soviet republics, we were able to observe the complex processes of understanding and perceiving new realities, including comprehension in the context of a retrospective historical analysis. The society was split into those individuals who continued, by way of good example, to appeal to the pages of Soviet history, and those people who having strongly condemned that period, as well as many of the conceptual history of science at that time, sought to exact a peculiar 'historical revenge' for the years of national humiliation. They feverishly tried and used some historical events and subjects to justify the thesis of singularity and exclusive nature, and sometimes of 'selectness' of one or another people. Excessive love for native history could be justified in moral terms, but as for the sphere of research, it usually led (and is leading) to extreme subjectivism (in particular, in trying by all means, 'to add to the age' of its history) and ultimately, to the opposition of particular nations to other people. However, in conditions of evident polyethnic nature of Uzbekistan and quite dramatic social and property stratification started in the society, how was it possible to reconcile the people who, in particular, differently interpreted the most important and key episodes of their recent and distant country's history? What could, at least to some extent, consolidate them?

It seems that one of the ways out of this situation was an attempt to appeal to the most brilliant, important pages of national history, which could bring people into accord, rather than disunite and keep them apart. It was necessary to remember that highlighting the key points in interpretation of historical events contributes at first instance to rational and friendly coexistence of people. Otherwise, there appears suspicion, prejudice, and negative cliches, which feature to be maintained a long while, escalate social tensions and generate conflicts. We were not supposed to forget that the fruits of some historical inquiries were often used in the current political and ideological polemics, being engaged by various political forces. And in this sense, a special responsibility rests not only on members of a political class, but, of course, on historians. However, it was important to convince people that the nation that truly has a rich cultural and historical heritage has the right to hope to overcome the temporary difficulties, and begin to create the necessary conditions for the positive development of society.

It should be noted that in Uzbekistan, this historical and cultural resource has been fully utilised. A thorough study and reinterpretation of national history based on new conceptual approaches has allowed members of different social and ethnic groups to find answers to many pressing issues that were of interest to them. The new version of national history cannot satisfy everyone even now. There will always be doubters and protesters. Nevertheless, this is also natural. In a normal society, there should be a place of alternative assessment and another look at those, or other events and occurrences of the past. However, whichever were the conclusions made by the researchers and ordinary people, it is undeniable that the ongoing process of intensive reanimation of national history could not but affect the growth of political and national consciousness of the population of the republic.

Today, society experiences the growing awareness of the fact that it is impossible to overcome the complex of the decline of the state, and national inferiority inherited by many peoples from the old times, in conditions of total social pessimism and disbelief. Obviously, the dynamic and positive development of society requires a certain optimistic spiritual environment. Therefore, it seems natural that at the so-called transition and critical stages of history, the national elites of those or other societies are trying to revive the original historical and cultural heritage of their people, and to focus their attention on the most significant events and examples from the past. One such historical event in Uzbek history, which exerts a serious impact on the evolution of social and historical consciousness, and of which the modern multinational people of the republic can be proud, is Jadidism—the movement of reformers in the early 20th century, who aimed at modernising the country, and its withdrawal from the state of stagnation and isolation.

It is known that in Soviet historiography, the Jadid movement was seen as problematic. In the interpretation of its reasons and essence, the national historians had to balance between the accusation of 'bourgeois nationalism', 'Pan-Turkism' and 'Pan-Islamism'. In most publications issued in those years, we used to find the Soviet era characterisation of the image of Jadidism as purely anti-people and reactionary movement was firmly established in the minds of people.[5] At the same time, all the evidence, and testimonies, which were not fit, the ideological framework was completely swept aside. At present, thanks to a new generation of Uzbek historians and detailed study of a large body of alternative sources, we have the opportunity to evaluate a different view of Jadidism and other important aspects of the country's history of national movements. We can claim that Jadids, under the colonial regime, had managed to gain confidence and trust of dozens or even hundreds of thousands of their compatriots as they came forward with ideas of social progress and inter-ethnic accord, religious tolerance, absorption of the modern type of civilisation, different model of behaviour, and finally, gaining the national sovereignty. The Jadids were also supporters of a system of government that could provide people with civil liberties and political rights effective in democratic states. Without impinging on the fundamentals of Islam, they endeavoured to convert a traditional Uzbek society, and adapt it to the realities of contemporary time. Today, independent Uzbekistan declares the secular and democratic way of development. In this regard, an appeal to such historical precedents as Jadidism seems particularly relevant.

This historical experience has shown that the progressively thinking part of the intellectual elite of the nation is capable, even in very difficult conditions of uniting people of different ideological orientations, social, ethnic, and confessional (religious) groups in the name of progress and decent life. Nowadays, in an array of intricate questions of Uzbek history, such problems also continue to provide the greatest impact on mass historical consciousness as ethnic and ethno-political processes ongoing in Central Asia—(1) spiritual, cultural, and scientific-intellectual heritage of the people in the region, (2) nationality policy of the Russian Empire and the Soviet power in Uzbekistan, (3) the national-territorial delimitation in Central Asia and its after-effects, and (4) the history of armed resistance against the Soviet regime (known in the past as the 'Basmachi movement').

In the context of contemporary realities among the topical subject matters, is a highly relevant theme of studying the evolution of political culture of the indigenous people and their elites in conditions of tough ideological confrontation and cultural isolation. It seems that today, it is also important to understand how the process of establishing and approving the new Soviet political and ideological priorities in our society took place; how was this process combined with existence of centuries-old traditional spiritual-and-moral values; who were those in our country, after the events of October 1917, and strengthening of the totalitarian regime that resisted mechanisms aimed at deformation of the public consciousness, and how did they perform. Poorly covered in the scientific literature has remained very ambiguous and contradictory—'post-Perestroika'—period in the history of Uzbekistan, when after many years of stagnation and intolerance, the first signs of freedom of speech and political pluralism appeared.

Thus, we can summarise that in the modern science of history of Uzbekistan, the contemporary historical research which, of course, has already achieved some positive results in the process of rethinking the past, there still remains 'unestablished bounds—unexplored positions' demanding for professionals serious investigations, reasoned, argumentative and correct scientific assessment. For this, the scientific community and many ordinary people are waiting with impatience.

Notes

1. A. Avtorkhanov, *Imperia Kremlya* (Sovetskii tip kolonializma), (Vilnius, 1990), p. 8.
2. *Cherez ternii*. Moscow, 1990, p. 362.
3. P.N. Milyukov, *Natsionalnyi vopros (Proiskhozhdenie natsionalnosti i natsionalnye voprosy v Rossii),* (Prague, 1925), p. 192.
4. M. Abuseitova, *Istoria Tsentralnoi Azii: kontseptsia i realnost. Materialy mezhdunarodnoi konferentsii^ Novaya istoria Tsentralnoi Azii. Pereotsenka istorii, sovremennye problemy i podkhody*, (Tashkent, 2004), p. 19.
5. See: K. Zhitov, *Pobeda Velikoi Oktyabrskoi sotsialisticheskoi revolyutsii v Uzbekistane.* Tashkent, 1957; *Pobeda Oktyabrskoi revolyutsii v Turkestane,* (Tashkent, 1958); I. Dodonov Kh. Inoyatov, *Pobeda Sovetskoi vlasti v Uzbekistane,* (Tashkent, 1967).

4. Transformation of *Baatyr* in the Formation of Nation-State in Kyrgyzstan

İlhan Şahin

The term '*baatyr*' meaning 'brave, hero' and 'valiant', is used in a wide geographical area and context in Central Asia.[1] In this connection, Kyrgyz society, both in the past and present, associates its nomadic culture primarily with its *baatyr's*. As far as it is understood from written and oral sources, the concept of *baatyr* emerged in Kyrgyz society together with the nomadic life style. It became not only a part of the national and cultural values but also an ideological factor in the communal security of Kyrgyz society. This article tries to explore the issue of 'heroism' in the context of Central Asian nations; it focuses particularly on the concept of *baatyr* in Kyrgyz society taking into consideration, how this concept was transformed in different eras and with the formation of the nation-state among the Kyrgyz people.

Baatyr in Pre-Soviet Times

It is worth emphasising that Kyrgyz society has two main social and political structures—On Kanat (Right Wing) and Sol Kanat (Left Wing). Each wing consists of clans called uruus. The clans are in turn divided into sub-clans known as uruk. Each clan is independent of one another, living in separate geographical locations.[2] Administratively these clans had been led by leaders, such as biy, bek, manap and datka. Here we can mention that *baatyrs* were leaders among the society, and at the same time, they were guards of the uruus. This meant that each uruu or clan had one or more *baatyrs* who were always together with the ordinary people.[3] In this respect, the central idea of this section is that in pre-Soviet times the traditional *baatyrs* of the Kyrgyz society emerged by themselves usually based on their own personal capacities, abilities and skills, as well as their heroic characteristics. That is, in the emergence of a *baatyr* in a clan, a person must possess strong physical, mental and leadership abilities. These abilities consisted of personal habits or deeds, such as gathering brave men called djigits around him, good horseback riding, and weapon usage.

The Manas *Baatyr* of Kyrgyz society is an accurate example for this case. As far as it is understood from the general text of the Manas epic, Manas is a talented, charismatic, and physically strong leader who emerged from the society by himself. According to the Manas epic, one of the most important features of Manas is that when he was thirteen years old, he gathered thirty nökörs (valiant) around him,[4] launched attacks against the Kalmyks, and united the dispersed Kyrgyz clans showing the most important features of a real leader. Indeed, the most popular expression related to Manas is:

Kulaalı taptap kuş kıldım	I made a Hawk out of a feeble bird
Kurama cıyıp curt kıldım	I made a nation out of dispersed people

There are also other political, social, and geographical reasons for the emergence of the *baatyrs*. One of the most important features is that each clan had an independent social and political structure and they needed fighters like *baatyrs* for self-protection. In this context, it is very useful to recall an expression thought to have originated with Asan Kaygy, a wise man and critic of the steppe who lived between the end of the 14th and middle of the 15th century, an expression which reflects the characteristics of a *baatyr*:[5]

Coodan suurup albasa	If s/he cannot take away from the enemy
Colun tosup barbasa	If s/he cannot cut a path to the enemy
Kalkka nazar salbasa	If s/he cannot take the responsibility of his people
Başın baylap barbasa	If s/he cannot face death
Baatırlıktan ne payda?	What is the use of being a *baatyr*?

This expression reflects some of the characteristics of a *baatyr* among Kyrgyz society in the past. Besides, a proverb related to the *baatyr* is 'er djigit el kamyn djeyt'. This proverb is very important because it bears a similarity in meaning with the expression of Asan Kaygy. In addition, we should not neglect the social and geographical factors in the emergence of a *baatyr*. In short, the *baatyrs* among the Kyrgyz were primarily responsible for the political security of the related clan, and as well as the protection of inhabited places in the region since it was a time when the weak could easily be eliminated by the 'strong' in intense struggles.

In giving further examples, from the middle of the 17th century Kalmyk attacks started to deeply affect Kyrgyz and Kazakh societies.[6] The *baatyrs* began to emerge in more specific areas, and of course, in considerable numbers. Thus, Djaiyl *Baatyr* and Er Soltonay *Baatyr* from the Solto uruu, Atake *Baatyr* from the Sarybagysh uruu struggled to unite the Kyrgyz clans against the Kalmyks. The Kalmyk attacks left unforgettable traces in the memory of the people. There is a famous expression that reflects a real event at that time: "Kazak kaiyng saap/ Kyrgyz Ysar Kölöpkö kachkanda." It is very clear from this expression that after the invasion of the Kalmyks, Kazakhs leaving their homeland suffered from hunger, and they drank the water of the beech wood. The Kyrgyz had to migrate through the (Hisor) and Kulyab (Kulab) areas to Tajikistan. Also, there is another expression among the Kazakhs related to this event: 'Aktaban shubyryndy' which means 'exodus on barefoot'. This expression is very important in the emergence of *baatyrs* under which conditions the above-mentioned heroes or *baatyrs* emerged.

Following the Kalmyk invasion, struggles began between the Kyrgyz and Kazakhs in the 1770s because of territorial issues. At that time some of the *baatyrs*, such as Ormon *Baatyr* and Törökeldi *Baatyr* from Sarybagysh uruu; Sadyr *Baatyr* and Alybek *Baatyr* from Saiak uruu, and Bürgö *Baatyr* from Kushchu uruu, emerged as distinguished people from their uruus, and played a significant role in the protection of their territorial areas. These struggles continued for a long time, followed by struggles with other nations. For instance, many local, regional, and national *baatyrs* appeared especially during the struggles with the

Chinese and Russians. It must in addition be taken into consideration that the emergence of these *baatyrs* was affected by internal factors, such as conflicts and struggles among the Kyrgyz uruus, as well.

As far as it is reflected in the epics of the Kyrgyz, being a *baatyr* in the Kyrgyz tradition is not only a feature for men. It is possible to find the names of some young girls or women as *baatyrs* in Kyrgyz epics and traditions. We can name Kyz Saikal,[7] Djanyl Myrza[8] and Kuialy *Baatyr*[9] as female *baatyrs*, for example. In the Manas epic, the female *baatyr*, Kyz Saikal, fights with Manas *Baatyr* in the battlefield. We can, therefore, say that the *baatyrs* are trusted persons who embody the moral values of Kyrgyz society.

***Baatyr* in Soviet Times**

Kyrgyz culture, including beliefs, habits, customs and traditions, as well as social and administrative institutions such as manap, bay, biy were banned in the earliest years of the Soviet system. There was an ideal of creating a new Soviet man in this embodiment of the Soviet Union. However, it is worth noting that the Soviet system began to benefit from the essential values of Kyrgyz society and kept these values alive for the success of the system over time. A typical example is the concept of the *baatyr*, which is why it was kept alive by the Soviet regime. On the other hand, some administrative and social institutions were banned by the regime. As far as it is understood the concept of *baatyr*, although it is a former institution, was seen as important for the future of the regime and especially in terms of establishing good relations with the local people. This is why the Soviet regime changed the concept of *baatyr* appropriately according to the needs of the system and integrated it into various areas.

In this context, the concept of *baatyr* was given a very important function for 'the creation of a new Soviet man', such as integrating, uniting and motivating people in moral values. The rewards related to the *baatyr* can be divided into three categories—(1) Geroi Sovetskogo Soyuza/Sovetter Soyuzunun *Baatyry* (Hero of the Soviet Union), (2) Geroi Sotsialisticheskogo Truda/Sotsialisttik Emgektin Baatry (Hero of Socialist Labour), and (3) Mat' Geroinya/*Baatyr* Ene (Mother Heroine).

Geroi Sovetskogo Soyuza (Hero of the Soviet Union)—the highest honorary title—was established by a decision made in the USSR on April 16, 1934. The title could be given to both Soviet civilians and soldiers for heroic acts. It was first given to a pilot, Anatoliy Lyapidevskiy on April 20, 1934. The last recipient of the award was diver Leonid Mikhailovich Solodkov, given on December 24, 1991. But at this time the Soviet Union had already collapsed. So he could not receive his award as a Soviet citizen. During the Soviet period over 12,000 persons were awarded this title.[10] There were also some Kyrgyz who received this title, such as Dair Asanov and Kalyinur Usenbekov. In appearance, this medal symbolises a five-pointed golden star, and this award could be received more than once.

Geroy Sotsiyalisticheskogo Truda (Hero of Socialist Labour) was a title that was established on December 27, 1938. It was an honorary title in the Soviet Union for exceptional achievements in economy and culture. In addition, according to instructions, a person who takes this title was given a medal known as the Lenin Ordeni as well as a certificate of honour. Besides, being an honourable citizen of the Soviet Union was highly appreciated and was accompanied by extra moral support as well. For instance, for those who were awarded this title more than once, a bronze sculpture was erected for them in their home countries. For example, among the *baatyrs* of the Kyrgyz Republic, a bronze statue was made for a kolkhoz worker, Zuurakan Kainazarova because she received the award three times. Over 20,000 people were awarded this title in the Soviet period. The last recipient was a Kazakh singer Bibigul Tulegenova on December 21, 1991.[11] Apart from Zuurakan Kainazarova, several Kyrgyz received this title, such as kolkhoz workers Kerimbübü Shopokova and Ülbüzkan Atabekova, shepherd Tashtanbek Akmatov and the famous author, Chingiz Aitmatov.

Mat' Geroinya (Mother Heroine) was a title established on July 08, 1944 and given to mothers of ten or more children. This title was given to 4,54,142 women between October 27, 1944 and November 14, 1991.[12] This honorary title for women was a gold star with pure silver as well as a certificate, which gave a number of privileges, such as the payment of public utilities and food supplies and other goods. Among the mother heroines of the Kyrgyz Republic are Gülbübü Mövküshova (13 children) and Zina Abdykasymova (10 children); they both gave interview to us.[13] In my opinion, since it was established at the end of the Second World War, this title could have been given with the hope of increasing the population.

Baatyr in Post-Soviet Times

Following the dismantling of the Soviet Union, public commemorations in different regions began remembering the *baatyrs* as the ancestors of Kyrgyz society. In this respect, here our main idea is that in the post-Soviet period, relatives of the *baatyrs* became the main vehicle for commemorating or rebirth of the concept of *baatyr*. As an example, it is worth noting the commemoration of Djarban (Jarban) by his relatives and the way they remember their *baatyr*. Because of very limited written sources related to Djarban, the following section is based on what his descendants and villagers say about him.

Revival of a *Baatyr*

Djarban has been revived in a village called Madaniyat, thus indicating the importance of the *baatyr* in Kyrgyz society. This village is in the Chui raion (district) of Chui province. There are 160 households in the village of Madaniyat in which 760 people live. Approximately 90 per cent of these people belong to those who say they are the descendants of Djarban. According to the villagers, Djarban who belongs to the Sarybagysh uruu (clan) used to live in the Atbashy region in the area of Naryn in the 17th century. The villagers tell that Djarban is named after the way he was born because they had made an operation for his birth.[14] Based on rumours, some researchers cite that Djarban and his people emigrated from Chui region to the mountainous regions of Naryn because of Kalmyk pressure.[15]

According to genealogy, the real name of Djarban, who is the son of Manap Biy, was Sütüke. In addition, the name of his brother was Sütöy. Djarban is a nickname for Sütüke, which is widely used by the inhabitants of the village of Madaniyat and especially by the descendants of Djarban.[16] His father Manap Biy was also a *baatyr*. Manap Biy is quoted as being a hero in the tribal conflicts between the Kyrgyz and Kazakhs. As far as it is understood, by this time the descendants of Djarban consisted of a subtribe called the Djarban uruu, which belongs to the Sarybagysh uruu. Around ten families are said to have immigrated from Atbashy to Chui area, among them some families known as the family of Tynalu uulu Belek, Tynalu uulu Bapy, Mambet Kazy and Mambet Kerim, etc.[17] These families maintain even at present a close relationship with their relatives who remained in Atbashy and other regions. This situation must be an indication of the time of the said immigration, which appears to have taken place in the 1930s. These years coincide with the establishment of kolkhozes and sovkhozes in the Soviet period. Here one should note that new villages and raions (districts) were established in this period. One of these villages is the village of Madaniyat. The early inhabitants of this village are those families who came from Atbashy. Thus, the village of Madaniyat was established by some members of the Djarban uruu. Later on, immigrants coming from different regions also settled in the village of Madaniyat. These latecomers belonged to some clans or sub-clans called Djetigen, Saiak, Monoldor, Manap and Djumash uulu. They joined the social network of the village called the Djarban Yntymagy, which means social and economic solidarity of the village in good and bad days (Jakshylyk and Jamandyk) like marriage and death.[18]

According to Abramzon, who conducted ethnographic field research in 1953-54, 80 per cent of the population of the village of Madaniyat consisted of people of the Djarban uruu belonging to the Sarybagysh uruu. Abramzon also indicates that six households from the same tribe were in the village of Ak-Beshim village in the Chui raion (district), seven households in Ataika village in the Bystrovska (Kemin) raion (district), four households in Ak-Beshim village in the Kulanak raion (district) in Naryn province, seventeen households in Koshoy-Korgon village in the Atbashy raion (district), and eight households in Djergetal village in the Naryn raion. Apart from these, 30 per cent of the population of the

Shamshy kolkhoz in the Kochkor raion (district) consisted of people of the Djarban uruu.[19] All of this shows us that the members of Djarban uruu are dissipated in a comparatively large geographical area.

Following the dismantling of the Soviet Union, in Kyrgyzstan local and regional activities reflect a return to Kyrgyz national traditions and culture. In this regard, the revival of a *baatyr* is being realised in the village of Madaniyat. One of the features of this village is that among the villagers there are many educated Kyrgyz, including businessmen and scientists, such as Oskon Osmonov, Salmoor Alymkulov, Ruslan Arzymatov, Mambet Kerimov, Kuban Beyshembayev, Altynbek Ismailov and Almaz Ismailov. Many of them are of Djarban descent.[20] These educated people led the villagers after 1991 to erect a commemorative monument in the village to honour the memory of 83 villagers who lost their lives in the Second World War. Later on, these pioneers led the villagers in the revival activity of the Djarban *Baatyr*. To this end, the villagers decided to raise a commemorative marble monument on which a representative picture was engraved.[21] This initiative and the respectful attitude of the descendents of Djarban prove that Djarban *Baatyr* has survived in the memory of the people. Here it is worth mentioning that the revival of Djarban owes much to the nomadic oral history of the Kyrgyz people. However, there was a problem in connection with the said monument: Djarban lived in the 17th century, and there was no drawing at hand. This problem was solved by using an earlier picture of one of the descendants of Djarban, namely Berdibek Ismailov, born in 1943. All expenses related to the construction of the monument were met by the villagers.[22]

The opening ceremony of the Djarban monument took place in 2003. On this occasion, all the relatives of Djarban living in Atbashy, Djumgal and Kochkor were invited to the ceremony. The presence of a crowd of Djarban descendants in the village of Madaniyat on this occasion shows clearly that not only the people keep their beliefs in their *baatyr* but also the privilege of being a 'Djarban'. This fact explains the continuing importance of tribal solidarity through the revival of *baatyrs*. Official representatives were also present at the opening ceremony. According to Kyrgyz tradition, on this opening a prayer and Koran reading. and a large banquet were organised.

Those who came to participate in the ceremony from Atbashy brought a horse offered for the meal during the banquet.[23] All of this constitutes a real example of the revival of a local *baatyr* during the post-Soviet period. As for the revival of Manap Biy, father of Djarban *Baatyr*, construction of a commemorative monument devoted to him began immediately after the building of the monument to Djarban *Baatyr*, According to the descendants of Djarban *Baatyr*,[24] Manap Biy was a more important, and distinguished *baatyr* compared to Djarban. In other words, while Djarban *Baatyr* has the character of being a local *baatyr*, Manap Biy is known as a regional *baatyr*. Here it is worth mentioning that more people than those who participated in the commemoration of Djarban were involved in the building of a monument for Manap Biy. In the end, the monument in memory of Manap Biy was constructed and placed at the entrance of Tokmok city.[25] This monument was also inaugurated with the presence of a large community and a great ceremony in 2009.

Two particularities attract attention when comparing the two monuments. The monument of Djarban *Baatyr* is in a village while the monument of Manap Biy is in a larger town capital of Chui province. The second point is that the Djarban *Baatyr* monument is smaller than the Manap Biy monument. This comparison shows that the people accept Djarban as a local *baatyr* and his father Manap Biy, as a regional and more important *baatyr*. The second important activity in relation with the revival of *baatyrs* in Kyrgyzstan in the transition period consists of the increase in publishing various articles and books, conferences and scientific gatherings. Thus, the background literature is being enriched. The main point to note is that the revival process of the *baatyrs* stems from the private initiatives of their descendants who meet the related expenses partly or fully. In this connection, publications and academic and popular meetings for various *baatyrs*, such as Djaiyl *Baatyr*,[26] Shabdan *Baatyr*,[27] Tailak *Baatyr*,[28] Nurdöölöt *Baatyr*,[29] Boronbai *Baatyr*,[30] Sadyr Ake,[31] Balbai *Baatyr*,[32] Baizak *Baatyr*,[33] Bürgö *Baatyr*,[34] Satykey *Baatyr*,[35] Alymbek Han[36] and Nüzüp Biy[37] are being organised. In the meantime, it is possible to find various publications related to Djarban *Baatyr* and his father, Manap Biy.[38]

Following the transition period, it seems that a strong interest in the revival of the concept of *baatyr* by the Kyrgyz state was not demonstrated in the early years of this period. However, an increasing interest can be seen over time. This may result from the creation and reestablishment of a new state. However, the Jogorku Kenesh (Supreme Council) took a decision on June 26, 1996 related to the state awards of the Kyrgyz Republic; it was approved by President Askar Akayev on July 10, 1996. Thus, the title of Kyrgyz El *Baatyry*, meaning Hero of the Kyrgyz People, was established by the Kyrgyz Republic. This title has started to be given to persons who made significant contributions to the country and people of Kyrgyztan and served for the future and independence of the Kyrgyz Republic. In addition, all rights and status in the Soviet Union related to the title have been preserved by the Kyrgyz state. Meanwhile, the title of *Baatyr* of the Kyrgyztani People was given to persons who gave superior service during the Soviet period. A medal of first degree called Akshumkar (White Eagle) and certificate of honour of the Kyrgyz Republic are given to the holders of this title. Several persons have received the title of *Baatyr* of the Kyrgyz people, such as Tugelbai Sydykbekov, Chyngyz Aitmatov, Turgunbai Sadykov, Salican Sharipov, Turdakun Usupaliyev, Sabira Kumushaliyeva, Asankan Cumakmatov and Mambet Mamakeev in the period of President Askar Akaev; Absamat Masaliyev, Tölögön Kasymbekov, Süyünbai Eraliyev, Sooranbai Cusuyev and Ernist Akramov in the period of President Kurmanbek Bakiev and Mirsaid Mirrahimov, Kuluypa Kunduchalova, Aliyasbek Alymkulov, Beksultan Djakiyev, Dooronbek Sadyrbayev, Iskhak Razzakov and Mitalip Mamytov in the period President of Roza Otunbayeva.[39] The most important feature of this title is that the official language in the medal and the text of the certificate is in the Kyrgyz language. Apart from this title, if a mother has at least eight children, she is given the title of '*Baatyr* Ene' meaning 'Hero Mother'.

Conclusion

The clan structure and the idea of belonging to a 'clan' played a very important role in the emergence of the *baatyr* in Kyrgyz society. Although Kyrgyz society at present displays a settled way of life, there still exists a sense of clan belonging, and the structure of the clan is still significant. Therefore, *baatyrs* were revived again after 1991 especially through the deeds of their descendants. In addition, this traditional concept, which is deeply rooted in hundreds of years, was effectively used in the creation of a 'new Soviet citizen' in the period of the Soviet Union. It is a fact that Kyrgyz society did not forget their traditional institutions at the time of the Soviet regime. It is clearly shown that after the collapse of the Soviet Union, the revival of the *baatyrs* was first initiated by their descendants. The pioneers of the revival and introduction of the *baatyrs* to the public are the related clans themselves. Djarban *Baatyr* is a typical example of this. Djarban is a hero who lived probably in the 17th century and currently he is the spiritual leader of his generation. They, specifically the descendants of Djarban in the village, say with pride that they are from the Djarban line. Even the people who live in other regions of Kyrgyzstan and who see themselves as the generation of Djarban still accept Djarban as their ancestor. This geographically widely spread generation of Djarban and their close relationships to each other shows that they were keeping tight solidarity bonds even in the oppressive times of the Soviets. Such a belonging to clan unity and solidarity definitely creates a social identity among the people. This kind of bond around a spiritual leader creates a basis for the formation of a larger union. The cultural aspects of these formations, specifically after 1991, must have played a very important role in the nation-state building of Kyrgyz society.

Notes

1. On the use and etymology of this word, see E. V. Sevortyan, *Etimologicheskiy Slovar Tyurkskih Yazykov*, (Moskva 1978), pp. 82-85.
2. For a field study on the geographical distribution, genealogy and ethnography of the Kyrgyz *uruus* in the 1950s see Ya. R. Vinnikov, "Rodo-plemennoy postav i raccelenie kirgizov na territorii Yujnoy Kirgizii", *Trudy kirgizskoy arkheologo-etnograficheskoy ekspedichii*, I, (Moskva 1956), pp. 136-181; S. M. Abramzon, "Etnicheskiy sostav kirgizskogo naseleniya Severnoy Kirgizii", *Trudy kirgizskoy arkheologo-etnograficheskoy ekspeditsii*, IV, (Moskva 1960), pp. 3-137.
3. On the one hand, the terms *er* and *alp* were sometimes used instead of *baatyr* in the epics of Kyrgyz society.
4. This expression related to this feature of Manas in the Sagymbay version of the Manas

epic is: "*Otuz nökör kashynda/Byiyl on üch djashynda/Azemil suunun bashynda*" (*Manas: Kyrgyz Elinin Baatyrdyk Eposu I Kitep*), (Bishkek 1995), p. 279, couplets: 658-660.

5. On this expression, see A. M. Eshiev, *Orto Türk Doorundagy Pedagogikalyk Oylor*, (Bishkek 2006), p. 254.
6. For more information on this matter, see I. Ya. Zlatkin, *Istoriya Djungarckogo Hanstva 1635-1758*, Moskva 1983; V. A. Moiseev, *Djungarskoe Xansvo i Kazakhi XVII-XVIII vv.*, (Alma-Ata 1991).
7. *Manas Sagymbai Orozbak uulu'nun Varianty*, II- Kitep, (Frunze 1980), pp. 49-69.
8. See *Sarindji, Bököi. Djanyl Myrza (A. Chorobaevin Aituusu Boyuncha)*, Bishkek 1998, pp. 209-372; *M. Musulmankulovdun Aituusu Boyuncha*, pp. 373-447.
9. B. Maksütov, *Seytek Baatyr Baiany*, (Bishkek 2007), pp. 130-162; A. Djaynakova, "Kuialy", *Manas Entsiklopediya*, I, (Bishkek 1995), pp. 358-359.
10. http://en.wikipedia.org/wiki/Hero_of_the_Soviet_Union
11. http://en.wikipedia.org/wiki/Hero_of_Socialist_Labour
12. http://en.wikipedia.org/wiki/Mother_Heroine
13. Gülbübü Mövküshova (1935-) is an inhabitant of Madaniyat village, Chui *raion* (district), Chui Province: interview on February 12, 2012, the village of Madaniyat, Kyrgyzstan; Zina Abdykasımova (1941-) is an inhabitant of Madaniyat village, Chui *raion*, Chui Province: interview on February 12, 2012, the village of Madaniyat, Kyrgyzstan.
14. Tentimish Ibraimov (1954-) is the head of Madaniyat Village Council, Chui *raion*, Chui Province: interview on February 12, 2012, the village of Madaniyat, Kyrgyzstan; Atyrkul Ibraimova (1959-) is an inhabitant of Madaniyat village, Chui *raion*, Chui Province: interview on February 12, 2012, the village of Madaniyat, Kyrgyzstan.
15. See Belek Soltonov, *Kyzyl Kyrgyz Taryhy*, (Bishkek 1993), pp. 102 and 1099; Doolotbek Saparaliev, *Vzaimootnosheniya kyrgyzckogo naroda s russkim i sosednimi narodami v XVIII* v., (Bishkek 1995), p. 29.
16. For the list of geneology related to the Djarban, see S. Attokurov, *Kırgız Sandjırası*, (Bishkek 1995), p. 122. Here this name is mentioned as only Djarban; also see S. M. Abramzon, Ibid, pp. 34-35 (the family tree of the Sarybagysh clan) and Belek Soltonoev, *Ibid*, pp. 102 and 109); S. A. Alymkulov, *Bardygy Özübüzgö Bailanyshtuu*, (Bishkek 2005), p. 28; Oskon Osmonov, *Manap Biy Degen Kim Bolgon, Manapçylyk Degen Emne?*, (Bishkek 2007) (on the last page of the booklet).
17. Asanbek Kakeev (1962-) is an inhabitant of Madaniyat village, Chui *raion*, Chui Province: interview on February 12, 2012, the village of Madaniyat, Kyrgyzstan; Kalbubu Ilebaieva (1961-) is an inhabitant of Madaniyat village, Chui *raion*, Chui Province: interview on February 12, 2012, the village of Madaniyat, Kyrgyzstan; Kanybek Abdykasymov (1961-) is an inhabitant of Madaniyat village, Chui *raion*, Chui Province: interview on February 12, 2012, the village of Madaniyat, Kyrgyzstan; Malika Usonova (1964-) is an inhabitant of Madaniyat village, Chui *raion*, Chui

Province: interview on February 12, 2012, the village of Madaniyat, Kyrgyzstan.

18. Kudaibergen Tatanov (1932-) is an inhabitant of Madaniyat village, Chui *raion*, Chui Province: interview on December 30, 2008, the village of Madaniyat, Kyrgyzstan; Nasip Tatanova (1938-) is an inhabitant of Madaniyat village, Chui *raion*, Chui Province: interview on December 30, 2008, the village of Madaniyat, Kyrgyzstan; Asanbek Kakeev; Ainura Omurakunova (1967-) is an inhabitant of Madaniyat village, Chui *raion*, Chui Province: interview on February 12, 2012, the village of Madaniyat, Kyrgyzstan.
19. See S. M. Abramzon, Ibid, p. 38. For a translation of this article into Kyrgyz, see S. M. Abramzon, *Kyrgızy cana Kyrgyzstan Taryhy Boyuncha Tandalma Emgekter*, (Bishkek 1999), s. 668 (The percentage related to the Shamshy kolkhoz is not mentioned in the Kyrgyz version).
20. Interview with Asanbek Kakeev, Tentimish Ibraimov, and Atyrkul Ibraimova.
21. Interview with Asanbek Kakeev, Ainura Omurakunova, andTentimish Ibraimov.
22. Interview with Tentimish Ibraimov and Asanbek Kakeev.
23. Suusar Karybekova (1954-) is an inhabitant of Madaniyat village, Chui *raion*, Chui Province: interview on February 12, 2012, the village of Madaniyat, Kyrgyzstan. Also interview with Ainura Omurakunova, Tentimish Ibraimov, and Asanbek Kakeev.
24. Interview with Tentimish Ibraimov and Atyrkul Ibraimova.
25. Interview with Tentimish Ibraimov and Atyrkul Ibraimova.
26. *Djaiyl Baatyr: Taryh, Uchur djana Kelechek, El Aralyk İlmiy-praktikalyk Konferentsiyanın Materialdarı*, (Bishkek 2006).
27. *Shabdan Baatır: Epoha i Lichnost*, (Bishkek, 1999).
28. Abdykalık Chorobaev, *Tailak Baatyr*, (Bishkek, 2002).
29. Emilbek Kaptagaev, *Nurdöölöt Baatyr Baiany*, (Bishkek, 2011).
30. Ernis Tursunov, *Boronbai*, (Bishkek, 2004).
31. Akmat Karybai uulu, *Sadyr Ake*, (Bishkek, 2002).
32. Ernis Tursunov, *Balbai djana Anyn Dooru*, (Bishkek, 1992).
33. *Baizak Tooke ulunun 175 Djyldygyna Karata Baizak Baatyr-Kemenger*, (Bishkek, 2003).
34. Kushubek Kachybekov, *Bürgö Baatyr*, (Bishkek 2003).
35. Kushubek Isan, *Satykey Baatyr*, (Bishkek, 2009).
36. Djanar Kenchiev, *Alymbek Han*, (Bishkek, 2004).
37. Djeenbek Alymbaev, *Nüzüp Biy*, (Bishkek, 2000).
38. S. A. Alymkulov; Oskon Osmonov.
39. Osmonakun Ibraimov (1954-), former State Secretary of Kyrgyz Republic (2000-05): interview on March 28, 2012, Bishkek city, Kyrgyzstan.

5. Manas as a Saviour in Times of Crisis

Yunus Emre Gürbüz

After independence, Kyrgyzstan had to struggle with massive problems and undertook radical changes for democratisation and liberalisation. The economic reforms, however, dissolved economic structure, which could not be replaced by a functioning private economic system. The reforms led to the collapse of economy in 1993-94. The first celebration of Manas was after the economic collapse and Akayev's dissolution of the parliament. The second celebration of Manas was in 2011 following the fall of Bakiyev in April 2010 after a bloody resistance and the tragic events in the south of Kyrgyzstan in June 2010.

These events of 2010 showed the importance of a common idea unifying the peoples of Kyrgyzstan. In the last two decades, Kyrgyzstan was struggling to replace the ideal of the Soviet period, the new Soviet man (*novy sovetsky chelovek*), with a new form of unifying identity. During the establishment of modern states civic and ethnic nationalisms[1] offer two different, even dichotomous approaches for state-building. For a multi-national republic like Kyrgyzstan, civic nationalism seems to be the way applied for the formation of the national identity, but ethnic nationalism is not very neglected. Kyrgyzstan's post-independence period shows tendencies of an official promotion of civic nationalism and a shy nationalism. This is represented in the official symbols of Kyrgyzstan. During the celebrations of independence, however, the epic hero Manas gained prominence shadowing all other national motives. The main event of the celebrations was the opening ceremony of the Manas Monument on the main square of the capital. The symbolical value of this opening is escalated by the fact that it replaced the Freedom Monument (*Erkindik*) on the very day the freedom was being celebrated. The replacement of statues manifested the sheer need for what Manas means. Similar to

1995, Kyrgyzstan had to be reminded once again that this is just one of the harsh periods in 'their long march in history', and only unity can help them to survive.

The Kyrgyz had no written history until the 20th century. Their past had been transmitted through oral literature, and the main source of it was the Manas Epic, which is full of stories telling the sufferings of the Kyrgyz people and their stubborn resistance. In the end, they had managed to survive against all odds. The epic, thus, presents the will to survive and the possibility to overcome the difficulties. In addition to that, it was also an epic tale about the unification of the Kyrgyz tribes under their leader Manas. This idea of unification in times of hardship is the solution put forward by the rulers of Kyrgyzstan. This need rose again after summer 2010. The relative silence of big official celebrations between 1995 and 2011, and the immediate rise of Manas might is affected by nationality policies as well.

This article aims to illustrate this process with examples about the celebrations. It also aims to show the changes in ethnic and civic positions in state policies determined by recent problems of Kyrgyzstan.

Recording of the Manas Epic and His Status as a National Hero

The epic was first identified by famous Kazakh scholar Chokan Valikhanov on May 26, 1856. He listened to some part of the epic and recorded it, which was the first record of the epic. He described the epic as 'an encyclopaedic collection of the folk myths, fairytales, legends, songs, and poems, which are grouped [sic] around the main epic hero Manas'. (…) This epic depicts the Kyrgyz people's way of life, customs, traditions, morals, religious rituals, geographical and medical knowledge, diplomatic relations with other countries and peoples.[2] This first impression about the Manas Epic as the source of all knowledge about the past and present life of the Kyrgyz still remains. Manas is understood as the greatest historical achievement of the Kyrgyz people. A writer asserts, "[o]ur ancestors did not leave after them grand pyramids, nor temples (…) However we are very proud that our ancestors created and preserved for us (…) the heroic epic 'Manas'."[3] It is argued, "It played the main role in self-preservation of [the] Kyrgyz

folk as the nation… It is a sort of a banner uniting people of Kyrgyzstan in the past and for the future... The main idea of the epic is the noble idea of unification of Kyrgyz people in their struggle against enemies."[4] As this citations shows, the epic in a way employs the role of history in building a nation.

The elevation of Manas to the source of Kyrgyz nationhood was strongly supported during the Soviet period. There are 33 records of Manas (as of 1995) and 30 of them were made during the Soviet period.[5] The Soviet historiography had indeed a negative attitude towards Khans and Begs, who were criticised as oppressive, feudal despots. Manas, on the other hand, had a very different position in the academic studies of Kyrgyzstan. While the study of rulers, like Kazakh Khans or Amir Temur, is being suppressed,[6] Manas was studied by many linguists, ethnographers, folklorists, historians and musicologists.[7] When the Kyrgyz tribes were acknowledged as the Kyrgyz nation in 1920s, Manas acquired a special position in forming the Kyrgyz nation.[8] It also helped that Manas was not a real historical figure, like other khans or begs criticised by the Soviet historiography. Many articles about Manas define the period of the epic as the period of 'military democracy',[9] which was presented as a more communalist period without oppressive feudal lords. These factors both enabled and reinforced the utilisation of the epic.

The Rising Symbolic Power of Manas

The employment of Manas in public places is not a novelty of the independence but it had started in the Soviet period. The name of Manas was given to the new airport opened in 1980,[10] and in 1981, a statue of Manas was erected in front of the building of Philharmony (built in 1980). Manas Epic enjoyed always a special status in Kyrgyzstan, but this was not a central place until 1995. For example, when the national symbols of Kyrgyzstan, such as the national flag (1992), anthem (1992) or state emblem (1994),[11] were being created, Manas was not honoured. The real celebration of Manas was triggered by the United Nations' decision in 1993 declaring that '1995 is the year that marks the millennium of the Kyrgyz national epic, Manas'.[12]

The celebration was initiated by the Kyrgyz state during the economic crisis after Akayev abolished the parliament in October 1994. Akayev declared that he had to abolish the parliament to enhance his power to fight the economic crisis.[13] As the democratic course of Kyrgyzstan was fading, celebration of Manas arose as a uniting force for the people. 1995 was also the year of parliamentary and presidential elections. The parliamentary election was in February and the presidential election was in December. The celebration of Manas, which was held in the summer of 1995, can be understood as an opportunity for strengthening the morale of the population. A festival was organised on the Talas Valley next to a mausoleum attributed to Manas (kümböz Manas). The celebration turned to be a national celebration with local contests on Manas recitation, carpet weaving (*shyrdak*) and nomadic tents (*bozüy*). In the capital Bishkek a special place was built for Manas (Historical-Ethnographical Manas Village); stamps were published by the National Post Office; conferences were organised in Bishkek and Turkey (Ankara and Konya).

In his opening speech of the conference, President Akayev underlined:

> "In these dire situations the Kyrgyz people 'by feeding [them] as babies and raising [them] as birds created a homeland by gathering various ethnic groups' giving birth to brave children with high spirit like Manas, strong, joyful; and there have been times, when they protected their homeland through bloody battles with the enemy and maintained their independence.[14] (...) The people, thus, even at times of trouble, did not lose the spirit of independence."[15]
>
> "... Today, on the eve of the third millennium, our destiny, our independence is in our hands, and when relations with other countries of the world are being established, it is sufficient to look back at the historical experience of our ancestors and their spiritual legacy. We have much to learn from them. Additionally the Manas Epic teaches us a lot. It is not hard to find [solutions] even to today's social, political, ethnic, ecological, philosophical problems ... in the epic."[16]
>
> "Manas, above all, shows that the Kyrgyz people has always been a people opening arms [to other peoples] for friendship and good neighbourhood."[17]

These passages demonstrate the need of Kyrgyzstan at a very special period. The main idea was that they had to overcome ages of hardship through unity. It is interesting that there was also stress on the friendship and generosity of the Kyrgyz for the peoples in need. The economic crisis of 1993-94 pushed many non-Kyrgyz citizens of Kyrgyzstan to migration.[18] Most of those Russian or German citizens were building the base of the qualitative workforce Kyrgyzstan needed. Additionally in 1990, a bloody ethnic clash had taken place between the Kyrgyz and Uzbeks in the south of the Kyrgyz SSR. In search of protecting the multinational character of Kyrgyzstan, Akayev put forward another slogan 'Kyrgyzstan is our common home'.

In spite of the fact that the Manas Epic was indeed ethno-centric, the need for sustaining the multinationality the multi-national features of the epic were underlined. The friendship between Manas and Almambet was mentioned by Akayev as a reference for deeply rooted Kyrgyz traditions of 'friendship of nations'. Almambet was a Kalmyk, that is, a member of Manas' archenemies, but this did not prevent them from establishing a strong friendship and military cooperation.[19]

A group of advisers worked on seven advises to form new tenets for the society. Akayev mentioned these in his speech during the celebrations in 1995.[20] They were named as the 'Seven Commandments of Manas':

- Unity and Cohesion of a Nation
- International Concord, Friendship and Cooperation
- National Honour and Patriotism
- Persistent Hard Work and Progress through Education
- Humanism, Generosity and Tolerance
- Harmony with Nature
- Consolidation and Protection of Kyrgyz Statehood

These commandments were added to schoolbooks as the foundations of the Kyrgyz culture instead of novy sovetsky chelovek of the Soviet period.

The criticality and popularity of the epic is also illustrated in the name of a university founded in 1995. The Kyrgyz and Turkish states signed an agreement to open a joint university in Bishkek under the name 'Kyrgyzstan-Turkey Manas University'. However, after 1995, the celebration and even the use of Manas in general lost the enthusiasm it achieved in 1995. The teaching of Manas continued as part of the school curriculum, and Manas also kept its popularity among the masses, but it lost the support among the elite it had found in 1995.

Erica Marat argues:

> "This is because Manas bears a profoundly ethno-centric identification of patriotism and emphasizes a spirit of defending the Kyrgyz nation from outsiders while befriending neighbouring nationalities. (...) The epic was perceived as an ethnically discriminating story which was not relevant to the present day. It raised discontent among Russians and lowered their trust in the state. The civic-based policy "Kyrgyzstan is our common home" competed with Manas as an ideology and enjoyed greater popularity in these sectors of the population."[21]

Two mottos of the Kyrgyz state at this period were Manas and 'Kyrgyzstan is our common home'. Because of Kyrgyzstan's multinational characteristic, it had to be careful in forming the nation-state. Manas was, therefore, introduced not only by stressing the unity of the Kyrgyz people but also with his generosity for the non-Kyrgyz tribes. However, it seems that it was not accepted by some part of the population; thus, it neither spread to all corners of Kyrgyzstan nor the celebrations were repeated with the same enthusiasm.

In the following years, the corruption and democratisation increased, the intensification of the presidential authority continued and it was even solidified through the new Constitution of 2003. Kyrgyzstan faced more hardships during the economic crisis (1998) and fierce fights with the Islamic Movement of Uzbekistan in Batken (1999-2000). From an objective point of view, Kyrgyzstan was in need of an exemplar figure like Manas. It can be understood basically as a way for the creation of a nation-state or as a manipulative tool to distract the attention of the population.[22] The celebration of Manas, however, was not repeated. The

Manas Village in Bishkek turned to an abandoned place, only visited by some newlyweds.[23]

The end of Akayev's regime came unexpectedly by a massive uprising in March 2005. The change of the president, however, did not bring about the expected democratisation, change of the Constitution, fight against corruption and nepotism. On the contrary, under the new president corruption, nepotism, centralisation of power and suppression of democratic rights intensified. The fading importance of Manas for the state was demonstrated by an event in 2009, when UNESCO declared that 'the Kirgiz [sic] ethnic minority in China, concentrated in the Xinjiang region in the west, pride themselves on their descent from the hero Manas', and it is added 'to the Representative List of Intangible Cultural Heritage on behalf of the People's Republic of China'.[24] This decision was of course protested by Kyrgyzstan, but Kyrgyzstan's unawareness until the decision was taken illustrated the official assessment of Manas.

The Year of Troubles: 2010

Manas as a spiritual source of power for the people rose after the events of 2010, but not right after. During the popular revolt in April 2010, 87 people died. This was a big number and especially in a country, where the capital punishment was abolished three generations ago (1947), killing of citizens by the state—although they were rising against the state—had a very negative effect on the people. This was followed by the ethnic clashes in the southern Osh and Jalalabad provinces in June 2010.[25]

There was even a more serious problem recognised by many experts on Central Asia—the cleavage between the north and the south of Kyrgyzstan.[26] First, President Akayev was from the north; second, President Bakiyev was from the south, and in their overthrow, the crowd from the other half of the country played a significant role. During the ethnic clash in the south, the problem rose because of the lack of authority of the interim government, mainly based of the northerners. During the formation of the coalition after the October elections, the government was formed by a party with their powerbase in the south (Ata-Jurt) and two other parties with their powerbases in the north (Social Democratic

People's Party and Republic). This was an attempt to cover all Kyrgyz people of Kyrgyzstan.[27]

In all this turmoil, when the decentralising factors were increasing, Kyrgyzstan was in need of a uniting ideological force. Manas still had a central place in the national symbolism, he was remembered and recited, new *manaschys* were supported and artistic or touristic drawings were produced, but Manas was not yet refurbished as the main uniting force for the people. As mentioned above it was probably not accepted by the elites in general. This was illustrated when in May 2011, an MP was publicly blamed for his criticism of Manas and calling him a bandit.[28]

The signs of changes in Kyrgyz policies were seen in President Otunbayeva's speech at the VII Peoples Kurultai of Kyrgyzstan on June 18, 2011, on the anniversary of the ethnic clashes in the south. President Otunbayeva denounced Akayev's policy of 'Kyrgyzstan is our common home'. She underlined:

> "Hoping for another Soviet internationalism, we—I mean first of all the authorities—but the People's Assembly of Kyrgyzstan, have not seen, that the situation has changed dramatically."
>
> "...I do not know any mono-ethnic state or a state based on ethnic exclusivity in the world. In all civilized and uncivilized countries the foundation of the state is the law, rather than ethnicity... The Kyrgyz Republic is inhabited by representatives of many ethnic groups, about 90 different ethnic groups and all of them (...) have exactly the same rights as Kyrgyz. (...) Kyrgyz language is a state language, and it must be the language of interethnic communication... the Kyrgyz history and culture are an important educational components."

President Otunbayeva clearly declared that they have to build a nation-state with its core as the Kyrgyz language and Kyrgyz culture. She also reminds that 'ethnic diversity it is our [their] wealth'. But after twenty years of using Russian language as the interethnic language, they did not achieve anything. The lack of unification was seen as the reason of ethnic clashes, and they should be solved through unification around the culture of the titular nation. She gives examples from European countries, where the education is on the titular nation's language.[29]

The Refurbishment of Manas for National Unity

The decision to raise Manas to a more prominent position was taken just a week later after the Kurultai and a bill was signed by the President Roza Otunbayeva to promote state support to manaschys, publication of Manas textbooks, 'renaissance of historical and cultural heritage' and erecting monuments of Manas.[30] President Otunbayeva remarked:

> "You shouldn't think about Manas epic as some tale... The main cultural heritage for Kyrgyz is Manas epic ...The epic is one of components [sic] of the Kyrgyz ideology as it reflects the history of the nation. Just Manas epic united Kyrgyz [sic]... The bill on Manas epic is a historical document which will allow keeping and developing cultural heritage and national ideology of the Kyrgyz nation."[31]

Following President Otunbayeva's speech, the bill was accepted by the parliament with compassionate declarations and the Kyrgyz parliament chose to reinvent Manas as the uniting force for the peoples of Kyrgyzstan. Later some historians and politicians put forward to abolish the Freedom Monument on the main square of Bishkek and to replace it by Manas. They claimed that a woman carrying a *tündük*, as it was in the case of the Freedom Monument, is an evil omen, and that it was the reason of Kyrgyzstan's troubled years.[32]

At the end of July 2011, just a month before the celebrations of the 20th anniversary of independence, the Kyrgyz government decided to replace the Freedom Monument with a Manas monument. As the state did not have sufficient sources, a fund raising campaign has been organised to collect the required US$ 6,27,000, which was a big amount for the state.[33] The 'true patriots of the country' were called for help.[34] At about the same period, some non-governmental organisations and young members of the parliament initiated a campaign to change the name of Bishkek to

Manas. Their declared reason was that 'the psychology of the people will change immediately with renaming'.[35] The name of Bishkek did not change, but the need to spread Manas' 'power of unification' continued. Prime Minister Atambayev declared that a Manas Monument would be installed in the biggest southern city, Osh. He said about the reason of it that they were doing this 'as a reminder of Manas' main commandment: the people of Kyrgyzstan are one and are made up of different peoples. He brought it together, and we must not allow it to be broken into pieces'.[36]

During the opening ceremony of the Manas Monument in Bishkek on the 20th anniversary of independence, Prime Minister Atambayev said that 'everything in this world is symbolic'. His speech was:

> "I want to mention that the statue of Manas arrived in Kyrgyzstan in kadyr-tun (sacred night of the Muslim fasting), and was installed on the sacred day of Orozo Ait [month of Ramadan]. (…) I am definitely sure that with the advent of Manas happiness, prosperity, unity and brotherhood will come in our country."
> "We must never forget the commandments of Manas, who always called for unity and brotherhood. He once managed to unite separate peoples in the Kyrgyz people."[37]

The cult of Manas with all these Islamic motives related to sacredness was revived because of crisis. The crisis this time seems to be related to the failure in building the Kyrgyz nation. The speeches during the celebrations of Manas show the seriousness of the north-south rift and secession. The slogans written at the bottom of the monument, are 'Generous Manas' and 'raised [them] as birds created a homeland by gathering [various] groups', which were also used by Akayev in 1995, and are closer to a civic notion of nationalism.

However, today the problem of decentralisation seems to be more acute than before. The newly formed government after the election of the Prime Minister Atambayev to Presidency also consists of mainly northerners. The opposition and the two main challengers of President Atambayev during the elections for Presidency are also from the south.[38]

Recently in January 2012, a big statue of Manas was opened in the city of Osh. With its height of 24 m, it is one of the biggest monuments of the world. Another statue was opened in Moscow in February 2012.

Conclusion

After the repeated events in the last two decades, it was recognised by President Otunbayeva and President (and former Prime Minister) Atambayev that the formation of a nation-state in Kyrgyzstan was not successful. When the disheartened generations were in need of hope, the image of Manas gained a central role again. Not only officially but also on the popular level Manas receives much attention. There is even a spiritual-religious group called Manas Ordo, whose members are thought to be 'touched' by the soul of Manas—similar to Shamans but with Islamic words and symbols as devote Muslims—and they are believed to posses magical powers to speak to spirits in order to heal persons. This sacredness is actually part of a general perception of Manas. For example, the manaschys (performers of Manas) are also thought to be touched by the soul of Manas, which gives them the 'magical ability' to remember and recite the long lines of the epic. Atambayev's speech during the opening of Manas Monument in Bishkek also refers to this understanding of Manas' spiritual power. Some people believe in this spirituality, which makes them receptive for the state's appraisal of Manas.

The end of the Soviet period created a vacuum for the foundations of a common identity or a moral base. The tools applied so far were not proved successful. Manas, which had always a significant position in presenting an ideology or moral basis for the people, gained now the central position with his monuments and references in public speeches of policy makers. He is expected to be a role model with his heroic deeds, and the ideals presented in the epic to replace the old communist ideals.

During the Soviet years, the traditional identities were replaced by the novoi sovietsky chelovek. Following the fall of the USSR, this secular notion of identity also had to be replaced. In a modern and secular world, where the religious and tribal identities had lost their former strength, the sense of being for any individual had to be replaced by a new form of bond.

The nationalised historiography in school education in most nation-states has a special mission to acquaint the future generations with the idea that they belong to a nation with a long and glorious past. The individual feels not alone but a member of a bigger and historical community. The epic can substitute the role, which nationalised histories are playing for students. The Manas Epic telling the story of a long struggle for survival and subsequent glory is very suitable for playing this role of history. Probably these factors lead Manas to a more prominent position in the official discourse, which has increased with the identification of the severity of the problems.

This time the crisis must have been seen as more critical, so that the ethno-centrality of the chosen symbol is not considered as binding. The apathy of the elites, which was the case after 1995, is less apparent. The recognition of multinational state sustains. Thus, in the example of Kyrgyzstan civic and ethnic nationalisms are not antagonistic. The priorities, however, are changing for the benefit of ethnic nationalism in order to become a nation. The unsolved problem and the main thread for Kyrgyzstan are identified as the destabilisation, and after twenty years of independence, the policymakers in Kyrgyzstan revise the national policies. In order to eliminate the threat of destabilisation, Kyrgyz nationality is expected to be strengthened, a solid ethnic core to be created, and other ethnic groups are to be united around this ethnic core. Manas, as an ethnic symbol, is at the centre of this need for the unification of the Kyrgyz people, but he is represented in a 'multinational' fashion not delimiting recent nationality policies only to ethnic nationalism.

Notes

1. Civic nationalism underlines the importance of citizenship in a country with shared political values and practices defined by the law. Ernest Renan defines nationalism in his prominent book "What is a Nation" (1882) as a "daily plebiscite dependent on the will of its people to continue living together". On the ethnic nationalism, on the other hand, nationality depends on ethnicity or "blood".
2. Ch. Ch. Valikhanov, "Assays [sic] about Jungaria". *Encyclopaedical Phenomenon of Epos "Manas"*. (Bishkek: Glavnaya Redaktsia Kyrgyzskoy Entsiklopedii Nauchno-Propagandistskiiy Delovoy Proekt "Muras", 1995), p.251.

3. Kanybek Imanaliev, *Kyrgyzstan. The Word about Homeland*, (Bishkek: Uchkun, 2004), p.38.
4. Imanaliev 2004, p.38.
5. S. Musaev, "The Epoch "Manas", *Encyclopaedical Phenomenon of Epos "Manas"*, (Bishkek, Glavnaya Redaktsia Kyrgyzskoy Entsiklopedii Nauchno-Propagandistskiiy Delovoy Proekt "Muras", 1995), p.291.
6. For more information about the evaluation of Amir Temur during the Soviet period, see Edward Allworth. *The Modern Uzbeks: From the Fourteenth Century to the Present; A Cultural History*. (Stanford: Hoover Institution Press, 1990), pp.242-248.
7. S. Musaev, This role of folklorists in forming a nation can be linked to the role given to folklorists by Hroch in his Phase A. See Miroslav Hroch. *Social Preconditions of National Revival in Europe*, (Cambridge: Cambridge University Press, 1985), p.277.
8. The first recording of Manas during the Soviet period was made between 1922-26, which was Sagymbai Orozbakov's version (Musaev 1995), p.291. In 1924, Kara-Kyrgyz Autonomous Oblast was formed. In 1925, "Kara-Kyrgyz" was changed to "Kyrgyz". In 1926, Kyrgyz Autonomous Soviet Socialist Oblast was declared, and in 1936, it acquired republican status under the name of "Kyrgyz Soviet Socialist Republic".
9. Musaev 1995, p.290; B.M. Unusaliev. "Kyrgyz Heroic Epos "Manas"". *Encyclopaedical Phenomenon of Epos "Manas"*. (Bishkek: Glavnaya Redaktsia Kyrgyzskoy Entsiklopedii Nauchno-Propagandistskiiy Delovoy Proekt "Muras". 1995), p.427.
10. B. Prokhorov, *Frunze. A Guide*, (Moscow: Raduga Publishers, 1982), p.36.
11. For the official explanation and years see: www.president.kg. Recently I was told by a Kyrgyz student that the falcon (*akshumkar*) at the center of the state emblem is the falcon of Manas. This does not correspond to the official explanation, but even if it represents Manas, this seems to be a very indirect symbol to remember Manas.
12. United Nations General Assembly, 49th session, Agenda item 12. 49/129. February 17, 1995. http://www.undemocracy.com/A-RES-49-129.pdf. For the decision see "Records of the General Conference". *Twenty-seventh Session, vol. 1*. Paris, October 25 and November 16, 1993:IV.13.22.III.5.a.xxi. http://unesdoc.unesco.org/images/0009/000956/095621e.pdf.
13. Rafis Abazov, *Historical Dictionary of Kyrgyzstan*, (Oxford: The Scarecrow Press, 2004), p.34.
14. Askar Akayev, "Açış Konuşması". Manas 1000 Bişkek Bildirileri. Ogün Atilla Budak (ed.). (Ankara: Atatürk Kültür Merkezi Yayınları, 1995), p.17.
15. Akayev 1995, p.19.
16. Akayev 1995, p.22.
17. Akayev 1995, p.22.
18. In 1993, 89,984 Russians, 11,740 Ukrainians, 11,148 Germans, and 9,468 Tatars left Kyrgyzstan (http://www.stat.kg/stat.files/din.files/census/5010015.pdf). In

the census of 1989, their population was as follows: 9,19,558 Russians, 1,08,027 Ukrainians, 1,01,309 Germans, and 70,068 Tatars (http://demoscope.ru/weekly/ssp/sng_nac_89.php?reg=11). Their population in 1995 was less because of the outmigration after the independence, but still these figures show that more than 10 per cent of Russians, Ukrainians and Tatars left Kyrgyzstan following the economic crisis in 1993.

19. There are still some Kalmyk villages in Kyrgyzstan on the south-western hills of Yssyk-Köl. There has been no enmity recorded against these Kalmyks, although in most versions of the Manas Epic they are the villain.
20. Akayev 1995, p.22.
21. Erica Marat, "National Ideology and State-building in Kyrgyzstan and Tajikistan", *Silk Road Paper*, Central Asia-Caucasus Institute, Silk Road Studies Program, January 2008:39. http://edoc.bibliothek.uni-halle.de/servlets/MCRFileNodeServlet/HALCoRe_derivate_00002229/National%20Ideology.pdf.
22. For the application of national symbols on a manipulative basis, see Eric Hobsbawm in Eric Hobsbawm & Terence Ranger (ed.). *The Invention of Tradition*, (Cambridge: Cambridge University Press, 1983), p.1 or Michael Billig. *Banal Nationalism*, (London: Sage Publications,1995), p.6.
23. Dennis Keen, "Ode to Manas". *The Spektator*. Bishkek, Kyrgyzstan. March 2011. No 10:12-13. www.thespektator.co.uk. In this article written in February 2011 the recent situation of the Manas village is defined as: "When the flurry of fun was over, the place was left to rot, almost forgotten." Here it is also mentioned that "in August [2010] ... it [the village] had received a facelift" and was painted in "rainbow" colours.
24. "Kyrgyzstan protests UNESCO's listing of Epic of Manas as Chinese" (October 2009) http://centralasiaonline.com/en_GB/articles/caii/features/entertainment/2010/02/20/feature-02
25. Based on personal observations of the author in Bishkek and discussions on web portals in June 2010.
26. "North" corresponds to the northern regions Chui, Naryn, Talas, Yssyk Köl and the capital Bishkek, "South" is used for Osh, Jalalabad and Batken regions.
27. In the first year of Bakiyev the same problem of North-south division pushed two forerunners, Bakiyev and Feliks Kulov to rule in tandem, but after a year and half the tandem was destroyed.
28. Tolgonai Osmongazieva, "Adilet Ayikeev: I can confirm MP Omurbek Abdyrakhmanov defamed Manas's dignity". 24.kg News Agency, July 08, 2011. http://eng.24.kg/community/2011/07/08/19148.html.
29. "Otunbayeva: Children of all nationalities after the primary school should have the Kyrgyz language". AkiPress, June 18, 2011; Otunbayeva: "No other Special Rights of Civilians in the Kyrgyz no" (speech at the Congress), June 18, 2011. http://www.

centrasia.ru/newsA.php?st=1308388620

30. Tolgonai Osmongazieva, "The President for Transitional Period of Kyrgyzstan signed the bill on Manas epic". 24.kg News Agency, June 28, 2011. http://eng.24.kg/community/2011/06/28/18930.html.
31. Tolgonai Osmangazieva, "You shouldn't Think Manas Epic as some Tale", *24.kg News Agency*, June 28, 2011. http://eng.24.kg/community/2011/06/28/18933.html.
32. Dina Tokbaeva, "Kyrgyz Folk Hero Replaces Freedom Monument". *Institute for War & Peace Reporting*. http://iwpr.net/report-news/kyrgyz-folk-hero-replaces-freedom-monument
33. Ulan Nazarov, "Manas Monument to Replace Bishkek Statue of Liberty", July 28, 2011.http://centralasiaonline.com/en_GB/articles/caii/newsbriefs/2011/07/28/newsbrief-14. The money was collected for two statues, Manas and Kyrgyz writer Chingiz Aitmatov, which were placed on two opposing sides of the main square.
34. "Kyrgyzstan, Purchased reputation", http://eng.24.kg/community/2011/08/03/19554.html
35. "The capital to be Renamed in Manas", August 01, 2011. 24.kg News Agency. http://eng.24.kg/bishkek24/2011/08/01/19489.html.
36. Alisher Karimov, "Regional Tensions Affect Kyrgyzstan as Election Approaches". http://centralasiaonline.com/en_GB/articles/caii/features/main/2011/10/25/feature-01.
37. "Prime Minister of Kyrgyzstan: The Installation of the Manas Monument is a way to a Bright Future". http://eng.24.kg/community/2011/08/31/20003.html.
38. Karimov, "Regional Tensions Affect Kyrgyzstan as Election Approaches".

6. Uyghur Historiography in Post-Soviet Kazakhstan

Ablet Kamalov

The Uyghurs, whose homeland is Xinjiang Uyghur Autonomous Region of PRC, are a diasporic community, and are spread out almost in all of the newly independent Central Asian states. The largest group is in Kazakhstan, where they moved from the seventh position in 1999 to the fifth position in 2010 in terms of ethnic composition, following the Kazakhs, Russians, Uzbeks, and Ukrainians. According to latest statistics of 2010, the total number of Uyghurs in Kazakhstan stands at 2,46,449 (1.54 per cent of a total population of the republic that is 1,60,36,075), out of which 1,55,156 have lived in Almaty oblast' (9.18 per cent of the oblast population), including 80,529 in the city of Almaty (5.7 per cent of the city population). Changes in the position of the Uyghur community as well as main challenges they face in post-Soviet period in Central Asian countries have been discussed elsewhere.[1] Nation building process in Central Asian countries, and construction of new identities embraced not only titular nations of the region, but also ethnic minorities—Uyghurs not being an exception. With the collapse of the Soviet Union and growth of the Chinese influence in Central Asia, Uyghurs revised their relationship with their historical homeland—Eastern Turkistan (Xinjiang), and rediscovered their sense of belonging to the Uyghur nation. At the same time, they also discovered their 'otherness' from their ethnic fellows in Xinjiang and closeness to the Central Asian nations. Shift from Soviet 'uniqueness' to a sense of being a part of a broader Uyghur nation occurring under the pressures of growing official nationalism of new Central Asian states, as well as formation of a transnational network of the Uyghur diaspora, shape Uyghur identity in the region. Ethnic conflicts in Central Asia and Xinjiang—the Uyghur-Han clashes in Urumchi in 2009 and Kyrgyz-Uzbek conflict in the Osh region of Kyrgyzstan in 2010 highlighted two factors shaping Uyghur identity in Central Asia—external and internal. In the first case, Central Asian Uyghurs demonstrated their solidarity with their ethnic brethren in Xinjiang, while the Osh ethnic conflict in Southern Kyrgyzstan prioritised a necessity of ethnic coexistence in the new nation-states and that of integration into local national units. The complex process of search for identity in post-Soviet Central Asia is reflected, among others, in historiography that is history writing of the Uyghurs.

This article intends to examine some aspects of the Uyghur historiography of post-Soviet Central Asia based on writings in independent Kazakhstan—(1) academic writings on Uyghur history of the last two decades in Kazakhstan, (2) growth of nationalist histories of the Uyghurs or mythological representation of the Uyghur history, (3) external reflections on the Uyghur history from the Kazakh and Russian perspectives, and (4) developing new fields of historical inquiry among the Uyghurs of Kazakhstan.

Academic Writings on Uyghur History in the Last Two Decades in Kazakhstan

Uyghur studies were institutionalised in Kazakhstan within the Academy of Sciences since 1947, when the Uyghur-Dungan section was set up to study language, literature, and history of these ethnic minority groups. Two separate divisions were created in 1963, with the Dungan division being transferred to the Kyrgyz Academy of Sciences in Frunze. The Soviet government promoted Uyghur studies to meet both internal and external demands. Within Kazakhstan, Uyghur studies provided guidance and service to develop educational and cultural institutions, while the academic work in this field also served the needs of the Soviet policy towards neighbouring Xinjang, where Uyghurs comprised an ethnic majority.

Uyghur studies reached its peak during its existence as a research institute within the Kazakh Academy of Sciences, under the directorship of two directors—G. Sadvakassov and K. Talipov. This institution functioned in the late Soviet period, and early years of the post-Soviet period (1986-96). It had made significant contribution when relations with China were eased, and there were frequent academic exchanges between the two countries and newer possibilities for internships in research and educational centres of Beijing and Urumqi.

During the initial years of the independence period, Uyghur studies in Kazakhstan received state support due to 'its own momentum'. Changes came up with Kazakhstan joining Shanghai Cooperation Organization in 1996, since when the institute has been closed and its remaining staff has been incorporated into the Institute of Oriental studies, thereby forming a Center for Uyghur studies. In contrast to the preceding periods, research projects of the Center of Uyghur Studies now mainly focus on historical relations between Kazakhstan and Eastern Turkistan (Xinjiang).[2] Publications of this centre largely are based on research done in the late Soviet period. These works include, among others, the work on Uyghur applied art and crafts of the Semirech'ye Uyghurs by R. Karimova,[3] who has been heading the Centre since 2007; Ablet Kamalov's work on the history of nomadic Uyghurs in the 8th and 9th century,[4] which has been translated into Persian;[5] a volume of works of G.Iskhakov;[6] A. Zul'yarov's research on Uyghur dwellings in Semirech'ye;[7] and G. Baratova's works on social and economic development of the Semirech'ye Uyghurs at the turn of the 19th and 20th century.[8] New projects of the last decades of the Center of Uyghur history have covered such themes as urban history of Eastern Turkistan,[9] Uyghur Muslim historical sources such as the Uyghur version of the work Tarikhi Rashidi by Mirza Muhammad Haidar,[10] Tarihi Amniya of Mussa Sairami,[11] an ongoing study of the manuscript of Taskira-i Bughra khan by Elvira Molotova, as well as Xinjiang's history of the first half of the 20th century,[12] history of the American and British diplomacy in Xinjiang before the communist regime,[13] as well as problems of the Uyghur community of Kazakhstan[14] and Uyghur historiography.[15] It is to be noted that some of the mentioned publications are the outcome of the projects funded not only by the Institute of Oriental Studies but also by other foundations.[16] In the new future, the Center plans to publish late Akram Anvarov's dissertation 'History of the study of Eastern Turkistan by Anglo-Indian travellers' (1812-1900)'.[17]

The first special school textbook on the history of the Uyghurs published by Daut Issiev in 1995,[18] designed as a textbook for middle school pupils in the Uyghur schools of Kazakhstan, was among the first in the series of academic writings. It was written in classical Uyghur language, and covered a period from ancient times through the Karakhanid Dynasty till early 13th century. The textbook became another attempt in the compilation of a general history of pre-Mongol Uyghurs and their homeland, that is, Eastern Turkistan.

Uyghur history writing in post-Soviet Central Asia is a marginal component in regional historiography. Academic research on the Uyghurs was conducted mainly in Kazakhstan, especially in the Soviet period. Few publications on Uyghur history and culture are indeed published in Kyrgyzstan and Uzbekistan.[19] Despite the changed priorities of the Kazakh national academia, Uyghurovedenia continues to be one of the important branches of knowledge, which, as before, reflected relations between China and Kazakhstan, on the one hand, and emergence of new nation-states, on the other. The number of works on Uyghur history in other Central Asian republics was quite limited.

Uyghur Nationalism and Growth of Uyghur Nationalist Histories in Central Asia

The emergence of new nation-states in Central Asia and the revival of new national identities marked a loss of Soviet identity. Not only titular nations but also ethnic minorities faced the dilemma of shifting identities. In the Soviet period, the Uyghurs were strongly aware of their uniqueness as 'Soviet Uyghurs' in contrast to the Uyghurs of China, who were perceived as 'oppressed people'. In post-Soviet Central Asia, the Uyghurs have re-discovered their ethnic links with Eastern Turkistan and have started thinking themselves as part of a bigger Uyghur nation, whose homeland has been occupied by the Chinese. The newly acquired independence of the Central Asian republics has stirred Uyghur nationalist sentiments and the desire to have their own independent state in Eastern Turkistan (Xinjiang). As a result, in the early years of independence, the anti-Chinese political movement was very strong among the Central Asian Uyghurs until China made a strong pressure on Central Asian governments and succeeded in suppressing public activities advocating 'Free Eastern Turkistan'. Cross-border relations with China resumed during the late Perestroika period, which became very intensive in the first decade after independence, resulted in the exchange of ideas and mutual influence among the Uyghurs on both sides of the border. Uyghur nationalism in Xinjiang not only grew because of political changes in Central Asia but also because publications in Xinjiang started addressed the aspect of Uyghur nationalism in Central Asia. It is quite interesting that while in the early Soviet period, the Soviet authorities assisted the development of education and culture in Xinjiang and nationalist ideas were exported to Xinjiang. In post-Soviet times, we observe a reciprocal process. Now the former Soviet Uyghurs who lost their 'advanced and progressive nature' have now become the users of the Uyghur language writings from Xinjiang. The best example of this is seen in the popularity of the nationalist history Uyghular (Uyghurs) by Turgun Almas, a Xinjiang Uyghur writer and historian. His book challenged the Chinese nationalist interpretation of the Uyghur history; he has offered his own version of their past and has glorified the Uyghur nation that was prohibited in Xinjiang as a nationalist version of history and the author was put under house arrest in Urumchi. Turgun Almas's book has been published in Almaty first in the Uyghur language in Cyrillic in 1993, then translated into Russian.[20] The book and repressive measures of the Chinese authorities had a reverse effect. It raised dramatically national consciousness of the Uyghurs—the book starting circulating in the underground and as a dissident literature it became extremely popular among the people who paid high price to loan rear copies of the book. The book also became popular among the Central Asian Uyghurs in early 1990s. It became the first case when, to the contrary of the previous time when Soviet Uyghur publications had a profound influence on the Xinjiang Uyghurs, Xinjiang publications started impacting Central Asian Uyghurs.

Cross-border Uyghur intellectual exchange proved to be quite complex, multi-facet, process. Not only did anti-Chinese ideas of the Uyghur nationalist publications reached Uyghur readers in Central Asia, but also those nationalist ideas, which were supported by Chinese ideology. The

Chinese interpretation of Uyghur history is based on the idea of a united Chinese nation (zhonghua minzu), which the Uyghurs are considered to be a part of. Therefore Chinese authorities tolerate Uyghur nationalist claims on Central Asian history, ascribing to them particular role in the region, for example, many well-known historical figures such as Al-Farabi, Al-Biruni, Alisher Navoi, etc., are represented as Uyghurs by origin. The Uyghur authors in Central Asia have borrowed such claims, and have circulated them in local publications, which have not only generated Uyghur nationalism but also Chinese nationalism for those Uyghurs who also share 'Chinese' affiliation. Thus, Chinese nationalist concept of zhonghua minzu benefits from the Uyghur nationalist interpretation of Central Asian and Uyghur history. One of the best examples of this complex ideology is a nationalist work Uyghurname by late Saut Abdrakhmanov (a former officer of the Eastern Turkistan Republic of 1944-49 who spent several decades in the Communist jails in Xinjiang and after migrating to Kazakhstan became one of the anti-Chinese Uyghur leaders). One can easily detect the influence of Xinjiang Uyghur publications in his Uyghur-centred vision of the Central Asian history.[21]

The growth of nationalist histories among Central Asian Uyghurs also reflects the search for a post-Soviet identity. The elimination of censorship in Kazakhstan has created the ground for popular nationalist histories among both the Kazakhs and ethnic minorities, including the Uyghurs. Often defined as 'alternative histories' (meaning 'alternative' towards official history), they construct an extremely distorted and falsified nationalist vision of the past. To have an insight into this sort of writings, it is necessary to mention the works by K. Daniyarov, who tried to substantiate the Kazakh origins of Chingiz Khan.[22] The subject of mythologisation of history in Kazakhstan is well examined and strongly criticised by leading Kazakh historians N. Masanov, Zh. Abylkhozhin, and I. Yerofeyeva in their joint research.[23] The process of mythologisation of history became the subject of several doctoral dissertations.[24] The mythologisation of history is seen by some scholars as an inevitable component of the nation building process. Nationalist histories presuppose a certain element of distortion as they are sometimes biased and represent falsified versions of the past. As an example of this approach to Uyghur history, the writings of Kasym Massimi who published four books on 'ancient' and 'medieval' history of the Uyghurs can be cited.[25] His approach to history is based on the arbitrary use of historical sources with an attempt to reanimate historical and contemporary legends and myths pertaining to the role of the Uyghurs in the history of Eurasia, including fantasised expressions like 'Continent Mu' which stated that ancient Uyghur Empire existed 17,000 years ago, and encompassed the huge territory including that of Europe.[26] Kasym Massimi attempts to 're-discover' the Chinese and Turkic sources by replacing the names of other ethnic groups (say, the Slavs, Iranians, Chinese and even American Indians) with the generic name 'Uyghur'. His work creates an image of a 'golden age' of the Uyghurs that is the genesis of all modern civilisations.[27] It worth mentioning here that publications in the Russian language such as those by Massimi have wider audience in comparison to the Uyghur language publications (for example, S. Abdrakhmanov's book), and therefore, evoke immediate reaction among its multi-ethnic readers.

The more modest version of nationalist history is offered by Kaharman Khozhamberdiev, who has published two books on Uyghur history so far—Uyghury v rakurse istorii (The Uyghurs from historical perspective), and Uyghury-Etnopotiicheskaya istoriya s drevneishih vremien do nashikh dney (The Uyghurs-Ethno-political history since ancient times to the contemporary period).[28] Kaharman Khozhamberdiev begins his narrative with the history of the nomadic Uyghurs and the Turfan Uyghur kingdom of the 9th to 13th century in the Tarim basin but gradually focuses more on the Uyghur national-liberation movement in Eastern Turkistan in the last few centuries. He has a rather Uyghur-centric vision and promotes the narrative of 'Uyghurstan', and idealises Eastern Turkistan/Xinjiang as homeland of the Uyghurs. As Uyghur leader in Kazakhstan, he closely co-operates with Uyghur political organisations of Europe and the US. He was a founder of the People's Party of Uyghurstan in September 2002, which has never been registered in Kazakhstan since the Law on Political parties bans parties along ethnicity.[29] Debates about the usage of the term 'Uyghurstan' instead of Eastern Turkestan as a means to designate the Uyghurs' historical homeland have continued all through the 1990s. After a decade, it is used much less intensively by Uyghur intellectuals, evidence of which can be seen in the title of recently published book by Dilinur Kassymova entitled Uyghuriya-Zagadochnaya, dalyokaya i blizkaya (Uyghuriya-Mysterious, distant and close).[30]

Uyghur History from Kazakh and Russian Perspectives

The nationalist version of Uyghur history tends to highlight the Uyghurs' achievements towards humankind. On the one hand, it shapes Uyghur national identity and on the other hand, it evokes anti-Uyghur feelings among other Central Asian nationalists. Kazakh nationalist writings are extremely critical of interpretations of Kasim Massimi and his search for the Uyghur origins of the Saka Golden man as representative of Kazakh nationhood. The roots of Uyghur-Kazakh antagonism apparently lie in different social and economic lifestyles of sedentary and nomadic people. The Soviet era ethnic identification sharpened the differences between these 'imagined communities' that has been long articulated in various debates about the historical past. This antagonistic approach was revealed during the debates about the ethnic origin of the present Kazakh Prime Minister Karim Massimov. Though Karim Massimov considers himself an ethnic Kazakh, the Kazakh intelligentsia does not recognize such claims, clearly shunning his Uyghur roots. Here, one is reminded of the forebodings of Ernst Gellner that nationalist feelings become especially strong when representative of the ethnic minority rules over a majority—that if the rulers of the political unit belong to a nation other than that of the majority of the ruled, this, for nationalists, constitutes a quite outstandingly intolerable breach of political property.[31] It should be said that this is actually the case in modern Kazakhstan when representatives of the Uyghur minority have been appointed to elite ranks, the first such case being that of Ismail Yussupov,[32] who had been the First Secretary of the Communist party of Kazakhstan in 1962-64. It was during the Yussupov period when negative images of the Uyghurs have been created due to the growing Kazakh nationalism. It seems not by chance that the Uyghur community has been involved in ethnic clashes in post-Soviet

Kazakhstan—clashes between Kazakh and Uyghur youth occurred in the village of Chilik (Shelek) of the Almaty oblast in November 2006. All this substantiates the argument of representation of Uyghur history in Kazakhstan—more tolerant in the Russian language publications and more radical in the Kazakh language publications. Anti-Uyghur articles frequently published in the Kazakh non-official press can be considered as a reflection of the struggle among political elite.

While analysing the Uyghur-Kazakh conflict in Chilik, the Chinese factor should not be ignored, that is, the involvement of the Kazakh *oralmans* (repatriates) from China in the conflict with Uyghurs may expose Chinese 'hands'. China accuses the Uyghur diaspora abroad of instigating secessionism among Xinjiang's Uyghurs. However, the tragic Uyghur-Han conflict in Urumchi of 2009, and Chinese bloody repressions of the Uyghurs have also evoked solidarity among the Kazakhs and the Uyghurs, an aspect that was demonstrated in public protest rallies in Almaty.

It is necessary to dissect aspects of Uyghur history, which are most often discussed in the Kazakh publications. There is a problem of continuity between modern and ancient Uyghurs who established their Empire in 744-840 AD contributing to the emergence of Turkic culture in Central Asia. Uyghur historiography does not doubt the continuity of Turkic tradition among the Uyghurs, which in a way idealises the 'golden age' of the ancient Uyghurs, which stimulates nationalist ideas as well as Uyghur ethnicity, but poses a problem for Chinese macro identity.

The Chinese authorities and the official historiography of the People's Republic of China have their own political interests in perpetuating the Uyghur claim—they substantiate the claim that ancient Uyghurs settled in Xinjiang (Eastern Turkistan) much later than the Han Chinese did. By taking the line of continuity between modern and ancient Uyghurs, they are able to articulate more strongly the migration of the nomadic Uyghurs to the Tarim basin after 840 AD, thereby, refuting the claims of the Uyghurs as an indigenous community of Xinjiang. According to the Chinese historians, the Han Chinese started settling in Western regions (Xi-yu) already during the Han Empire. The migration theory of the nomadic Uyghurs to Xinjiang (Eastern Turkistan) became a means of solidifying the Chinese claim that the historical homeland of the Uyghurs is present day Mongolia, while Xinjiang has been an integral part of China since ancient times.

Unlike in China, where both Uyghur and Chinese historiographies mention that the origin of the modern Uyghurs is linked to the nomadic Uyghurs, the Turkology studies in newly independent Central Asian states tend to underestimate the historical role of the Uyghurs and in a wider sense tend to gloss over their own histories. In Kazakhstan, the continuity of traditions between modern and ancient Uyghurs is denied to such an extent that even in school textbooks on the history of Kazakhstan, there has been hardly any reference to Uyghur history. Some of the Kazakh authors like Karzhaubay Sartkhozhauly deny existence of the Uyghur Empire, and has arbitrarily re-named it as 'the united khanate of the Turks'.[33]

Criticism of the Uyghur representation of their history is reflected in the publications of the most ardent pro-Chinese sinologists of Kazakhstan—Konstantin Syroyezhkin for example, who advocates the Chinese imperial interpretation of the Uyghur history based on depiction of Xinjiang as an integral part of China since times immemorial.[34]

Politicisation of the Uyghur history and its negative representation in local mass media construct an image of Uyghurs as a pariah group. This attitude is expressed when the Kazakhs call them 'people without motherland, without flag', the latter symbolising absence of statehood (stateless nation). The negative nationalist attitudes towards Uyghur ethnic minority in Kazakhstan should not be essentialised. The stereotypical representation of Uyghurs as separatists and terrorists due to the involvement of Chinese propaganda has been revealed by the Kazakh scholar Bakhytzhamal Bekturghanova in her sociological research—'Uyghur extremism in Central Asia: myth or reality'?[35]

From National Narrative to Local History: New Trends in Uyghur Historiography in Kazakhstan

The contest among national histories in post-Soviet Central Asia has been recently called as 'a war between histories'—also reflected in contemporary history writing in Kazakhstan. The collapse of the Soviet Union and liberalisation of the public life have revealed new perspectives among historians. Access to archival sources, absence of censorship (as it was already mentioned), and minimalisation of banned themes opened possibilities of diversified research. Many themes, which were banned in the Soviet period, have now become well-researched subjects. With regard to the Uyghur history, revision of history can be applied to such themes as the Soviet-Xinjiang relations, the Soviet role in suppression of the Muslim uprisings in Xinjiang in the 1930s, its involvement in establishing of the Eastern Turkistan Republic (ETR) in the three prefectures of Xinjiang neighbouring Soviet Kazakhstan in 1944-1949. The traumatic experience of repression of the Uyghurs of Semirech'ye by the Bolshevik contingents of Murayev in 1918 was commonly assessed in Soviet historiography. Only in post-Soviet Kazakhstan it has become possible to discuss a tragedy called by Uyghurs 'Atu pajiasi' (tragedy of shooting), and create a monument in memory of thousands of people killed by the Bolsheviks.

Another new trend in Uyghur history writing in the last decade is the development of local history of Uyghur villages and urban neighbourhoods of Kazakhstan. Local history writing in Soviet Central Asia was well structured within the domain of kraevedeniye (local area studies), which has been the dominant theme in all local museums at the institutional level, and has involved local historians who have been working for educational and cultural organisations, including local schoolteachers of history. The main feature of local histories produced in the Soviet period was that they were have been written 'from above': not only local history writing was organised and control by the Communist party and the government, but the content of local histories represented generalised vision on the past based on local 'materials'. Writing history of the Uyghur villages of Kazakhstan for the first time was initiated in 1972, when a publishing house 'Kazakhstan' printed a book entitled Yeŋilanyan yeza (A renewed village) of two authors M. Roziev and M. Mamat'yarov. The book depicted the history and current situation in one of the biggest Uyghur villages in Kazakhstan—Chong Aksu (Big Aksu), located in the Uyghur district of the Almaty oblast'.[36] It should be noted here that in the beginning of the 20th century, there were 99 Uyghur settlements in Semirech'ye altogether, most of which were united within the new administrative region called 'Uyghurski rayon' in 1935. The main aim of the book on Chong Aksu village was to illustrate achievements of the ethnic minorities of the Soviet period. The idea of renewal of the Uyghur village became a central one in the book and this idea was later applied to the history of the village Ghalzhat. Another example of local history of the Soviet period is highlighted in the book Güllång olka (A blossomed region) by Arziev Hashim that was published in 1987. The book also praised the socialist system in the entire Uyghur rayon.[37]

Histories on the Uyghur villages and neighbourhoods have increased considerably in the last decade. During this time were published histories of villages Ketmen, Baiseit, Qariturug, Malivay, Dovun, Shunqar, Qoram, a town of Zharkend/Yarkend, Almaty neighbourhoods Druzhba (Dostyq) and Sultanqorghan (Almaty-1).[38] These publications show growing interest of the local Uyghurs in the history of neighbourhoods. This interest can be compared with heroisation of the past so widely spread among the Central titular Asian nations, which in post-Soviet period started constructing memory of local heroes—baatyrs through writing their genealogies (shezhere), local histories and erecting monuments across the country. Unlike the Soviet samples of history of the Uyghur villages most of the new publications are by enthusiastic representatives among the local intelligentsia, which resembles the pattern of alternative histories. Most of the histories of the Uyghur villages and neighbourhoods contain not only historical narration, but also biographies of prominent figures who have originated from those places; some include popular stories, poetry, and poems related to the locations. From this perspective, they represent histories written 'from below'. Principles of writing history 'from below' are demonstrated explicitly in the history of present day Almaty neighbourhood 'Sultanqorghan' (Almaty 1), which has been set up by the Taranchi Turks (Ili Uyghurs) in 1871 when the Russian Empire resettled the rule of the Ili Taranchi Sultanate from Kuljia to the northern vicinities of the city of Verny. Being the oldest Uyghur neighbourhood in Almaty, 'Sultanqorghan' (specific name used only by the Uyghurs) had experiences of every phase—the Russian imperial, Soviet and independence periods. What was a kolkhoz 'Parizhskaya kommuna' (Paris commune) in the early Soviet period became Almaty's urban territory in 1959.

Unlike other similar histories, the book 'Sultankurgan-istoriya v litsakh' (Sultanqurghan—History in Personalities) was written in Russian. Its author emphasised that the book was not 'written following strict canons of literature genre, there is no scrupulous precise academic order of historical events'.[39] The book offers a collection of photographs of the villagers followed by texts. These pictures and texts represent life stories of concerned individuals, sometimes superficially, and with much detail about everyday life of the village/neighbourhood. The work *per se* does not belong to the oral history genre.

Histories of the Uyghur villages and neighbourhoods in Kazakhstan reveal a sense of local belonging rather than an overall national identity among the Kazakhstani Uyghurs who comprises an ethnic group with its own specific historical past, different from the rest of the far bigger Uyghur nation. This re-discovery of the local has been strengthened by the local Uyghur press, especially the newspaper 'Uyγur avazi' (former 'Kommunizm tuγi') in Kazakhstan, which focuses on the life of the community as well as some other newspapers that are in circulation within the smaller administrative units in the Almaty oblast.

Conclusion

Post-Soviet historiography of the Uyghurs reflects the changes that have occurred in the status of this transborder ethnic minority and new relations with its historic homeland—Eastern Turkistan (Xinjiang) that was ruled by China. Being a part of Uyghur studies (Uygurovedeniye), which is concentrated now only in the Centre of Uyghur studies at the Institute of Oriental Studies in Almaty, Uyghur history writing in Central Asia has been marginalised as a field of academic inquiry. Academic research is being held mainly in Kazakhstan with its largest Uyghur community, where Uyghur studies were funded by the Soviet government since 1947.

New trends in Uyghur history writing in post-Soviet Kazakhstan refer, on one hand, to broadening the subject area covering now previously closed topics, such as Bolshevik massacres of the Taranchi population in 1918, Soviets interference into Xinjiang internal affairs, such is backing up Eastern Turkistan Republic of 1944-49, etc. on the other, growth of nationalistic perception of the past. The latter is a result of overall process of nation building process in the region, which has been pushed forward by independence of the Central Asian republics. Nationalist writings on the Uyghur history mark further development of the Uyghur national narrative constructed in the Soviet times. This narrative challenges the Chinese perception of Uyghur history as an integral part of Chinese history; at the same time, it experiences invisible impact of the Chinese historiography which promotes Uyghurs' claims for particular role in cultural history of Central Asian—this substantiates a special role in Central Asian past of the Chinese nation (zhonghua minzu) which, according to the Chinese national concept, Uyghurs are a part.

The dual loyalty of the Uyghurs of Central Asia—to the Uyghur nation, a major part of which resides in historical homeland (Eastern Turkistan/ Xinjiang), and to their host countries—is expressed in writings that have addressed general problems of a national history and developing local history of the Uyghurs. The latter trend in Kazakhstan can be illustrated by local history of the Uyghur villages and neighbourhoods as a popular field of research.

Certainly, discussion of the Uyghur historiography in post-Soviet Central Asia cannot be limited to the Kazakh case. It should be examined within the context of the processes occurring not only within Kazakhstan but also at regional and global levels. This may address the question of regional and transnational dimensions of history writing. At the same time, a comparative approach seems to add another perspective to the overall discussion of Uyghur historiography in post-Soviet Central Asia.

Notes

1. Ablet Kamalov, "Uyghurs in the Central Asian Republics. Past and Present", in Colin Mackerras and M. Clarke (eds.), *China, Xinjiang and Central Asia. History, Transition and Crossborder Interaction into the 21st century*, (London-New York: Routledge, 2009), pp.115-132; Sean Roberts. 'Dawn of East': A portrait of a Uyghur Community between China and Kazakhstan, in I. Beller-Hann, M.C. Cesaro,

R.Harris, J.S. Finley (eds.), *Situating the Uyghurs between China and Central Asia*, 2007, pp.203-217; Kamalov, 'Uighur community in 1990s Central Asia. A Decade of Change', in Touraj Atabaki and Sanjot Mehendale (eds.), *Central Asia and the Caucasus. Transnationalism and diaspora*, (London-New York: Routledge, 2005), pp.149-168.

2. Discussed in Ablet Kamalov, *Uyghur Studies in Central Asia: A Historical Review*, Asian Research Trends, New Series, no. 1, (Tokyo: Toyo Bunko, 2006), pp.3-32.
3. Risalat Bibi Karimova, *Traditsionnie khudozhestvenniye remesla i promysly uigurov* [Traditional Uyghur art crafts and individual works]. (Almaty: Daik-Press, 2005).
4. Ablet Kamalov, *Drevniye uigury VIII-IX vv [Ancient Uyghurs VIII-IX cc]*, (Almaty: Nash Mir, 2001).
5. Ablet Kamalov, *Tarihi umumi uygurstan [General history of Uyghurstan]*. Centre of Documentation of the Ministry of Foreign Affairs, (Tehran, 2002).
6 Gegel Iskhakov, *Issledovaniya po uygurovedeniyu [Uyghur study research]*, (Almaty: Nash Mir, 2005).
7. Adilzhan Zul'yarov, *Yattissu uiyurliri [Semirech'ye Uighurs]*, (Almaty: Nash Mir, 2009).
8. Galina Baratova, *Sotsialniy i ekonomicheski story Uighurov Semirech'ya v kotse XIX - nachale XX vv. [Economic and economic system of the Semirech'ye Uyghurs in the end of the XIX – beginning of the XX centuries]*, Kandidat nauk dissertation in History, Almaty, 1988; G. Baratova, 'Uigury v Kazakhstane i Srednei Azii v XIX-XX vv (dinamika chislennosti) [The Uyghurs of Kazakhstan and Central Asia during the XIX-XX cc. Dynamics of population growth]', *Izvestiya Natsional'noi Akademii nauk Respubliki Kazakhstan*, Seriya obshestvennykh nauk. №6, 1994; Galina Baratova, *Sotsialniy i ekonomicheski story Uighurov Semirech'ya v kotse XIX - nachale XX vv. [Economic and economic system of the Semirech'ye Uyghurs in the end of the XIX – beginning of the XX centuries]*, Kandidat nauk dissertation in History, Almaty, 1988.
9. Risalat Bibi Karimova, Srednevekovaye goroda Vostochnogo Turkestana [Medieval towns of Eastern Turkistan], Avtoreferat doktorskoi dissertatsii, (Almaty, 2008).
10. Dilshat Raikhanov, *Mirza Muhammad Haidar. Tarikhi Rashidi* [Tarikhi Rashid by Mirza Muhammad Haidar, prepared for publication by D.Raikhanov], (Almaty: Nash Mir, 2004).
11. Zufiyam Karimova, *Musa Sayramidyng 'Tarih-i amniya' shyghamasy – Shyghys Turkistan halqining tarihynyng Derek kozi (XIX ghasyrdyng ekinshi zhartysy) [The work 'Tarihi-i amniya'by Mussa Sairami as a source on history of the peoples of Eastern Turkistan (second half of the XIX century)]*, Aftoreferat kandidatskoi dissertatsii, (Almaty, 2010).
12. Turkestan Vostochny, *Vostochny Turkestan v tsivilizatsionnykh protsessakh [Eastern Turkistan in civilizational processes]*, (Almaty: Nash Mir, 2010); Kommunar Talipov, 'Alihan tura Saghuniy Qumul qozghlingi haqqida', in Y. Azamatov (ed.)., *Tarikh*

Savaqliri Yaki Ötmüshsiz Keläch\u00e4k Yoq [History lessons or There is no future without past], (Almaty: Nash Mir, 2010), pp. 17-28; Kommunar Talipov, 'Chong tarihiy väqialar shahidi [Eye witnesses of the great historical events]', *Uiyur avazi*, (Almaty, January 24, 2003), pp. 8-9.

13. A. Kamalov, 'Vostochno-turkestanskaya Respublica v zapisyakh britanskogo diplomata Valtera Grekhema' [Eastern Turkistan Republic in the writings of the British diplomat Valter Graham]', *Shyghys*, 2, 2004, pp. 67-75; A. Kamalov, 'Uyghur Memoir Literature in Central Asia on Eastern Turkestan Republic (1944-49)', in Yasushi Shinmen, Jun Sugawara, James Millward (eds.), *Studies on Xinjiang Historical Sources*, Toyo Bunko, (Tokyo, 2010), pp. 257-278; A. Kamalov, 'Eastern Turkistan and British Xinjiang Relations During 1930s', in P.L. Dash etc. (eds.), *India and Kazakhstan. Silk Road Synergy Continues*, (Delhi: Academic Excellence, 2011), pp. 219-229.
14. W. Clark and A. Kamalov, 'Uighur migration across Central Asian frontiers', *Central Asian Survey*, 23(2), 2004, pp. 167-182; Ablet Kamalov, 'Uyghur Nationalism and Islam: A historical perspective', in W.J. Burszat, T. Kamusella and S. Woijciechowski (eds.), *Nationalisms across the Globe. An overview of Nationalisms in state endowed and stateless nations*, vol. II, School of Humanities and Journalism, (Poznan, 2006), pp. 533-550.
15. Ablet Kamalov, 'The Uyghurs as a part of Central Asian commonality: Soviet Historiography on the Uyghurs', in I. M.C. Beller-Hann, R. Cesaro and J.S. Harris (eds.), *Situating the Uyghurs between China and Central Asia*, (London-New York: Ashgate, 2007), pp. 31-45.
16. Outcomes of the Eurasia Foundation funded project have been published in Syroyezhkin Konstantin (ed), *Sovremenniy Sinjan i ego mesto v kazakhstansko-kitaiskih otnosheniyah [Modern Xinjiang and its place in the Kazakhstani-Chinese relations]*, (Almaty, 1997).
17. Akram Anvarov, *Istoriya izucheniya Vostochnogo Turkestana anglo-indiyskimi puteshestvennikami (1812-1900) [History of the study of Eastern Turkistan by Anglo-Indian travellers (1812-1900)]*, Aftoreferat kandidatskoi dissertatsii, (Leningrad, 1992).
18. Daut Issiev, *Uiyur tarihi [Uyghur history]*, (Almata: Zhazushy, 1995).
19. Tursun Nabijan, *Voprosy politicheskoi istorii uygurov v kitaiskoi istoriografii (Questions of political history of the Uyghurs in the Chinese historiography)*, Moskwa, 1998 (published in Bishkek); Zhalilov Omonbek, *Ofoq Hozha manoqibi*, (Andijon: 'Hayot' Nashriyoti, 2001).
20. Almas Turgun, *Uygurlar [The Uyghurs]*, Shinjang nashriyati, Urumchi, 1991; Almas Turgun, *Uygurlar [The Uyghurs]*, Qazaqstan, (Almata, 1993); Almas Turgun, *Uygury [The Uyghurs]*, (Almaty: n/p, 1996).
21. Abdrahkmanov Sbit (Sabit Uyghuriy), *Uyghurname*, (Almaty: Nash Mir, 2005).

22. Kalibek Daniyarov, *Alternativnaya istoriya Kazakhstana [Alternative history of Kazakhstan]*, (Almaty: Kainar, 1998).
23. N.E. Massanov, Zh.B. Abylkhozhin, I.V. Yerofeyeva, *Nauchnoye znaniye i mifotvorchestvo v sovremennoi istoriografii Kazakhstana [Academic knowledge and mithologization in modern historiography of Kazakhstan]*, (Almaty: Daik-Press, 2007).
24. Anuar Galiev, *Etnolopiticheskiye protsessu u tyurkskikh narodov: istoriya i myifologizatsiya [Etnopolitcal processes among Turkic peoples: history and mythologization]*, Aftoreferat doktorskoi dissertatsii, (Almaty, 2010).
25. Kassym Massimi, Plemennoye ob'yedineniye 'Uyghur', *Istoriya Uigurskoi derzhavy. [Tribal union 'Uyghur'. History of the Uyghur power]*, Almaty, n/p, 1998; Kassym Massimi, Istorya Uyghurskoi derzhavy, *Golubiye tyurki. Istoriko-khronologicheskiye issledovaniya. [History of the Uyghur power. Blue Turks. Historical khronological research]*, (Almaty, n/p, 2000); Kassym Massimi, *Istoriya Uyghurskoi derzhavy. Istoriko-khronolgicheskoye issledovaniye [History of the Uyghur power. Historical-chronological research]*, (Almaty, n/p, 2002); Kassym Massimi, *Istoriya uyghurov i facty o kreposti Por-bazhyn [History of the Uyghurs and facts of the citadel Por-Bazhyn]*, (Almaty: Nash Mir, 2011).
26. James Churchward, *The sacred symbols of Mu*, (New York, 1933).
27. Anthony Smith, 'The 'Golden Age' and National Renewal', in G. Hosking, G. Schopflin (eds.), *Myth and Nationhood*, (London: Hurst and Company, 1997), pp. 36-59.
28. Kaharman Khozhamberdiev, *Uyghury v rakurse istorii [The Uyghurs from historical perspective]*, Qazaqstan zhoghary mektebi, Almaty, 2001; Kaharman Khozhamberdiev, *Uyghurs (ethnopotiicheskaya istoriya s drevneishih vremion do nashikh dney) [The Uyghurs (ethno-political history since ancient times though current days]*, (Almaty: Nash Mir, 2010).
29. Oka Natsuko, 'Transnationalism as a Threat to State Security? Case Studies on Uighurs and Uzbeks in Kazakhstan', in U. Tomohiko (ed.) *Empire, Islam, and Politics in Central Eurasia*, (Hokkaido University, Sapporo, 2007), p. 366.
30. Dilinur Kassymova, *Uyghuriya. Zagadochnaya, dalyokaya i blizkaya [Uyghuriya. Mysterious, distant and close]*, (Almaty: Nash Mir, 2012).
31. Ernst Gelnner, *Nations and Nationalism*, (London-New York: Blackwell Publishing, 1983), p. 1.
32. Yoldash Azamatov (ed.), *XX asir mayandiliri [Outstanding persons of the 20th century]*, (Rond, Almata, 2005), pp. 129-137.
33. Karzhaubay Sartkhozhauly, *Ob'yedinenniy kaghanat tyurkov v 745-760 godakh [The united khanate of the Turks in 745-760]*, (Foliant, Astana, 2002); Ablet Kamalov, 'O nekotorykh problemakh istorii srednevekovykh uygurov [On some problems of the history of medieval Uyghurs]', in *K novym srednevekovym standartam v razvitii*

obshestvennykh nauk v Tsentralnoi Azii [Towards new standards of social sciences development in Central Asia], (Almaty: Daik-Press, 2006), p. 229.

34. Konstantin Syroyezhkin, *Mify i realnost' etnicheskogo separatism v Kiteye i bezopasnost' Tsentralnoi Azii [Myths and reality of ethnic separatism in China and security in Central Asia]*, (Almaty: Daik-Press, 2003).
35. Bakhytzhamal Bekturghanova, *'Uygurskii extremism' v Tsentral'noy Azii: mif ili real'nost'? ['Uyghur extremism' in Central Asia: myth or reality?']*, (Almaty: Kompleks, 2002).
36. M. Roziev and M. Mamat'yarov, *Yeŋilanyan yeza [A renewed village]*, Qazaqstan, (Almaty, 1972).
37. Hashim Arziev, *Gullängän olkä [The blossomed region]*, Qazaqstan näshiyati, (Almata, 1987).
38. Mukhtar Abdurakhmanov, *Konlumgha yeqin kishelar*, Almuta, 2005 (history of the village Qoram); Minamjan Abdurakhmanov, *Shungqar va shungqarliqlar [Shungqar and shungqar villagers]*, 2012 (history of the village Shungqar); Omarzhan Bavdinov, *Ochmas izlar [Tracks which will not erased]*, (Almata, 2008) (history of the village Bayseit); K. Ismailov, *Bu bizning parzimiz [This is our debt]*, (Almata, 2004) (history of the village Qaraturuq); Bakhrimjan Glavdinov (ed), *Azhdattin avladqa [From ancestors to decendents]*, Idan, Almuta, 2010 (history of the village Malybay); Ghainiddin Kurvankulov, *Kurvankul ve uning avlatliru [Kuvankul and his descendents]*, (Almaty: Nash Mir, 2008), (history of the village Dovun); Qadyrdan Razaqqov, *Nazughum iz qaldurghan zhut [The villages where tracks have been left by Nazughum]*, (Almata, 2004) (history of the village Ketmen); Hemtakhun Tokhatsunov, *Omrim avlatqa chiraq [My life is light for descendents]*, Mir, Almuta, 2008 (history of the village Dovun); Akram Qadiry, *Kolumdin kalghini shu [This is what I can do]*, Almata, 2010 (history of the village Qoram); Selimakhun Zainalov, *Zhut atisi [Farther of the community]*, (Almata, 2009) (history of the neighbourhood Druzhba/Dostyq, Almaty); *Zolotaya dolina [Golden valley]*, (Almaty, 2005) (Album on the Uyghur district); Sadyrzhan Yunusov, *Qutluq diayar – guzel Yarkand [Sacred lands – beautiful Yaknand]*, (Nash Mir, Almata, 2004) (history of the town Yakand/Zharkend); Assim Qassim, *Uiyur nahiyasi – dostluq vadisi [Uyghur region – a valley of Friendship]*, Mersal baspa uyi, (Almata, 2005) (history of the Uyghur district).
39. Imarzhan Kadirov, *Sultanqurghan - istoriya v litsakh [Sultanqurghan – history in faces]*, n/p, (Almaty, 2009), p. 3.

7. Kyrgyzstan: Back to Being 'The Island of Democracy'

Pınar Akcali

This article aims to look at the prospects of Kyrgyzstan for being successful in terms of establishing a better functioning, even consolidated democracy after many turbulent political events of the post-Soviet era. When the Soviet Union had collapsed in 1991, most observers looking at the five Central Asian republics believed that Kyrgyzstan had the best shot in terms of democratic transition and consolidation. The country, under the leadership of its first president Askar Akayev, took ambitious and quick steps in realising a regime change from a totalitarian one-party system to a democratic one. In terms of many freedoms, Kyrgyzstan was far ahead than any other Central Asian republic; it was thus labelled as 'the island of democracy' standing alone in a 'sea of authoritarian regimes' surrounding the country. Akayev organised many referendums in order to realise certain constitutional changes as well as several presidential and parliamentary elections with more than one candidate or party running in it.

However in time, Akayev's support started to fade away and he would be replaced by a popular uprising in 2005 by Kurmanbek Bakiyev, who followed Akayev's path in terms of organising referendums and elections. He, however, met the same fate and was forced to leave power in 2010. Part of the reason why these initially very popular leaders were ousted from office was related to the public resentment caused by the fact that they both took effective measures to concentrate executive power in their hands, mostly by constitutional amendments.

Since Bakiyev's fall, however, many positive steps towards further democratisation were taken in Kyrgyzstan; the steps included Rosa Otunbayeva's coming to power as an interim president, constitutional changes adopted by the June 2010 referendum (with which the presidential powers were reduced and a parliamentary system was introduced, first in Central Asia), and the election of Almazbek Atambayev as the new president of the country. Atambayev now has the chance to determine the country's future trajectory in terms of democratisation. He has to act, however, within a political framework that was shaped by the legacies that the three leaders before him had left.

This article, rather than giving an account or a description of the political developments that took place in post-Soviet Kyrgyzstan leading up to the adaptation of the 2010 Constitution, attempts to analyse their impact on the country, in terms of the possibility of becoming 'the island of democracy' in the region once again. In this framework, it first looks at the legacies of Akayev, Bakiyev, and Otunbayeva. Then it proceeds with Atambayev's prospects for being successful in laying down the foundations of a consolidated democracy as well as the challenges that he has to face. In the final part, both the comparative advantage of Kyrgyzstan and some of the recent developments, which may pose certain potential problems for further democratisation of the country are analysed.

Akayev's Legacy

Askar Akayev was elected by the deputies of the Supreme Soviet as the first president of the country on October 28, 1990.[1] Soon after he came to power, Akayev proved himself a leader committed to change in political, economic, and social spheres of life. He declared Kyrgyzstan's future goal to be a multi-party republic in which several political and economic reforms would take place. Akayev omitted the labels of 'Soviet' and 'socialist' from the republic's official name and restored the capital of Kyrgyzstan as 'Bishkek' from its Soviet version, Frunze. In these early months of his rule, Akayev proved himself a different leader as compared to others in the region, not coming from a professional political background. However, his popularity among the people would increase enormously when he denounced the coup attempt against the Soviet leader Mikhail Gorbachev organised by the hardliners of the Communist Party of the Soviet Union (CPSU). Akayev clearly sided with Gorbachev, risking his own political career, as a similar coup was also attempted against him by the Kyrgyz hardliners. Surviving this failed attempt, Akayev further increased his support.

In the early years of independence, Kyrgyzstan experienced many basic liberties under Akayev's rule, such as freedoms of speech, press, and assembly. Principles like separation of powers and checks and balances were also much more visible in the country. Furthermore, Kyrgyzstan was one of the most ambitious republics in the region to adopt speedy economic reforms.[2] During the 15 years of Akayev's rule, five referendums were conducted in 1994 (twice), 1996, 1998, and 2003; three parliamentary elections were held in 1995, 2000 and 2005; and four presidential elections took place in 1990, 1991, 1995, and 2000.[3] It must be pointed out that in almost all of these elections, there were more than one candidate and/or more than one political party. Despite the fact that there were electoral frauds and heavy use of administrative resources for favouring Akayev and pro-presidential parties in these elections, they nevertheless can be seen as important experimentations with the *sine quo non*-condition of democracy—peoples' involvement in the process of electing their leaders. Likewise, the referendums gave the people yet another similar opportunity in which their 'opinion' was asked, even if these referendums produced 'pre-determined' outcomes.

As early as 1995-96, however, Akaeyv started to resort to authoritarian policies for the sake of political stability in his country, which had limited natural resources, and few alternatives for economic prosperity. In such a political atmosphere, elections and referendums turned out to be used more frequently for increasing executive (presidential) power, rather than for consolidating democracy. People, already suffering from economic hardships started to resent Akayev's now more visible tendency toward authoritarianism.

The Aksy events took place in such an environment. Aksy is one of the poorest regions of the Jalalabad oblast in southern Kyrgyzstan in which most people were poor farmers planting potatoes and herding their sheep. On January 05, 2002, the parliamentary deputy of Aksy, Azimbek Beknazarov, who was born and raised here, was put under custody. He was charged with 'abuse of power or service position or excess of power'.[4] His arrest, however, took place soon after his protest against a border agreement that Akayev had made with China because of which Kyrgyzstan ended up giving away some territory. Beknazarov's arrest resulted in mass protests in Aksy. On March 17, 2002, the police opened fire against the demonstrators, killing five.[5] Although eventually Beknazarov was released, the Aksy events can be considered as the beginning of the end for Akayev.[6] After 2002, people's resentment toward Akayev and his rule increased considerably, resulting in his eventual downfall by public riots that started soon after the first round of the fraud parliamentary elections in February 2005. The riots resulted in Akaev's ouster from power in March of the same year, an incident commonly known as the 'Tulip Revolution'.[7]

What was Akayev's legacy as the first president of Kyrgyzstan who ruled the country for 15 years? Firstly, there is this legacy of holding regular and relatively competitive elections (despite frauds) as well as referendums in which the issues were 'referred to' the people. Akayev initially allowed the functioning of an environment in which many economic, political, and cultural freedoms were quite extensively enjoyed. Kyrgyzstan was also much more open to the outside world—that is how the country started its path of democratic transition. Even when Akayev shifted towards authoritarianism, comparatively speaking, Kyrgyzstan remained way ahead of other Central Asian countries in terms of democratisation. All these factors contributed to a legacy of change, transition to democracy, and openness to new ideas and practices.

The second most important legacy of the Akayev era was the impact of the Aksy events. After Aksy, people gained a very important political experience: protests do actually matter and work. They could make their voices heard; demands met; and will to be realised via such actions. They learned that they can change things and make a difference. As Radnitz suggested, in a way these events 'set the stage for national mobilization of 2005' by demonstrating to the people that 'mobilization was possible and effective'.[8] Therefore, 'before there was the Tulip Revolution, there was Aksy'.[9] As such, this previous successful experience indicated 'the power of precedent' and had a direct impact on the emergence of the

Tulip Revolution.[10] In other words, "It was the Aksy protests that showed that mobilization was possible in Kyrgyzstan. There was no such example anywhere else in Central Asia. ... [Aksy] empowered the people and shaped the elite's reaction to other revolutions."[11] It can, therefore, be concluded that by being the 'precedent' of the Tulip Revolution of 2005, the Aksy experience demonstrated that the support of the people was essential for the leader(s) to continue to stay in power.

A final legacy of Akayev being partially related to Aksy is the way in which he left power. After Aksy, he promised not to use force against the people. Keeping his promise, he ordered the troops not to open fire against the demonstrators during the 2005 uprising. His fall from power, therefore, was not accompanied by bloodshed, and as such, a relatively peaceful transfer of power, which was a remarkable experience for a new country.

Bakiyev's Legacy

When Kurmanbek Bakiyev came to power after Akayev's fall in 2005, the political atmosphere in the country had totally changed. Firstly, Bakiyev had to take into account the impact of the accumulation of 15 years of initial experimentation with democracy via elections and referendums. During Bakiyev's five years of presidency, there was one referendum in 2007; two presidential elections in 2005 and 2009; and one parliamentary election in 2007. As such, it can be suggested that Bakiyev acted within the framework of Akayev's legacy in terms of such experimentations with democracy. However, he had to go far beyond that in order to meet people's now highly raised expectations in the post-Akayev era. Bakiyev also took over all of the negative aspects of Akayev's rule, such as concentration of power at the hands of the president, nepotism, and corruption. People had hoped that Bakiyev would bring solutions to such problems. After all, he had resigned from his post as the prime minister in order to protest the Aksy shootings three years earlier.[12] Furthermore, he had emerged as one of the most prominent figures of opposition to Akayev.

However, instead of solving the problems that brought the end of Akayev, Bakiyev added even more to them. He was involved in higher levels of nepotism and corruption, allegedly having direct links with some criminal mafia groups. He was also not successful in balancing ethnic interests and ethnic balance, increasing the tensions between the Kyrgyz and the Uzbeks.[13] Furthermore, his rule turned out to be even more authoritarian than Akaev's. As Beshimov suggested:

> "Bakiyev viewed (Akayev's) liberal predictions as a weakness and took the course of consolidating his own personal power. To this end, he subjugated all other branches of power to the presidency, removing even the weakest remaining checks and balances, and became increasingly hostile toward democracy and human rights. When he announced that he would protect his power by violence if necessary, he rang the death knell for peaceful and legitimate regime change."[14]

Otunbayeva's Legacy

Rosa Otunbayeva was an experienced diplomat who had served as an ambassador to the US during 1992-94, then as an ambassador to the UK during 1998-2001. Between 2002 and 2004, she was the deputy to the UN Secretary-General's special representative for the conflict in Abkhazia, Georgia.[15] However, she would emerge as one of the most influential opposition figures prior to the fall of Akayev, when she had been denied permission to run for parliament in the 2005 elections due to the 5-year residence criterion. Her case became more striking as she was on the ballot with President Akayev's daughter Bermet from the same constituency.[16] People believed, quite in line with the claims of the opposition parties, that this denial was yet another way of political repression on the part of Akayev on his rivals.

Once Bakiyev was ousted and Otunbayeva became the interim president, she took her place among the rather different political elites as compared to the previous ones. Otunbayeva, similar to the other members of the interim government, developed a plan to make sure that all political parties would have an equal chance in real competitive elections. Likewise, these new elites also wanted 'to create a precedent for a peaceful and lawful transfer of power in Kyrgyzstan, after years of corrupt and authoritarian rule'.[17] It has also been suggested that Otunbayeva and the members of the government took certain effective measures so that the executive power would not be concentrated at the hands of the president. Soon after the ouster of Bakiyev, it was decided that Otunbayeva's term of office would end by the end of 2011, and that she would not run for the presidential elections scheduled for October 2011.[18]

Another major development, which took place under Otunbayeva's rule, was the preparation of the new constitution, which significantly limited the presidential powers and made a shift to a parliamentary democracy, despite challenges coming from the supporters of Bakiyev.[19] In the new constitution, the powers of the president are decreased and those of the prime minster are increased. The president also has to work together with the parliament. According to Otunbayeva, the new constitution 'present[ed] a new system of checks and balances and a fresh and sober look at the judiciary'.[20] She also stated that this constitution 'built the first-ever new state model in Central Asia' to be followed by neighbours 'sooner or later'.[21]

The 2010 constitution was put to a nationwide referendum on June 27, 2010 and was favoured by 90.55 per cent of the voters, with a total turnout rate being 70 per cent.[22] The document makes a very clear emphasis on separation of powers in Article 3, Paragraph 2, by stating 'separation of state power' as one of the basic principles of Kyrgyzstan's political regime.[23] The constitution also clearly states in Article 5, Paragraph 2 that 'no part of the population, no association, and no separate person shall have the right to monopolise power in the state. Usurpation of state power shall be considered as a gravest crime'. In this framework, the presidential term of office is limited to one period of six years. As Article 61, Paragraph 2 states: "One and the same person may not be elected twice." Furthermore, it is now possible for the parliament (the Jogorku Kenesh) to impeach the president or adopt decisions on early dismissal of the president from office due to health reasons (Article 66). Upon dismissal from office, 'the President may be brought to criminal liability' (Article 67, Paragraph 2). The president does not 'have the right to call early elections of the Jogorku Kenesh or dismiss the Government' (Article 68, Paragraph 2).

The president also has no right to initiate legislation (Article 79), and has no real veto power, but some delaying power of 14 days over legislation, except for republican budget and taxes (Article 82). As for the Jogorku Kenesh, it has 120 deputies elected by proportional representation for a period of five years (Article 70, Paragraph 2). The Jogorku Kenesh is the responsible organ to call presidential elections and introducing changes to the present constitution (Article 74, Paragraphs 1&2).

As can be seen from such developments, Otunbayeva's legacy may have a very positive impact on the future prospects of Kyrgyzstan's democratic development, despite her short term of office as the country's third president. Otunbayeva set up a very good example in terms of 'opening the possibility for Kyrgyzstan to have the first peaceful transfer of power in Central Asia'.[24] Otunbayeva's rule, being both legal and legitimate, introduced important changes to the country's political regime. It has also been suggested that her willingness to leave office in 18 months as had been decided, resulted in increase in her popularity. After the 2011 presidential elections, she was greeted by many Bishkek residents with roses in their hands chanting 'Thank you Rosa'![25]

Prospects for Atambayev

Almazbek Atambayev became the president of Kyrgyzstan in the presidential elections held on October 30, 2011, getting 63 per cent of the votes cast. His main rivals, the leader of Butun Kyrgyzstan Adakhan Madumuradov and the leader of Ata-Jurt Kamchybek Tashiev, both got 14 per cent of the votes.[26] Born in 1956, Atambayev is a relatively young but quite experienced politician who entered the elections as the leader of the Kyrgyzstan's Social Democratic Party. He had previously served as the Prime Minister of Kyrgyzstan.[27]

One major priority of Atambayev is fighting corruption. According to him, "Corruption threatens Kyrgyzstan with [a] third revolution it will not survive."[28] As such, immediate practical measures need to be taken in order to restore order. If that cannot be achieved, 'people will grow tired'. According to Atambayev:

> "We cannot expect a solution to find itself. If we do not start working right now, Kyrgyzstan will lag behind every developed state in the medium-term future. ... Public officers are involved in corruptive practices. No matter how much we conceal the truth, corruption blooms in this country. We rank 166th amongst 180 states by corruption level, which is almost the last place. Some deputies boast of corruptive links. It is strange that some of our public officers are dollar millionaires; where does their wealth come from? I must tell all deputies, officials and government members that thieves will go to prison."[29]

In addition to fighting corruption, Atambayev also aims to bridge the divisions among the people of Kyrgyzstan along ethnic as well as regional lines. During his election campaign, he focused on the importance of unity in the country.[30] His main election campaign slogan, 'Kyrgyzstan is for all' clearly indicated where he stood on this issue.[31] One other clear attitude Atambayev adopted is a pro-Russian foreign policy, a choice that is supported by a majority of the people.[32] According to some analysts, 'it's clear that [Atambayev] is going to show the Russians more goodwill' as compared to the previous leaders of the country.[33]

Atambayev has started its term of office in a relatively more democratic political environment, mostly thanks to Otunbayeva's positive legacy. One of the most important developments in Kyrgyzstan over the course of months after Bakiyev's fall has been the way in which elections are held. Both the parliamentary elections in October 2010 and the presidential elections in October 2011 were 'fairly free and transparent' as compared to the ones held in previous years.[34] Even though some shortcomings and irregularities were reported, these were not significant and extensive enough to affect the outcome of the elections, which took place in a much transparent environment than ever.[35] As Marat indicated, the OSCE 'praised the peaceful and orderly manner in which the elections were conducted'.[36] Furthermore, as Tuigunaaly Abdraimov, the head of the Kyrgyz Central Elections Commission (CEC), indicated, the CEC was instructed 'to look into the crudest irregularities reported' and 'if they prove true, to cancel the voting results in [such] districts'.[37]

Another related issue that needs to be addressed is the general negative attitude on the part of the Kyrgyz leaders to change the constitution, unlike the first two presidents of the country. For example, parliamentary speaker Akhmatbek Keldibekov said in a meeting that 'the constitution is not a dogma, but one should not change it too often'. According to him, in order to preserve national stability and unity, 'compliance with the fundamental law and constitutional norms is a topical goal of the entire society of Kyrgyzstan'.[38] One other important step was taken in December 2011 when the Jogorku Kenesh discussed the creation of a national torture prevention centre. As the United Nations Special Rapporteur on Torture and Cruel, Inhuman and Degrading Treatment or Punishment, Juan Mendez indicated, "It doesn't matter what form the centre will take place ... the important thing is that it [will] function."[39] One recent development is related to a new policy to foster ethnic peace between the country's Uzbeks and the Kyrgyz. Local government in Osh, in an attempt to 'heal wounds' left by the violent clashes in June 2010,[40] tries to bring the two communities together by mixed marriages. As Gulmara Erkolova, a state employee at the city hall in Osh, indicated these couples become eligible for payment of approximately US$ 2,000, an amount that can be used for a variety of needs of the newlyweds.[41]

Challenges for Atambayev

Despite all such positive developments, however, Atambayev faces several important political challenges as well. One of the most important challenges that Atambayev has to deal with is the potential threat of tension between the Kyrgyz and Uzbek populations of the country, which had resulted in bloody ethnic clashes on two occasions. The first such occasion took place back in 1990 in the city of Osh. Being the second largest city in Kyrgyzstan after Bishkek, Osh has a sizeable Uzbek population. As Liu suggests:

> "Because Osh is squeezed between mountains to its immediate south and the border with Uzbekistan to its immediate north, land use for agriculture, industry, mahalla [neighbourhoods] (mostly Uzbek) and apartment complexes (Kyrgyz, Russian, Uzbek and others) have been in a perpetual zero-sum deadlock."[42]

The immediate triggering event of the first Osh conflict was also related to the scarcity of land. In April 1990, some nationalist minded Kyrgyz youth activists from the Osh-aimagy organisation directed 500 appeals to local authorities for the allocation of land for Kyrgyz families. When their demands were not met, they threatened that they will start seizing the land for themselves. Eventually the local authorities agreed to give an agricultural field that belonged to an Uzbek collective farm for housing purposes to the Kyrgyz. This decision angered the Uzbeks and dramatically increased the tensions between the two communities.[43] Eventually in June 1990, the tensions escalated into bloody ethnic clashes between the Kyrgyz and the Uzbeks in Osh because of which more than 200 people died.[44]

However, there were deeper resentments between the Kyrgyz and the Uzbeks in the country. From the perspective of the Kyrgyz, the Uzbeks had 'all the best jobs in the retail and consumer sector'.[45] So the Kyrgyz 'resented the relative wealth and prominence of the local Uzbeks' controlling at least 80 per cent of the city's trade.[46] The Uzbeks, on the other hand, claimed that despite their economic and demographic dominance in Osh, they were underrepresented in the country's political life.[47] Therefore, prior to the Osh incident, there were several tensions between these two communities that had socioeconomic reasons.[48]

In the post-Soviet era, such tensions continued to be influential, eventually culminating in the second bloody ethnic incident between these two communities in June 2010, again in the city of Osh. In the predawn hours of June 10-11, youth gangs from the two communities gambling in a casino in Osh started arguing with each other. Soon the conflict escalated into a fighting on the street with others joining in. Upon false rumours that an Uzbek mob raped 12 Kyrgyz girls and killed three, anger among the Kyrgyz increased. By early morning, attacks on Uzbek neighbourhoods started with counterattacks on the part of the Uzbeks soon following.[49] When the clashes could finally be taken under control by June 15, at least 435 people were dead and over 2,000 others were injured.[50]

In addition to the clashes between the ethnic groups in Kyrgyzstan, there are divisions among the Kyrgyz people themselves. Commonly known as the north-south divide, this type of regionalism can be considered as the natural outcome of geographical conditions of the country, which separates these two regions from each other with high mountains. This separation would have direct impact on the development of different cultures, traditions and world views of the people.[51] Broadly, up north where Bishkek, Issyk-Kul and Talas are located, people are a lot more Russified and secular, using Russian as their first language and retaining Soviet influences; whereas down south where Osh, Jalalabad, and Batken are located, people are more under the influence of Islam as well as their customs and traditions.[52] Furthermore, it has been suggested that even during the Soviet era such traditional ties of tribal and regional nature could not be eradicated.[53] To make things even more complicated, there are further sub-divisions among the people living both in the north and in the south.[54]

However, it must also be kept in mind that economic factors play a major role to exacerbate the differences and tensions between these two regions. The north has been more developed as compared to the south where population density and unemployment are more commonly seen. Under such economic conditions, drug trafficking and radical Islamic activities also concentrate in the south.[55] As has been suggested by Lewis, "For the most part, however, the reality of these divisions was only instrumentally about the issues of identity and culture: in general the key dynamic of the north-south cleavages was about access to resources and rent-seeking state positions".[56]

This structure has an impact on the political power struggles in post-Soviet Kyrgyzstan as well. As Ryabkov suggested, since 1991, northern and southern elites 'have played different roles' in the political life of the country.[57] Since tribal and regional loyalties proved to be resilient, the political process in Kyrgyzstan 'is dominated by a hidden power struggle between major clans that represented traditional rivalries'.[58] In the post-Soviet era, although there were some attempts on the part of the central leaders to reduce the importance of regionalism, for most part it turned out to be the case that 'power in Kyrgyzstan was, and would remain, regionally based'.[59] As put forward by Beshimov, "In order to survive, Kyrgyz leaders need to work cleverly with and balance among clans and regional groups. But this is very hard to do—it requires superb flexibility and personal strength."[60]

Conclusion

Despite all odds and all incidents of political instability, such as the downfall of two presidents and ethnic clashes, Kyrgyzstan continues to be the most successful country in Central Asia 'doing much better' in terms of moving towards a more democratic system.[61] As Anderson suggests, the country 'retains a considerable degree of social pluralism and a more open political space than any of its Central Asian neighbours'.[62] Many scholars also indicate that civil society institutions can function more freely in this supportive environment of free expression and tolerance.[63]

Soon after Akayev came to power, he would call his country 'an oasis of democracy' and 'an island in the midst of a tempest, which could, however, be suppressed by high seas'.[64] Some of the recent developments after the fall of Bakiyev seem to be hopeful indicators of Kyrgyzstan regaining its ground as the 'island of democracy'. The country took effective measures to curb executive power after two decades of painful experimentation with democracy. As was explained above, since 1991 Kyrgyzstan has been challenged with several incidences of political instability, despite the major concern on the part of the leaders on political stability. However, it must also be kept in mind that, authoritarian regimes, which are seemingly more 'stable', may be faced with much bloodier, sudden and dramatic power changes. As for Kyrgyzstan, the incidents of 2002, 2005, and 2010 may simply be 'safety valves' to keep the country together without being drifted into a civil war and to keep a more democratic regime intact in the long-run. In other words, experimentations with democracy (with all its ups and downs) may, in the long-run, provide a more solid base on which Kyrgyzstan can become a real island of democracy as compared to seemingly stable Turkmenistan, Uzbekistan and Tajikistan. Kyrgyzstan paid a heavy price in all of the above-mentioned incidents of instability and it seems as if these unfortunate events had a positive impact on the development of democracy in the country. The new leaders seem to be aware of the dangers of repeating the mistakes of Akayev and Bakiyev in terms of concentrating executive power. As Beshimov points out: "Now a new crop of politicians needs to show they're able to practice what for this country is a new kind of politics, and pave a road to peaceful change of power, through fair elections. They have a chance to challenge the assumption that their country is destined—by location and historical circumstance—to tyranny and violence."[65]

Recent developments that took place in Kyrgyzstan since Bakiyev's ouster are critical for the country's future path toward democratisation. Some experts suggest that the political actors in Kyrgyzstan are getting used to the new system of parliamentary governance in which most decisions are made by the legislative, rather than the executive, making political compromises and consensus inevitable.[66] However, despite all positive developments, the new era may have its own challenges, such as establishing a stable, functioning coalition. For example, just one day after the presidential inauguration of Atambayev, the parliamentary faction leader of Kyrgyz Social Democratic Party Chynybai Tursunbekov announced that his party was leaving the parliamentary coalition.[67] According to Social Democrats, the contradictions of the coalition 'had become irreconcilable'.[68] Such 'irreconcilable contradictions' among the parties of the new Kyrgyz parliamentary regime have the potential threat of yet another type of political instability. Prior to the break-up of the coalition, an expert said:

> "The constitution does not state in clear and specific terms who is responsible for what. The different institutions may come to a working arrangement on how power is to be distributed. If that doesn't happen, conflicts will arise. The current governing coalition will fall apart, followed by attempts to build a new one. If that doesn't work, parliament will be dissolved and we will be back to elections and confrontation. I don't think many people want that."[69]

To conclude, it is possible to suggest that the people of Kyrgyzstan are fed up with confrontations, instabilities and ethnic clashes. Now is the country's chance to go back to being an 'island of democracy' once again. This new era presents both an excellent opportunity and a major challenge for Atambayev and the parliament. In case they both refrain from making the same mistakes of Akayev and Bakiyev, Kyrgyzstan may succeed in consolidating its democracy and as such may set an example for the region as an 'oasis' of democracy.

Notes

1. Giampaolo Capisani, *The Handbook of Central Asia: A Comprehensive Survey of the New Republics*, (London: I. B. Tauris, 2000), p. 208.
2. Peter L. Roudnik, *The History of Central Asian Republics*, Greenwood Press, Connecticut, 2007, pp. 150-151. For a detailed analysis of the developments in Kyrgyzstan's first decade after independence, see John Anderson, *Kyrgyzstan: Central Asia's Island of Democracy*, (The Netherlands: Harwood Academic Publishers, 1999), pp. 22-63.
3. For a detailed account of these referendums and elections see, Dinara Murzaeva, *Transition to Democracy in Post-Soviet Kyrgyzstan: Leaders, Citizens and Perceptions of Political Legitimacy*, (Ankara: METU, 2011).
4. Scott Radnitz, 'Networks, Localism and Mobilization in Aksy, Kyrgyzstan,' *Central Asian Survey*, 24 (4), 2005, p. 410.
5. David Lewis, "The Dynamics of Regime Change: Domestic and International Factors in the 'Tulip Revolution'", in Sally N. Cummings (ed.), *Domestic and International Perspectives on Kyrgyzstan's Tulip Revolution: Motives, Mobilization and Meanings*, (London: Routledge, 2010), p. 45.
6. For a detailed analysis of the Aksy events, see Scott Radnitz, 'Networks, Localism and Mobilization in Aksy, Kyrgyzstan,' *Central Asian Survey*, 24 (4), 2005, pp. 405-424.
7. For a detailed analysis of the Tulip Revolution, see Sally N. Cummings (ed.), *Domestic and International Perspectives on Kyrgyzstan's Tulip Revolution: Motives, Mobilization and Meanings*, (London: Routledge, 2010).
8. Radnitz, 'Networks, Localism and Mobilization in Aksy, Kyrgyzstan,' p. 406.
9. Radnitz, 'Networks, Localism and Mobilization in Aksy, Kyrgyzstan,' p. 405.
10. Bermet Tursunkulova, 'The Power of Precedent,' *Central Asian Survey*, 27 (3-4), 2008, p. 349.
11. Tursunkulova, 'The Power of Precedent,' *Central Asian Survey*, 27 (3-4), 2008, p. 359.
12. Tursunkulova, 'The Power of Precedent,' *Central Asian Survey*, 27 (3-4), 2008, p. 357.
13. Yaşar Sarı, 'Kırgızistan'da İktidarın El Değiştirmesi: Akayev ve Bakiyev'in Düşüşü,' *Orta Asya ve Kafkasya Araştırmaları*, 5 (9), 2010, p. 29.
14. Bakyt Beshimov, "Kyrgyz Democracy's Narrowing Window of Opportunity,"

at Transitions Online, 12141615, October 10, 2010, http://ehis.ebscohost.com (Accessed on February 02, 2012). For a detailed analysis of political developments that took place prior to the fall of Akaev and Bakiyev, see Yaşar Sarı, 'Kırgızistan'da İktidarın El Değiştirmesi: Akayev ve Bakiyev'in Düşüşü,' *Orta Asya ve Kafkasya Araştırmaları*, 5 (9), 2010, p. 27-47.

15. Bermet Tursunkulova, 'The Power of Precedent,' *Central Asian Survey*, 27 (3-4), 2008, p. 360.
16. Tursunkulova, 'The Power of Precedent,' *Central Asian Survey*, 27 (3-4), 2008, pp. 353-354.
17. Erica Marat, "Kyrgyzstan Marks the First Peaceful Transfer of Power", *Eurasia Daily Monitor*, vol. 219 (December 2011), pp. 7-9, at http://ehis.ebscohost.com (Accessed on February 24, 2012).
18. Sarı, 'Kırgızistan'da İktidarın El Değiştirmesi: Akayev ve Bakiyev'in Düşüşü,' *Orta Asya ve Kafkasya Araştırmaları*, 5 (9), 2010, p. 41.
19. Columbia Electronic Encyclopedia, 6th Edition, "Roza Otunbayeva," December 01, 2011, at http://ehis.ebscohost.com (Accessed on February 24, 2012).
20. "Kyrgyz Constitution Cannot be Altered for 20 Years," Rosa Otunbayeva. Interfax, Central Asia Business News, May 16, 2011, at http://ehis.ebscohost.com (Accessed on February 02, 2012).
21. "Kyrgyz Constitution Needs to be More Specific," President Rosa Otunbayeva. Interfax, Russia & FSU General News, May 05, 2011.
22. "New Kyrgyz Constitution Favored by 90.55 % Voters, Official Results," Interfax, Military News Agency, 16095863, July 02, 2010 at http://ehis.ebscohost.com (Accessed on February 02, 2012).
23. Unless otherwise indicated, all references to the 2010 Constitution are taken from the Unofficial translation from Russian was done by the EU-UNDP Project on Support to the Constitutional and Parliamentary Reforms and OSCE/ODIHR. This translation is available at: http://www.wipo.int/wipolex/en/text.jsp?file_id=254747 (Accessed on February 24, 2012).
24. Erica Marat, "Kyrgyzstan's Presidential Elections: As Good as it Gets in Central Asia," November 02, 2011, at http://www.cacianalyst.org/?q=node/5657/print (Accessed on February 06, 2012). For more information on the electoral outcomes, see www.shailoo.gov.kr
25. Marat, "Kyrgyzstan Marks the First Peaceful Transfer of Power".
26. Marat, "Kyrgyzstan's Presidential Elections: As Good as it Gets in Central Asia".
27. Timur Toktonaliev, "Now That He's Won, Atambayev Must Start Delivering," November 08, 2011 (IWPR/UNIVERSAL), at http://www.universalnewswires.com (Accessed on February 06, 2012).
28. "Corruption Threatens Kyrgyzstan with Third Revolution it will not Survive," President Atambayev. Interfax, Military News Agency, 16095863, January 30, 2012,

at http://ehis.ebscohost.com (Accessed on February 24, 2012).

29. "Corruption Threatens Kyrgyzstan with Third Revolution it will not Survive," President Atambayev.
30. Marat, "Kyrgyzstan Marks the First Peaceful Transfer of Power".
31. Marat, "Kyrgyzstan's Presidential Elections: As Good as it Gets in Central Asia".
32. For an account of such opinions, see Erica Marat, "After Winning Elections Atambaev Focuses on the US Transit Center," Eurasia Daily Monitor, vol. 8, Issue 208, pp. 6-8, November 03, 2011, at http://www.jamestown.org (Accessed on May 09, 2012).
33. Toktonaliev, "Now That He's Won, Atambayev Must Start Delivering".
34. Marat, "Kyrgyzstan's Presidential Elections: As Good as it Gets in Central Asia".
35. Toktonaliev, "Now That He's Won, Atambayev Must Start Delivering".
36. Marat, "Kyrgyzstan's Presidential Elections: As Good as it Gets in Central Asia".
37. "Atambayev Wins Kyrgyz Presidential Election – Head of Central Elections Commission (Part 2)," Interfax, Russia & FSU General News, October 31, 2011, at http://ehis.ebscohost.com (Accessed on February 24, 2012).
38. "Kyrgyz Constitution Needs to be More Specific," President Rosa Otunbayeva. Interfax, Russia & FSU General News, May 05, 2011, http://ehis.ebscohost.com (Accessed on February 24, 2012).
39. Erkin Kamalov, "Kyrgyz Parliament Considers Creating Torture Prevention Centre," December 06, 2011, http://centralasiaonline.com/en_GB/articles/caii/newsbriefs/2011/12/06/newsbrief-05 (Accessed on February 06, 2012).
40. Information on these clashes will be provided in the next part.
41. Nicolas Tanner, "Kyrgyzstan Urges Long-time Uzbek-Kyrgyz Enemies to Marry," Washington Times/Universal, December 06, 2011, at http://www.universalnewswires.com/centralasia/viewstory.aspx?id=10862 (Accessed on February 06, 2012).
42. Morgan Y. Liu, "A Central Asian Tale of Two Cities: Locating Lives and Aspirations in a Shifting Post- Soviet Cityscape", in Jeff Sahadeo and Russell Zanca (eds.), *Everyday Life in Central Asia: Past and Present*, (Indiana: Indiana University Press, 2007), p. 68.
43. John Anderson, *Kyrgyzstan: Central Asia's Island of Democracy*, (The Netherlands: Harwood Academic Publishers, 1999), p. 20; Morgan Y. Liu, "A Central Asian Tale of Two Cities: Locating Lives and Aspirations in a Shifting Post- Soviet Cityscape", in Jeff Sahadeo and Russell Zanca (eds.), *Everyday Life in Central Asia: Past and Present*, (Indiana: Indiana University Press, 2007), p. 68.
44. *Kyrgyzstan: Then and Now*, (USA: Lerner Publication Company, 1993), p. 36.
45. John Anderson, *Kyrgyzstan: Central Asia's Island of Democracy*, (The Netherlands: Harwood Academic Publishers, 1999), p. 19.
46. Gene Huskey, "Kyrgyzstan: the Politics of Demographic and Economic Frustration", in Ian Bremmer and Ray Taras (eds.), *Nations and Politics in the Soviet Successor States*, (Cambridge: Cambridge University Press, 1993), p. 406.

47. Huskey, "Kyrgyzstan: the Politics of Demographic and Economic Frustration", p. 406; Michael Kort, *Central Asian Republics*, Facts on File, (New York, 2004), p. 154.
48. Sarı, 'Kırgızistan'da İktidarın El Değiştirmesi: Akayev ve Bakiyev'in Düşüşü,' *Orta Asya ve Kafkasya Araştırmaları*, 5 (9), 2010.
49. Bruce Pannier, "Audio menu Internet TV Kyrgyzstan: Anatomy of A Conflict," July 02, 2010, at http://www.rferl.org/content/Kyrgyzstan_Anatomy_Of_A_Conflict/2089464.html (Accessed on February 07, 2012).
50. "Kyrgyz Speaker Proposes Admitting Head of International Commission Probing June 2010 Clashes," Interfax, Russia & FSU General News, July 02, 2011at http://ehis.ebscohost.com (Accessed on February 07, 2012).
51. David Lewis, "The Dynamics of Regime Change: Domestic and International Factors in the 'Tulip Revolution'", in Sally N. Cummings (ed.), *Domestic and International Perspectives on Kyrgyzstan's Tulip Revolution: Motives, Mobilization and Meanings*, (London: Routledge, 2010), p. 52; Yaşar Sarı, 'Kırgızistan'da İktidarın El Değiştirmesi: Akayev ve Bakiyev'in Düşüşü,' *Orta Asya ve Kafkasya Araştırmaları*, 5 (9), 2010, p. 31.
52. Michael Kort, *Central Asian Republics*, Facts on File, New York, 2004, pp. 151-152.
53. Seçil Öraz, 'Tribal Connections within the Political Processes: the Case of Kyrgyzstan', *Orta Asya ve Kafkasya Araştırmaları*, 1 (2), 2006, p. 89.
54. Lewis, "The Dynamics of Regime Change: Domestic and International Factors in the 'Tulip Revolution".
55. Although not seen as a major problem as compared to countries such as Uzbekistan and Tajikistan, radical Islam constitutes another major threat for Kyrgyzstan. The country had its own share of events challenging its political system. One of the most widely known incidents took place in 1999 when the guerilla forces of the Islamic Movement of Uzbekistan (IMU) infiltrated into the Batken region of Kyrgyzstan and killed at least 18 government troops and took some Kyrgyz police officers, four American geologists and four Japanese tourists hostage (see Michael Kort, *Central Asian Republics*, Facts on File, New York, 2004, p. 161). Some scholars point out that this was one of the most important developments which weakened Akaev's rule, as Kyrgyz security forces proved to be inefficient in fighting with IMU militants and the government had to ask for help from other countries. As such, Kyrgyzstan developed a negative image as a country that cannot protect even its own territory, contributing the rise of several doubts in the minds of the people about its future (see Yaşar Sarı, 'Kırgızistan'da İktidarın El Değiştirmesi: Akayev ve Bakiyev'in Düşüşü,' *Orta Asya ve Kafkasya Araştırmaları*, 5 (9), 2010, p. 33).
56. Lewis, "The Dynamics of Regime Change: Domestic and International Factors in the 'Tulip Revolution".
57. Maxim Ryabkov, "The North-South Cleavage and Political Support in Kyrgyzstan", in Sally N. Cummings (ed.), *Domestic and International Perspectives on Kyrgyzstan's*

Tulip Revolution: Motives, Mobilization and Meanings, (London: Routledge, 2010), p. 77.

58. Öraz, 'Tribal Connections within the Political Processes: the Case of Kyrgyzstan'.
59. Pauline Jones Luong, *Institutional Change and Political Continuity in Post-Soviet Central Asia: Power, Perceptions and Pacts*, (Cambridge: Cambridge University Press, 2002), p. 165.
60. Bakyt Beshimov, "Kyrgyz Democracy's Narrowing Window of Opportunity," at Transitions Online, 12141615, October 10, 2010, http://ehis.ebscohost.com (Accessed on February 02, 2012).
61. Peter L. Roudnik, *The History of Central Asian Republics*, Greenwood Press, Connecticut, 2007, p. 149; Richard Pomfret, *The Central Asian Economies Since Independence*, (New Jersey: Princeton University Press, 2006), p. 86.
62. Anderson, *Kyrgyzstan: Central Asia's Island of Democracy*, p. 23.
63. Kelly M. McMann, "The Civic Realm in Kyrgyzstan: Soviet Economic Legacies and Activists' Expectations", in Pauline Jones Luong (ed.), *The Transformation of Central Asia: Sates and Societies from Soviet Rule to Independence*, (USA: Cornell University Press, 2004), pp. 244-245; Erkinbek Kasybekov, "Government and Nonprofit Sector Relations in the Kyrgyz Republic", in M. Holt Ruffin and Daniel Waugh (eds.), *Civil Society in Central Asia*, (USA: University of Washington Press, 1999), p. 71; Erica Marat, "March and After: What has Changed? What has Stayed the Same?", in Sally N. Cummings (ed.) *Domestic and International Perspectives on Kyrgyzstan's Tulip Revolution: Motives, Mobilization and Meanings*, (London: Routledge, 2010), p. 7.
64. Giampaolo Capisani, *The Handbook of Central Asia: A Comprehensive Survey of the New Republics*, (London: I. B. Tauris, 2000), p. 212.
65. Bakyt Beshimov, "Kyrgyz Democracy's Narrowing Window of Opportunity," at Transitions Online, 12141615, 10 October 2010, http://ehis.ebscohost.com (Accessed February 2, 2012).
66. Marat, "Kyrgyzstan Marks the First Peaceful Transfer of Power".
67. Asyl Osmonaliyeva, "Kyrgyz Parliamentary Coalition Collapses," December 02, 2011, at http://centralasiaonline.com (Accessed on February 06, 2012).
68. Asker Sultanov, "Atambayev Joins Talks on New Parliamentary Coalition," December 05, 2011, http://centralasiaonline.com/en_GB/articles/caii/newsbriefs/2011/12/05/newsbrief-06
69. Toktonaliev, "Now That He's Won, Atambayev Must Start Delivering".

8. Kyrgyzstan: Achievements and Problems

R.G. Gidadhubli

Since its independent existence (during the last two decades), Kyrgyzstan has achieved major successes in political and economic fields. At the same time, it has sustained severe economic downturns, regional upheavals, two revolutions, and high ethnic tensions. Among the Commonwealth of Independent States, this tiny Central Asian country, though not very richly endowed with resource potentials, has to its credit the distinction of the membership of World Trade Organization (WTO). Equally significant is the fact that the country has brought about constitutional changes—from the Presidential form to the Parliamentary form of government. With this view, it is worthwhile to examine some of the latest developments in this Central Asian country.

Ethnic Issue

Factional differences, which have persisted over decades between the majority Kyrgyz and the Uzbeks in the southern region of Kyrgyz Republic, resurfaced recently. The tragic event became evident in the contemporary history of Kyrgyzstan in June 2010 when the country suffered the worst form of violence in which about 2,000 people were killed or wounded, and about 4,00,000 people were displaced, seeking shelter in the Jalalabad region in bordering Uzbekistan. The Ferghana Valley, where violence occurred, is a tinderbox of ethnic conflicts, and has borders with three Central Asian States—Kyrgyzstan, Uzbekistan, and Tajikistan. In fact, the borders were arbitrarily drawn in the 1920s under Stalin's rule. Apart from the Kyrgyz population who are dominant in number, Uzbeks have been living here for several decades and are actively engaged in economic activities such as agriculture and commerce while Kyrgyz were mainly in mountainous regions and were traditionally nomadic. During the

Soviet era, there were not many conflicts, on any large scale, except some on issues of sharing land and water; they were controlled by Moscow. Analysts have argued that the conflicts in June 2010 were mainly caused by groups who had vested interest in creating problems for the present government.

Referendum

Even as the aftereffects of June 2010 violence were felt, the country had made significant achievements in sociopolitical and economic fields. It was highly creditable that the Interim government of the Kyrgyz Republic in the Central Asian region headed by Rosa Otunbayeva successfully held the promised Referendum on June 27, 2010 though the environment was extremely difficult. In fact, there were divergent views expressed on the desirability of holding it. An International human rights organisation criticised the timing of referendum contending that hardly 15 days earlier the country witnessed ethnic violence. On the other hand, the UN, and the leaders of Russia and the US were of the view that the Referendum would legitimise the claim of the Interim government, which had come to power in April 2010 after violent protests leading to the ouster of the former president Kurmanbek Bakiyev who is in exile in Byelorussia. In fact, the decision to hold the Referendum was taken much before the violence in April 2010 soon after the Interim government assumed office. Rosa Otunbayeva was determined to hold it even as the country was struggling to bring normalcy to the situation. The government lifted the curfew and strong security arrangements were made for holding the Referendum, which was peaceful. In fact, to prove her contention and determination, she cast her vote in the city of Osh, which was the epicenter of bloodshed. Thus, Rosa Otunbayeva has created history by being the first woman in the Central Asian region to head the government and by holding the referendum to establish her authority as a leader acceptable to the country.

Hence, there was high appreciation for the referendum, which was monitored by about 70 international observers and media personnel from several Western countries, Russia and former Soviet Republics, Shanghai

Cooperation Organization, etc. and the observer of the Organization of the Security and Cooperation of Europe (OSCE) opined that the voting was 'Fairly Transparent'. About 70 per cent of voters from the northern part and about 50 per cent of southern part took part, indicating wide participation in referendum, and negating allegation of possible manipulation and falsification of election. The Interim government, which was called 'Caretaker Government', claimed legitimacy with the support of about 65 per cent supporting it in the Referendum which was more than the minimum of 50.1 per cent required by law.

By holding the referendum, Rosa Otunbayeva won only half the battle. The country was facing several problems and challenges. Firstly, the threat of violence persisted since several criminal elements including drug mafia groups, which were active and initiated violence, by arson and looting in the second week of June had not been eliminated. Ethnic differences between the majority Kyrgyz and the Uzbeks, which contributed to the clashes, persisted even as the Interim government had tried to reduce the animosity that triggered conflict. Secondly, there were forces in the country, which were not accepting the verdict of referendum and tried to create problems for the government. The ousted President Kurmanbek Bakiyev who is hiding in exile in Byelorussia since April 2010 and his family members including his son Maksim and his three brothers who were alleged to have financed and planned violence in the second week of June 2010 tried to trigger violence again to prevent legal action being contemplated by the Interior government. There are allegations that they have amassed wealth at the cost of the country through corrupt practices. Hence, their intention was to prevent smooth functioning of the government so that they could come back to power.

Thirdly, individuals and parties openly expressed their views against policies of the government. Moreover, Niyazov apart from alleging that there were mass falsification of voting even warned that the 'consequences could be unpredictable'. This was very serious and could mean possibility of threats of repeated violence and even political agitations by his party causing instability to the Interim government. As per reports, these former leaders could be having strong links with some sections of the security forces in the southern part of country, which could be used as it was alleged during the violence in June 2010. Thus, money power and muscle power were used to frustrate the programmes of the Caretaker government.

Fourthly, according to some analysts, fundamentalist forces including the Islamic Movement of Uzbekistan were reported to be part of groups escalating violence and have been active in Central Asia including in the Ferghana Valley comprising part of Uzbekistan, south Kyrgyzstan, and Tajikistan to destabilise the peace by creating violence. The president of Kazakhstan Nursultan Nazarbayev expressed his concern about the possibility of ethnic disturbances in Central Asia. Fifthly, the government had to face major challenges of economic development, which were quite formidable. Because even before taking over the reigns of government, the Kyrgyz economy was experiencing crisis due to mounting external debt, high inflation, energy deficit, decline in industrial and agricultural production, high rate of unemployment, widening economic disparities, and so on. The violence had worsened the economic situation since the new government needed huge resources not only for reviving economic development but also for the rehabilitation of lakhs of refugees who had returned to their hometowns. The economic damage caused by violence has been enormous.

Rosa Otunbayeva rightly opined that the solution to the problems was for the country to be given time to calm down and leave quarrels behind, to digest all ethnic process that were going on in the country with an economy in transition and a tumultuous political life. She advised strongly that all the Kyrgyz must find a formula of cohabitation, a system of coordination where everyone would feel comfortable and find his or her place. In all fairness, it needs to be stated that in comparison to other Central Asian states, Kyrgyz state has a strong civil society and growing role of political parties. Some analysts opine that historically the Kyrgyz nationality has democracy in the blood and during the last two decades, it is shown that the Kyrgyz people are in favour of open democratic rule. These positive factors will enable the country to overcome problems and challenges.

Another important achievement is that the government adopted a new Constitution, which proposed to convert Kyrgyzstan from the present presidential form to a parliamentary one in which the powers of the president were to be drastically reduced. Elections were held and a new government has been formed, thus establishing that normal political situation prevails in the country. The leadership of the country needs to be given due credit because there were 100 parties in this small country of 3.5 million population with diversity of ethnic groups and interests. There are not only ethic differences, which are quite strong, there are also differences among clans even within same ethnic group of Kyrgyz between North and South. Thus, getting the consent of parliament was a major challenge. Notwithstanding several constraints, the government was able to get the approval for constitutional changes, which are unique among the CIS for which the leadership of Kyrgyzstan needs to be credited.

New Government

The Kyrgyz Republic has witnessed regime changes during the last two decades, which is in sharp contrast to other Central Asian States. Looking back in 2005 the then Kyrgyz president Askar Akayev and his government were overthrown because of accusations of mismanagement. In fact, this tiny Central Asian State was a victim of color revolution in 2005 known as Tulip Revolution subsequent to the Rose Revolution in Georgia and Orange Revolution in Ukraine in 2004. As a result, there had been a demand for constitutional reform caused by political and constitutional crisis when Kurmanbek Bakiyev took over presidency. Kyrgyzstan has attempted in bringing about changes in the constitution to work out a balance within the political system.

In December 2011, the Kyrgyzstan state ushered in a new political era with a new government after the election was held as per the provisions of the new Constitution. This is a coalition government, which brings together four parties—Respublika, the Social Democratic Party, Ar-Namys, and Ata-Meken. On December 24, 2011 Omurbek Babanov, the leader of the Respublika Party, was appointed as the prime minister. The wealthy, Moscow-educated 41-year old has vowed to fight widespread corruption and to focus on boosting prosperity. Rosa Otunbayeva is not in power, and thus, the Kyrgyz state has shown that it is an exception in Central Asia, which is known for its long-serving leaders, many of whom have not left the presidency for two decades. The new cabinet has many experienced professionals as also some old faces that have served under various previous cabinets. For instance, Saparbek Tynaev, who at 63 has taken over as agriculture minister, served as a deputy minister from 1996 through 2001 under former President Askar Akaev. Newly appointed Finance Minister Akylbek Zhaparov held the same portfolio under President Kurmanbek Bakiyev in 2006. Likewise, the new deputy Prime Minister Aali Karashev had served in the same post during the Bakiyev era. As opined by some analysts, there will be continuity in the policies of the new government and radical changes are unlikely. However, there are reservations by some critics about the possibility of introducing much needed reforms. Moreover, the Kyrgyz state has also become a victim of inter party rivalries. For instance, in December 2011, the speaker of Kyrgyz parliament Akmatbek Keldibekov resigned on allegation of links with criminal elements. But his supporters clamed that it was blackmail and demanded that Omurbek Tekebaev of Ata-Meken (Fatherland) party who also leads the party's parliament faction, should resign, which shows that inter-party rivalries persist.

Economic Achievements and Constraints

Kyrgyzstan is a relatively less developed mountainous country with a dominant agricultural sector. Cotton, tobacco, wool, and meat are the main agricultural products, although only tobacco and cotton are exported in some quantity. Industrial exports include gold, mercury, uranium, natural gas, and electricity. The economy depends heavily on gold exports—mainly from the output at the Kumtor gold mine.

Looking back, the breakup of the former Soviet Union was sudden and unexpected, and hence, the Central Asian States were not prepared to deal with this situation. Therefore, the economic decline in the first decade of independence was enormous particularly for small states such as the Kyrgyz Republic and Tajikistan. This is evident from the fact that Gross Domestic Product declined by about -5 to -20 per cent per annum in the 1990s with equally sharp decline in industrial production. Hyperinflation was ranging between 800-2,000 per cent per annum in the first half of the 1990s, and unemployment was ranging between 20-30 per cent of labor force. As a result, about 40-50 per cent of population went below poverty line, and the country experienced huge external debt.

At the same time following independence, Kyrgyz leaders took progressive policy measures in carrying out market reforms, such as an improved regulatory system in economic management and land reforms in agriculture. Notwithstanding economic problems, the Kyrgyz leaders undertook various economic reform policy measures including some of aspects of controversial Shock Therapy (ST). In 2004, the former deputy prime minister J Otarbayev justified that ST was a positive step. The Kyrgyz Republic also set up Free Economic Zones (FEZs) in Bishkek, Naryn, Karakul, etc. to attract foreign capital, joint ventures, and so on. The Kyrgyz government provided incentives for investment, simplified customs, and registration procedures. Apart from these reform policy measures, Kyrgyzstan was one of the first countries to implement full current account convertibility, which helped the country to be granted the membership of the WTO in 1998. In fact, Kyrgyzstan was the first Commonwealth of Independent States (CIS) country to be accepted into the World Trade Organization.

After overcoming the crisis period of the 1990s, Kyrgyzstan reported a 5-6 per cent annual average GDP growth during the 2000-08. This was confirmed also by Ben Slay, a Senior Economist for the UNDP Bureau for Europe and the Commonwealth of Independent States. In fact in 2005, the Bakiyev government and international financial institutions initiated a comprehensive medium-term poverty reduction and economic growth strategy. Moreover, Bishkek agreed to pursue much needed tax reforms, and in 2006, the country became eligible for support under the scheme of the Heavily Indebted Poor Countries (HIPC). As a result, the government made steady strides in controlling its substantial fiscal deficit, nearly closing the gap between revenues and expenditures in

2007-08. GDP grew at about 8 per cent annually in 2007-08, partly due to higher gold prices internationally, but slowed down to 2.3 per cent in 2009. The overthrow of President Bakiyev in April 2010, and subsequent ethnic clashes, left hundreds dead and damaged infrastructure. Shrinking trade and agricultural production, as well as political instability, caused GDP to contract to about 3.5 per cent in 2010, which is evident from the data given in table-1. The fiscal deficit widened to 11 per cent of GDP, reflecting significant increases in crisis-related spending, including both rehabilitation of damaged infrastructure and bank recapitalisation. Hence, progress in reconstruction, fighting corruption, restructuring domestic industry, and attracting foreign aid and investment are key to future growth.

In 2011-12, agricultural sector accounted for about 21 per cent, industry 28 per cent while services about 51 per cent in the total GDP. This shows that during the last two decades there has been a major change in the composition of GDP since during the Soviet era, the industry accounted for the largest share while services sector was the lowest. One reason for the high growth of service sector is that the Kyrgyz Republic has emerged as the largest service provider in the Central Asian region. This is a new development with high potential as rightly asserted by the then governor of Osh province in 2006. A major problem that is persisting is the underdevelopment of the country which is evident from the fact that even at present about one-third of the population is below poverty line in the country which has about two and half million labour force. Agriculture accounts for about 48 per cent of population, and service sector has about 40 per cent and industry a mere 13 per cent of labour force. Officially, the unemployment rate is about 18-20 per cent but in reality it is about 25-30 per cent of the working age group of population.

So far as the financial position is concerned, in 2010 the total revenue was US$ 1.262 billion against expenditure of US$ 1.496 billion, thus, having deficit of about US$ 234 million, which is about 5 per cent of budget as per some western estimates. The country also faces high inflation, which though officially claimed to be about 9 per cent, but actually it could be about 15 per cent during the last few years. The main branches of industries are small scale enterprises dealing with manufacture or parts of machinery, textile units, food processing, cement, shoe making, wood cutting, refrigerator repairs, furniture making, electric motors, mining of gold, rare-earth metals and so on. In 2010 officially industrial growth rate was estimated at about 9.8 per cent, and Kyrgyzstan registered exports valued at about US$ 1.783 billion and imports US$ 2.981 billion. Thus, the country had huge negative balance of trade. While main items of exports are cotton, wool, meat, tobacco, gold, mercury, uranium, natural gas, hydropower, machinery, and shoes, the major items of imports are oil and gas, machinery and equipment, chemicals, foodstuffs, and so on. The major trading partners are Russia, China, Kazakhstan, Uzbekistan, the UAE, etc.

Kyrgyzstan's external debt has been increasing over the years estimated approximately at US$ 3.738 billion in 2010, which was about US$ 3.467 billion in 2008. At present, it seems the debt has exceeded US$ 4 billion. The reserves of foreign exchange including gold reserves in 2010 were US$ 1.72 billion and have been increasing over the last two decades. 2011 was good for the growth of agricultural sector partly caused by high prices for food, which promoted agricultural production and benefited the farmers. However, it might cause problems for a large section of the population including the urban poor. "The agricultural sector faces the greatest challenge because it is more difficult to attract large-scale foreign direct investment for crop production," as opined by an independent researcher Dr. Tony Pizur who has specialised in economics from the International University of Kyrgyzstan. It is important to note that the Kyrgyz Prime Minister Almazbek Atambayev in January 2012 made the claim that Kyrgyzstan would see its gross domestic product increase by 6.3 per cent, a figure that may have surprised many in a nation where infrastructure and businesses were largely destroyed by recent riots. Nevertheless, experts say that the projection is not unrealistic. Another factor that might help Kyrgyz economy is its gold resource potentialities. Kyrgyzstan expert and University of Minnesota professor Dr. Kathleen Collins said Kyrgyzstan will also benefit from the surge in gold prices. In her opinion, "(Atambayev's) projections are probably based on the increased prices of gold, a major driver in the growth of the Kyrgyz economy". Apart from gold, which dominates Kyrgyzstan's exports, significant growth can also be achieved in agriculture and electricity.

Kyrgyzstan, which is not endowed with hydrocarbon resources, depends upon hydropower generation from its Toktogul hydropower plant. The prospects of electricity generation depend upon the level of water in this Toktogul dam, which marginally changes from year to year. For instance, one Central Asia expert opined that in 2011 Kyrgyzstan would have enough scope for electricity generation considering the high water level in the Toktogul dam. At the same time, it is important that the government seems serious about reducing theft, corruption and other shenanigans in the energy sector.

The prospects of economic development of Kyrgyzstan depend upon the industrial sector. In fact as opined by Collins, Kyrgyzstan is in desperate need of is reinvestment in its manufacturing sector, which never recovered after following the dissolution of the Soviet Union in 1991. Hence, the new government needs to create stable political conditions and favourable economic incentives for Foreign Direct Involvement (FDI) to build up its manufacturing sector. While only about 12 per cent of Kyrgyzstan's workforce is employed in the manufacturing sector, it accounts for roughly a quarter of the economy's GDP. In fact, the manufacturing industry is not the only sector that can benefit from an improved business environment. Improving the overall business and investment climate and increasing the level of corporate confidence in Kyrgyzstan are necessary to increase the number of small- and medium-sized enterprises to engage the Kyrgyz workforce, which is increasing overtime.

Considering the fact that there is a major problem of unemployment, which forces lakhs of people to go to Russia for jobs, the Kyrgyzstan government needs to create more job opportunities in the country itself. It can be possible by giving importance to manufacturing sector attracting capital and new technology, which alone can create jobs and wealth. In the opinion of international experts who are also associated with the organisations providing assistance to Central Asian States,

Kyrgyzstan succeeded in attracting business groups which were doing well in the past and that can be done again. However, the fact that some cases were there when they were taken over by the government officials, which affected investment climate for foreign capital and technology, affecting economic environment as a whole. In fact, Kyrgyzstan has a unique regional advantage because of its WTO membership, which it can use to attract investment and access a vast number of markets.

Problems and Prospects

The new government under Almazbek Atambayev's Presidency faces several problems even as there are reasonable prospects for development in the years to come.

Firstly, as the country continues to struggle to regain its economic footing and to solidify the stability of its newly adopted parliamentary system, its economic future depends upon factors that are beyond its control and remains uncertain. For instance, a major economic problem facing Kyrgyzstan and other CAS is the lack of regional economic cooperation. Realising the importance of regional cooperation, during the last about two decades, Kyrgyz Republic has consistently supported and actively participated in regional organizations including the Commonwealth of Independent States (CIS), Central Asian Union (CAU), Economic Cooperation Organization (ECO) and Shanghai Cooperation Organization (SCO). Similarly, the Kyrgyz Republic joined Eurasian Customs Union formed by the Russian Federation and Kazakhstan, and Central Asian Free Trade Area (CAFTA) since 1993. It is a member of CAREC Program since 1992 of the Asian Development Bank (ADB).

Regional cooperation is essential and ideal for economic development of all Central Asian States and being a small country with limitations of resource potentialities, Kyrgyz Republic realised the significance of regional cooperation. However, several analysts are skeptical about the practical performance and implementation of policies adopted by the regional organisations in Central Asia. For instance, according to Martin C. Spechler, meetings and decisions taken at the regional bodies are often more likely end up as rhetorics and not much progress is made in reality. The Kyrgyz Republic is a victim of this phenomenon because very often, there is lack of complementarity among the CIS and even the CAS and by asserting their sovereignty and independence, they have adopted protectionist policy measures affecting the spirit of regional co-operation and development. A very glaring example has been the persisting problem arising out of on-going conflicts among the CAS in sharing of water between upstream and downstream countries. Similarly, hydrocarbon energy scarce Kyrgyzstan and Tajikistan which are small and upstream states have been the worst affected in the region.

Secondly, on the social front the situation has worsened by such problems as regionalism possibly because as some analysts allege that President Atambayev has established his team without taking into account regional factor, which seems to have fuelled the already prevailing tensions between Kyrgyz and the Uzbeks.

Thirdly, on the external front, the present Kyrgyz president has been trying to strengthen relations with Turkey by his visit to that country, with which there are historic and ethnic cultural ties for centuries. As opined by some analysts by this policy approach he is trying to search for counter-balance against Russia and the US. However, this is rather simplistic approach and might be pragmatic for the country in the end. This is because he visited Russia also in March 2012 after presidential election, and profusely praised Putin on his victory. He specially mentioned that Kyrgyzstan would always strengthen ties with Russia. In fact, political and economic ties between Kyrgyzstan and Russia are always close and cordial. During his visit to Moscow, Atambayev also met the Russian President Dmitri Medvedev who stated that stability in Central Asian countries was of utmost importance for Russia amid growing pressure on Syria and Iran the Central Asian region. Ahead of Atambayev's trip, the Kyrgyz finance minister Akylbek Japarov met Russian leaders in Moscow seeking urgent external financial support considering problems that Kyrgyzstan has been facing to secure a loan of some US$ 107 million within the framework of the Eurasian Economic Community, an organisation within the CIS led by Russia.

Fourthly, it is important to note that Kyrgyzstan has the unique distinction of giving concessions to both Russia and the US for their military bases during the last over a decade. Apart from strategic location and considerations, Kyrgyzstan also benefited from the money it receives as a part of rent from both these countries. Sometimes, there are bureaucratic problems affecting normal functioning of this arrangement. For instance, in March 2012, Kyrgyzstan had to remind Russia about the non-payment which was granted by Russia. According to the Kyrgyz Defense Ministry, Russia holds a US$ 15 million debt before Kyrgyzstan for leasing its military facilities, which might further help the country to tide over the critical financial problems. On the other hand, as per reports the US, which also has a military base at Manas, near the Kyrgyz capital Bishkek, pays around US$ 150 million every year without any delays, which was reported by news agency 'Kabar' in March 2012. This has immensely benefited Kyrgyzstan. But allowing military base to the US has been a sensitive issue to both Russia and China. Hence, as of now to keep its relations close and cordial with Russia and China, the Kyrgyz president Atambayev has stated that the US air base at Manas will not stay in Kyrgyzstan after its lease expires in 2014. Since the base is a key strategic staging post for the US military in Afghanistan, the final outcome will ultimately depend upon the geopolitical situation as it unfolds in the region in the years to come.

References

1. R.G. Gidadhubli, 'Economic Development of the Kyrgyz Republic: Performance and Prospects' in K. Santhnam and Ramakant Dwivedi (eds) *India-Kyrgyz Relations Perspectives and Prospects,* (New Delhi: Anamaya Publishers, 2008).
2. Anita Sengupta, 'Tulip Revolution and Constitutional Reforms in Kyrgyzstan' in K. Santhanam and Ramakant Dwivedi (eds) *India-Kyrgyz Relations Perspectives and Prospects.*
3. Imtiyz ul Haq, 'Economic Transition in Central Asian Republics: Problems and Prospects' in Mushtaq Kaw (ed) *Central Asia Continuity and Change,* (University of Kashmir, 1999).
4. E. Trusin, 'Basic Problems of Market Transition in Central Asia' in Boris Rumer (ed) *Central Asia and the Global Economy,* (New York: Armonk, 2000).
5. Tursunay Usubalieva-Oktai 'International Trade Development of Kyrgyzstan Within

the Central Asian Region' in Ajay Patnaik and Tulsiram (ed) *Globalisation and Eurasia*, (New Delhi: KW Publishers Pvt. Ltd., 2010).

6. R.R. Sharma, 'Political System and Democratic Discourse in Central Asia: A View from Outside'. In J.N. Roy and B.B. Kumar.(eds) *India and Central Asia Classical to contemporary Periods*, (New Delhi: Concept Publishing Company, 2007).
7. R.G. Gidadhubli, 'Turmoil in Kyrgyzstan-Powerplay of Vested Interests' *Economic and Political Weekly*, (Mumbai, July 2010).
8. R.G. Gidadhubli, 'Will Kyrgyzstan Make History in Central Asia?' *Freedom First Weekly*, (Mumbai, July 2010).

9. Democratization of Political Structure in Kazakhstan

Mukesh Kumar Mishra

In the pre-1991 period, the Central Asian elite were among the conservative elements of the Soviet political establishment which strongly resisted Mikhail Gorbachev's policy of *Glasnost* (openness) and democratization. Even during *Perestroika*, the Central Asian leaders perceived the emergence of various opposition parties and groups in their Republics as a direct challenge to their position and power. They were preoccupied with the idea of preventing "unproductive and damaging reforms" and of consolidating their power without democratization and radical changes in political and state institutions. This, however, did not stop the discussion of possible "models of development" for the Central Asian Republics (CARs), which dominated the intellectual discourse in the region throughout the 1990s. It was especially intensive in Kazakhstan, Kyrgyzstan and Uzbekistan on the eve of the dissolution of the Soviet Union and during the first stage of independence. A number of developmental models were floated - the Turkish secular political model versus the Iranian theocratic model, the Chinese model of gradual economic reform versus Russia's shock therapy model etc- to mention a few.

In each of the five countries of Central Asia - Kazakhstan, Kyrgyzstan, Tajikistan, Turkmenistan and Uzbekistan, political institutions of democratic government and market-oriented economies were adopted soon after these nations attained independence in 1991. As these countries entered the first stages of transition, the leaders of each of the Central Asian countries spoke in favor of the establishment of democratic institutions and secular government. Following independence, each of them adopted a constitutionally limited, representative form of government and a legal and regulatory framework in accordance with international standards. Today, Kazakhstan and Kyrgyzstan seem to be making steady progress towards the development of democratic or quasi-democratic polities. Kazakhstan can take pride in certain achievements, having avoided the bloody chaos of a civil war like that in Tajikistan and the dictatorial backsliding as in Turkmenistan and, to a lesser degree, in Uzbekistan. The current Constitution of the Republic of Kazakhstan, approved through a national referendum in August 1995 and ratified in September 1995, replaced the previous constitution of 1993. The Constitution provides for a democratic, secular state and a Presidential system of government. State governance is divided among the executive, legislative and judicial branches. The President is considered the supreme authority of the state. In October 1998, the Constitution was amended to provide for a 7-year Presidential term instead of 5 years. However, in 2007 the term of the President has reverted back to 5 years from the existing 7 years starting from 2012. The first election under the amended constitution was held in January 1999 which resulted in the re-election of President Nazarbayev.

However, in January 2011, the lower house of Kazakhstan's parliament adopted a nation-wide appeal to President Nursultan Nazarbayev for holding a referendum to extend his presidential term until December 2020. The initiative group supporting the referendum submitted signatures of 5 million Kazakhs, from all over the country, to the Central Electoral Commission. This was considered to be more than a half of Kazakhstan's voters. In accordance with the Constitution of Kazakhstan, the first President could run for the post of head of state for an unlimited number of times. However, this referendum was rejected by the Constitutional Court and Presidential election took place in April 2011 in which Nazarbayev was re-elected. Kazakhstan achieved success in building its national institutions and developing its economy. Kazakhstan leadership understands that it is important to continue with the experience of a young democracy as it has also been playing a role on the global stage such as the Chairman of the OSCE in 2010 and OIC in 2011. Such developments in the democratization process of Kazakhstan have given the country a new identity in the post-Soviet world, which needs to be examined.

It is against this background that this paper seeks to examine the process of democratization in Kazakhstan in the post-1991 period, with particular focus on the reforms in the country's political structure. It appears that although the Kazakh government does crack down on some opposition groups and newspapers, the country has a strong basis on which it could move towards democratization. As such it also highlights the challenges in the democratic development of the country.

Background

Possessing abundant hydrocarbon resources and buoyed by high oil prices, Kazakhstan's economy has out-performed its regional competitors.[1] When we talk about political development in Kazakhstan, it is about the process of democratization. President Nazarbayev identifies seven fundamental elements of democratization and political liberalization which are necessary for political reform in Kazakhstan.[2]

- The electoral process must be honest, representative and encourage the fullest participation of candidates and voters. Free and fair elections are at the heart of any democracy and Kazakhstan should be no exception. Quoting a popular proverb Nazarbayev argues that 'The people seldom speak but when they speak they never make mistakes.' Elections are the manifestations of people's verdict. Our goal should be clear: to make the upcoming national elections a model for free and fair elections. According to Nazarbayev, Kazakhstan should develop 'a comprehensive step-by-step programme of election of leaders at all levels'.
- The second major element underlined by the President in the political democratization package is the strengthening of the role of parties in the country's political system. Political parties are the basic building blocks of democracy and the need of the hour is to help them grow and develop. The President also encourages international groups and non-governmental organizations to come to Kazakhstan to educate and train the political parties. Calling upon all parties, regardless

of their political orientation, he urges them to respect and preserve political and inter-ethnic stability in the country as the future of the State system and democracy depends on this.

- For stability and succession of power in Kazakhstan strengthening and providing autonomy for *Majilis* and Senate seemed appropriate to the President. The President believes in the greater responsibility of the Parliament to build up a responsive government in the coming years. Representation by political parties according to proportional representation will make the *Majilis* better reflect the full spectrum of political views in Kazakhstan. The President proposes that to ensure representation of a broader range of ethnic and religious minorities of the country in Parliament, some of the Presidential appointees to the Senate shall be from candidates recommended by the People's Assembly.
- A key element of democratization is recognized as strengthening the role of non-governmental organizations in building a civil society. A democratic structure does not in itself guarantee a democratic society. Democracy depends on private voluntary institutions which allow citizens to be politically involved, aware enough to volunteer their services and express their grievances to advocate their interests. To ensure that civic groups can operate freely, the Ministry of Justice has been asked to simplify registration and supervision procedures for domestic and international non-governmental organizations who wish to work in Kazakhstan, thus encouraging and accelerating operation.
- The President acknowledged an independent judiciary as the pillar of a democratic society. An autonomous judicial system is absolutely necessary, which would decide issues on their merits and would be free from corruption. The training process of judges should be improved. Vigorous enforcement of the recently enacted Anti-Corruption Law was stressed. It was also pointed out that the Higher Judiciary Council should not be headed by the President.[3]
- Nazarbayev emphasized the building of a free, uncensored and independent press. According to him the Government should

consider the free access of journalists to information not as a favour of the Government but as its commitment to public opinion. The work to remove any remaining impediments to a free press from the nation is accorded importance. The privatization process of many state publishing houses and the availability and increase in the number of independent mass media means the growth of openness in society.

- The progress of the society can be measured by its attitude to women. The President therefore intends to increase the role of the Council on Problems of Family, Women and Demographic Policy or reorganize it into a Special Commission on women's issues. It must become a Chief Advisor both to the President and the Government in solving important problems pertaining to this sphere. It is necessary to increase women's representation in all branches of authority. This is a question of social equality.

President Nazarbayev insists that his observations are based on a survey of the situation in his country and the world scenario. He is of the opinion that some forces including those who are skillfully hiding behind the mask of pseudo-democrats in public tend to become more authoritarian. He expressed his belief that 'Only a free democratic society will be a guarantor of our stable and happy life in the near future. My nation deserves freedom in this terrible and bloody century.[4]

Constitutional Reforms

The post-independence government was structured by the 1993 constitution with a strong executive parliament and judiciary. The constitution formalized the enhanced powers that President Nazarbayev assumed upon the dissolution of parliament in early 1995. It continued the previous constitutional definition of Kazakhstan as a unitary state with a Presidential form of government. The President is the highest state officer, responsible for forming the government, subject to parliamentary approval, and appointing all other republican officials. The 1995 constitution expanded the President's powers to introduce and veto legislation. The President has the powers to appoint the council of Ministers, headed by a Prime Minister and several state committees. In October 1995, Nazarbayev himself assumed the portfolio of the Ministry of National Security. In early 1996, after Nazarbayev had reshuffled the government in October 1995, the Council of Ministers included the heads of twenty-one ministries and nine state committees, the Prime Minister being Akezhan Kazhegeldin[5].

The President is the sponsor of legislation and the guarantor of the constitution and of the proper functioning of government, with the power to override the decisions and actions of local authorities and councils. The only grounds on which a President can be removed are infirmity and treason, either of which must be confirmed by a majority of the joint Upper and Lower House of the new parliament. The 1993 constitution created a unicameral parliament, which was to replace the 350 seat Supreme Soviet when the mandates of its deputies expired in 1995. The 1990 parliament, which was composed of the former communists, was dissolved early under the pressure of President Nazarbayev in December 1993 in order to pave the way for a smaller and presumably more flexible parliament. Under the 1995 constitution, the parliament consisted of two houses, the Senate and the *Majilis*, both operating in continuous sessions.

The judiciary system is the least developed of Kazakhstan's three branches of government. The constitution retains the provision of Presidential appointment of all judges in the republic. Whereas the 1993 constitution specified the terms of service for judges, the 1995 document made no mention of length of service, suggesting that judges would serve at the discretion of the President[6] . Under the constitution of 1993, lines of judicial authority were poorly defined, in part because the republic had three 'highest courts', the Supreme Court, the State Arbitrate Court and the Constitutional Court employing a total of sixty six senior judges. The 1995 constitution makes no provision for the State Arbitrate Court Provisions, for the new judiciary clearly subordinates all other courts to the Supreme Court, which has a consultative role in appointing senior judges[7] .

It is to be noted that the reform period in Kazakhstan's political system began immediately after its independence. Transition to democracy commenced under difficult conditions: the country was then experiencing socio-economic crisis due to decline in industrial and agricultural production, hyperinflation (up to 3,000 per cent) and drastic decline in living standards. After the collapse of the USSR, former Soviet states experienced a crisis situation. Kazakhstan too experienced the same and tried to overcome the problems related to democratization of political institutions, so as to strengthen the political system in Kazakhstan. In accordance with the 1995 Kazakh constitution, the government exercises the executive power. The government is composed of the Prime Minister, the deputy ministers, heads of the government departments, ministers and Chairpersons of state committees.

According to Act 166 of the Kazakh Constitution (1995), the government works out the basic socio-economic directions of the state policy, its defense preparedness and security, ensures social order and organizes their implementation. The government presents the state budget to the parliament. Among other functions performed by the government, mention may be made of tabling laws in the *Majilis* (Parliament) and administration of state properties, working out measures for conducting foreign policy; guiding the activities of the ministers, state committees, other central and local executive organs, keeping vigilance on the actions of the ministers and state committees as well as on other central and local executive organs of the republic and the appointment and removal of the heads of the central executive organs not forming part of the government. In short, the government is liable to discharge functions entrusted to it by the constitution, laws and acts of the President[8] .

The new constitution of 1995 preserved the extensive executive powers of the President and also abolished the post of Vice President. The Supreme *Kenges* was replaced by a bicameral Parliament, comprising a 47 member Senate (the Upper Chamber with 40 members elected by Kazakhstan's regional administrative bodies and seven appointed by the President) and 67 directly elected members of *Majilis*.[9] The Constitutional Court was replaced by a Constitutional Council, whose decisions are subject to a Presidential right of veto. The Constitution retained Kazakh as the state language but guaranteed the development of all other languages, making Russian the language of inter-ethnic communication.

Notwithstanding the sufficient authority regarding the implementation of the executive powers, the government is extremely dependent on the President. A number of mechanisms are incorporated in the constitution through which the President is in a position not only to form the government in the manner he considers fit but also to influence its day to day functions. According to the constitution, the President of Kazakhstan being the head of the state remains the key figure to which all executive powers are subordinated. The President, with the consent of the parliament, appoints the Prime Minister; removes him from his post, determines the structure of Government on the recommendation of the Prime Minister, appoints and terminates from the post all its members all implying to a high degree of personal influence of President on the composition of the government. In general, the level of participation of the President in the government formation in Kazakhstan is compared with the prerogatives of the President of the Russian Federation in regard to the government formation.

In 2007, the Parliament of Kazakhstan underwent its most radical transformation over a decade when seats were added to both senate and *Majilis*, with the latter body elected exclusively through a system of proportional representation, with nine members elected from within the 400 member Assembly of Peoples D. 1998.[10] But it is noteworthy that the concentration of power in the hands of an experienced statesman and administrator like Nazarbayev during the critical years of transition has proved fruitful for Kazakhstan which has withstood the difficulties in its economic and socio-political transition. As an outcome of the 2007 amendments, the key powers are transferred from the President to the Parliament. The new changes were aimed at increasing Parliament's authority in forming the Government, thus reducing the powers of the President.

The Constitution also authorises ethnic groups to form 'National Cultural Centers' committed to protecting their cultural heritage. However, it prohibits the formation of public associations or political parties based on ethnic, religious, or nationalist agendas. Nazarbayev has used his personal patronage to create symbolic institutions of ethnic representation, such as the Assembly of Peoples of Kazakhstan, established in 1995. Its members are nominated by the officially recognized national cultural centres and by the President, who also serves as the Assembly's Chairman. Lacking juridical power or a representative base, the Assembly serves as an instrument for co-opting leading ethnic figures into the existing political system. Its members are encouraged to engage in cultural activities and steer clear of politics.[11]

Political Structure

According to President Nazarbayev stability inside Kazakhstan and stability for Kazakhstan in its neighborhood requires the pursuit of at least seven elements.[12]

- First, fully consolidated national independence. Twenty years of statehood in a neighborhood that Kazakhstan inhabits does not guarantee permanent national independence and state integrity. The cultivation of a distinct Kazakh identity and the construction of Kazakh statehood, the fully liberated self from the lingering influences of centuries of imperialist dominance is a multi-generational project.
- Two, effective state institutions. Whatever the level of democratic development, if it is to retain its legitimacy, the government must provide its citizens with the basic necessities D. 1998. These include personal security, justice, social services and economic opportunity. Moreover, official corruption and abuse of office must be combated, as office-holding should not be a means of personal enrichment. In fact, Transparency International recently upgraded Kazakhstan, by 15 places in its index on corruption.
- Third, balanced economic development. As an emerging power in the region, Kazakhstan must invest in the kind of economic development that benefits broader sectors of the population and promotes the emergence of a class of entrepreneurs, professionals and local leaders who can accelerate the country's development in the coming years.
- Four, growing political competition. Kazakhstan needs to become

more responsive to the changing structure of society in order to harness the expectations of different interest groups. Here, the parliamentary elections in 2012 were important for several reasons: moving the country from a presidential to a more mixed presidential parliamentary system; an opportunity for greater competition among several political streams, political parties and interest groups; more extensive public debate on policy and politics; and, very importantly greater involvement of a new generation of citizens in public life and political life.

- Five, effective national security. The state must provide credible protection from the security threats that challenge Kazakhstan's integrity and stability: whether this is international jihadist terrorism, organized crime and trafficking, resource disputes between Central Asian countries, or environmental disasters.
- Six, international economic integration. Kazakhstan's integration with global markets and increasing economic diversity will attract business and commerce from all corners of the globe. Here, Kazakhstan's international balancing—or "multi-vector policy" as it is known—is not only important politically but also economically. Its ambitions to develop East-West infrastructure and commerce should be supported, including the highway and railway projects designed to link China with Europe.
- Seven, balanced regional cooperation. This not only concerns the larger powers—the United States, Russia, and China from which Astana can benefit—but also the smaller Central Asian states, where joined projects in a host of domains from water management, cross-border crime fighting, to trade and infrastructure development must be developed and sustained, and other nearby countries in Central and South Asia, including Afghanistan, increasingly engaged.

Recent Presidential and Parliamentary Elections

Kazakhstan's Presidential election of 2005 became an important milestone in Kazakhstan's history with implications for the future and the wider region. In September 2005, Kazakhstan's President Nursultan Nazarbayev had declared his commitment to ensure the forthcoming election to be 'free, fair and transparent'.[13] US Secretary of State Condoleezza Rice, on a visit to Astana earlier in October 2005, said 'with the Presidential election in December 2005, Kazakhstan has an unprecedented opportunity to lead Central Asia toward a future of democracy and to elevate US-Kazakhstani relations to a new level'. Nazarbayev was re-elected for a new term in the Presidential election held on 4 December 2005 receiving the support of more than 90 per cent of those who voted.

It is believed that Nazarbayev drew lessons from the Presidential elections in other transitional countries in Central Asia. In other elections in democratic and semi-democratic regimes in the CIS, incumbent Presidents lost office. This happened to Kravchuk of the Ukraine and Shushkevitch of Belorussia in 1994 in spite of their emphasis on 'patriotism' and anti-Russian sentiments.[14] And it was not possible to use the same jargon in multi-ethnic and multicultural Kazakhstan. Second, the Kazakh elite widely perceived the Russian Presidential elections as deceitful accompanied by a high level of corruption and a very expensive election campaign. Although Boris Yeltsin won the elections in Russia, he and his regime lost both moral and political grounds. Third, the experience of neighbouring Kyrgyzstan showed that the best way to assure victory is to follow some democratic procedures (like conducting relatively free elections). As such, the Kazakh ruling elite followed the Kyrgyz model during the December 1995 Presidential elections by banning strong potential and undesirable candidates from the registration process.

Like 2005, Kazakhstan's Presidential election of 2011 too proved to be a major boost to the political stability in the country. Nazarbayev was re-elected for a third term with 95% of the votes and 90% turnout, against three nominal candidates. It is to be noted that Nazarbayev called the early poll after rejecting parliament's vote for a referendum to extend his term until 2020, bypassing presidential elections scheduled for 2012 and 2017. It may also be recalled that at the time of his re-election in 2011, Nazarbayev gave indications that conditions were ripe for moving from a single-party to a multi-party parliament. In order to achieve that goal, on January 15, 2012, pre-term elections were held for the 107-seat *Majlis*, the parliament's lower chamber. The country-wide voter turnout was recorded as 75.5 percent of all the registered voters. As per the report of the Central Electoral Commission, the final tally of the vote was as follows: The presidential party Nur Otan [Fatherland's Light] garnered 81 percent of the votes cast; the party Ak Zhol [Bright Path], 7.5 percent; and the Communist People's Party (CPPK), 7.2 percent .[15] While these parties cleared the required 7 percent representation in the parliament, four other parties could not meet that benchmark. As such Nur Otan got hold of 83 seats, Ak Zhol eight seats, and the CPKK seven seats, out of the 98 contested seats in the parliament. On January 16, 2012, the remaining nine seats were allocated by the Assembly of the People of Kazakhstan (a consultative body of ethnic groups) to representatives of ethnic minorities.

Conclusions

To conclude, the technocratic model and the programme of reforms make Nazarbayev's regime quite different from the regimes of Turkmenistan and Uzbekistan, and from that of Russia. Nazarbayev did not ignore democratic procedure. However, he limited this 'procedure' within certain framework and his 'rules of the game'. Nazarbayev and some other Central Asian Presidents have been emphasizing on 'Asian values' and the peculiarities of Central Asian democracy. Besides, the policy of manoeuvres and compromises with different social, ethnic, tribal and political groups, and the moderate technocratic programme of reforms, allows Nazarbayev to broaden the social and political base of the President of Kazakhstan.[16] His flexibility has attracted wide social support in Kazakhstan and even the Russian ethnic community voted for Nazarbayev which is evident from his re-election as the President in both 2005 and 2011 elections. Further, the recently concluded parliamentary elections point to a successful accomplishment of Kazakhstan's goal of moving from a single-party to a multi-party parliament. It can rightly be concluded that this political opening, that has come about due to the decision of the state leadership, marks one step ahead in an evolutionary process of broadening political representation, correlated with the diversification of Kazakhstani society itself. Undoubtedly, the credit goes to viable constitutional reforms in the country which keep the pace of democratic political development going.

Notes

1. Martha Brill Olcott, "Democratization and the Growth of Political Participation in Kazakhstan', in Karen Dawisha and Bruce Parrot (eds) *Conflict, Cleavage, and Change in Central Asia and the Caucasus*. Cambridge: Cambridge, 1997, p. 211
2. Nursultan Nazarbayev, 'On the Situation in the Country and major Directions of Domestic and Foreign Policy: Democratization, Economic and Political Reform for the New Century', Parliamentarian speech delivered by President Nazarbayev, Almaty, 30 September 1998.
3. Nazarbayev, 'On the Situation in the Country and major Directions of Domestic and Foreign Policy: Democratization, Economic and Political Reform for the New Century'.
4. Nazarbayev, 'On the Situation in the Country and major Directions of Domestic and Foreign Policy: Democratization, Economic and Political Reform for the New Century'.
5. Glenn E. Curtis, *Kazakhstan: A Country Study*, Washington: Library of Congress. 1996. Human Rights Watch, 2001, 'Memorandum: U.S. Policy in Central Asia', May 2001, United States.
6. Curtis. *Kazakhstan: A Country Study.*
7. Curtis, *Kazakhstan: A Country study.*
8. D. Galyamova, 'Division of Powers in Kazakhstan: Constitutional Experience of Independent Development', *Contemporary Central Asia*, vol. 11, no 3, December 1998, pp. 27–37.
9. Galyamova, 'Division of Powers in Kazakhstan: Constitutional Experience of Independent Development'.
10. Anthony Clive Bowyer, 'Parliament and Political Parties in Kazakhstan', *Silk Road Paper*, John Hopkins University–SAIS. Washington DC. 2008
11. Adel E. Abbishev, 2002. *Kazakhstan in Focus: Ten Years of Independence*, Almaty: Center for Foreign Policy and Analysis, 2002.
12. Janusz Bugajski, *Event Summary* The Future of Kazakhstan after the Presidential Election May 12, 2011 Carnegie Endowment for International Peace, Washington, DC.
13. OSCE/ODIHR, 'Interim Report', OSCE Office for Democratic Institutions and Human Rights Election Obsevation, 2004.
14. K Wolczuk, 'Presidentialism in Ukraine: A Mid-Term Review of the Second Presidency', *Democratization*, vol. 4, no. 3, 1997, pp. 152–171.

15. Kazinform, 17 January 2012.
16. Rafis Abazov, 'The Presidential Elections in Kazakhstan', Contemporary Central Asia, vol. 3, no. 2, D. 1998. 1999, pp. 22–33.

10. Foreign Policy of Uzbekistan: Bilateral and Multilateral Dimension

Mirzhoid Rakhimov

Adopting International Relations

During the 1980s, the presence of a systemic crisis, aggravated ethnic conflicts, complicated socioeconomic and managerial crisis became evident in the Soviet Union. However, the process of gaining real national sovereignty was intensified in many former Soviet republics. In March 1990, the first secretary of the CPSU Central Committee Mikhail Gorbachev was elected President of the USSR. On March 24, Islam Karimov was elected President of Uzbekistan through voting in the Supreme Council of the USSR. In June 1990, the Declaration of Independence of the Republic was adopted, whose purpose was not only to declare its new legal status, but to proclaim at a broad international level the sovereign rights of building an independent state.

It should be noted that the new leadership of Uzbekistan made one of the first attempts to establish and maintain its own international relations. In particular, President of Uzbekistan visited India (August 17-19, 1991), where he met with President R. Venkataraman and Prime Minister of India Narasimha Rao and signed two Agreements on trade, economic and scientific-technical cooperation and Agreement in the field of culture, arts, education, tourism, sports and media.[1] This visit, in fact, was the first for the new leadership and took place during the complex and tendentious processes ongoing in the USSR. In particular, in August 1991, Mikhail Gorbachev, President of the USSR, was forcibly removed from office and a State Committee was established on the Extraordinary Situation in the USSR (GKChP) headed by Vice-President G. Yanaev. At this time, Uzbek President was on visit to Delhi and upon his arrival, he was met in Tashkent not only by official person of the republic, but also military generals sent from the centre. But the official news media of the time do not mention the presence of generals.

As is well known the GKChP's coup collapsed, and at the 6th Session of the Supreme Council of the Republic held in the end of August 1991, the Constitutional Law 'State Independence of the Republic of Uzbekistan' was adopted. After that, Uzbekistan has consistently and deliberately formed a coherent system of organisation and an independent foreign policy. The Ministry of Foreign Affairs was reorganised into the Ministry of Foreign Economic Relations and the University of World Economy and Diplomacy was founded. Other state institutions of the political system were also involved in the implementation of the foreign policy in Uzbekistan. In particular, the Committee on International and Inter-Parliamentary Affairs at the Legislative Chamber and the Committee on International Relations of the Upper Chamber of Parliament—the Senate, were formed. However, the President of Uzbekistan defines the main directions of domestic and foreign policy.

As we know, however, the end of the 20th century was characterised by significant geopolitical changes and transformations of the entire system of international relations. As a new subject within the sphere of international relations, Uzbekistan was also in touch with the realities and complexities of world politics. The Republic is located in the center of an important geopolitical region—Central Asia, which is one of the priorities of distinct non-coincident geostrategic interests of the leading world and regional powers. Central Asia and the Caspian region possess large reserves of energy. Also relevant remains the question of Afghanistan as a source of instability and threat to security. These factors are of great significance in determining the foreign policy interests in Central Asia, including Uzbekistan, covering both bilateral and multilateral diplomacy.

Bilateral Relations and Its Challenges

In the context of bilateral relations, the Uzbek government voiced its interest in developing mutually beneficial relations with Russia, China,

Germany, the US, Japan, India, Korea, and other countries. Relationships between Uzbekistan and Russia can be divided into several periods. The first period is between 1992 and 1995, when Russia's foreign policy was considered pro-Western, and the Central Asian region was given marginal significance, what was often emaphasised by many Russian and foreign scholars.[2] The second period covers the time interval between 1996 and 1999, when Russia began a more active policy towards Central Asia. This period is characterised by the intensification of relations between Russia and Central Asia, in particular, the Russian-Uzbek relations. The relationships between countries became even closer with Vladimir Putin's arrival in the Russian Government, and with his election as President.[3] This period is the third stage and relations covered, above all, the intensification of political dialogue, economic cooperation, and mutual concern about the threat of international terrorism in both Russia and Central Asia. The two sides signed contracts 'strategic partnership between Russia and the Republic of Uzbekistan' (2004) and 'the allied relations between Russia and the Republic of Uzbekistan' (2005), as well as between the two countries there are more than 200 bilateral documents regulating cooperation in different fields—military, political, economic, humanitarian, and others. The Republic of Uzbekistan is one of the main trade partners of Russia in Central Asia. If in 2006 the trade turnover between the two countries amounted to about US$ 3 billion,[4] in 2010 it was US$ 6.4 billion.[5] However, a number of problems still exist. In particular, there does not exist a clear Russian policy in Central Asia in general and in individual countries of the region. Russia has different opinions and positions—from concepts of normal inter-State attitudes to imperial ambitions. Unfortunately, the media and public institutions of the Russian Federation frequently project one-sided and at times, biased information about the processes taking place in Central Asia.

An important trade partner of Uzbekistan is China, with which strategic partnership has been established, and an important feature of the process of development of relations between them is the continuous deepening of political dialogue. Mutual visits at the summit level have become regular, for example, the President of the Republic of Uzbekistan

Islam Karimov paid visits to China in 1992, 1994, 1999, 2005, 2001, 2006, and 2010. Dynamics of trade turnover is growing constantly, thus, in the first half of 2009, turnover of commodities with China reached US$ 881.3 million, the export of Uzbekistan US$ 167.6 million, and import US$ 713.7 million.[6] At the end of 2011, the trade turnover accounted for more than US$ 2 billion. In its policy in Central Asia, China holds as priorities the expansion of trade and economic contacts with the countries of the region on a bilateral and multilateral basis, maintaining a close policy dialogue with the possibility of an extended economic presence preserving the balance between political forces and stability in Central Asia. The strategic importance of Central Asia for China, in opinion of Chinese experts, is now more evident in the economic sphere.[7]

Important for Uzbekistan and other Central Asian countries is the relationship with the US in the context of co-operation with the developed Western countries, in carrying out democratic reforms in the region and the development of economic transformations. The US declared Central Asia to be a zone of top strategic interests and its relations with the countries of Central Asia had certain difficulties and problems. After the terrorist attack in the US on September 11, 2001, the Central Asian countries were among the first countries to sympathise with the US. The Central Asian countries—Uzbekistan, Tajikistan, and Kyrgyzstan—agreed to the military use of their infrastructures in the antiterrorist campaign in Afghanistan.

The US and Uzbekistan developed close political relations, as was demonstrated in March 2002 during the visit of President of Uzbekistan to Washington, where he met with US President George W. Bush, who expressed his gratitude to Uzbekistan.[8] Following years, Uzbek-US relations passed through several transformations and difficulties. Since 2008, official visits to Tashkent from US intensified, including the visit of the US Secretary of State Hilary Clinton in December 2010. According to the US, their key partners in Central Asia were Uzbekistan and Kazakhstan; the latter ones expected that the relationships between the parties should be based on mutual understanding and mutual benefit. The US should avoid the approach of double standards, as well as cooperate with other major and regional countries in solving the problems of Central Asia, including the problems of terrorism and religious extremism, gradually developing cooperation in terms of democratic and economic reforms.

Priority is given to the relationship between Central Asia and the EU. In its development, it went through several stages. The first stage covers the beginning of the 1990s, when the EU and countries of the Central Asian region only started establishing their own relationships. Since July 1999, the second stage had begun with coming into force of the 'Partnership and Co-operation Agreement' (PCA) signed between the parties in 1996. The increased interest of the EU in Central Asia is partly due to increasing European role in international processes.[9] The third stage in the relations between the EU and Central Asia falls on 2007, when under the programme of the EU Presidency, Germany initiated a new programme to extend political cooperation with countries of Central Asia. Adopted for the period 2007 to 2013, the new strategic Programme of the EU towards Central Asia, gave special importance to the expansion of political and economic cooperation. This strategy was endorsed by Central Asian countries.[10] The Central Asian countries also showed increased interest in expanding cooperation with the EU at all levels and in all areas. Specific actions have been agreed and are already being implemented based on bilateral agreements on key regional issues such as education, legal regulation, water supply, and environmental protection.

Together with the PCA, another important instrument of EU policy in the region is associated with the implementation of the TACIS technical assistance programme, which aims to support the implementation of economic reforms and the establishment and maintenance of political ties between the partner countries. It should be noted that in the relations between the EU and Central Asian countries, special attention was attached to cooperation in the field of education. Representatives of universities and research institutes of Central Asian countries participated in such programmes and projects of the EU as Tempus, Erasmus Mundus and others. The EU countries have been active in Central Asia at the national level. For example, German humanitarian

Foundation DAAD, Konrad Adenauer Foundation, DBB-International, Volkswagen and Ebert Foundations, Goethe Institute, as well as universities have been active in cooperation with universities, research centers and government agencies.

There have been certain shortcomings in relations between the EU and Central Asia, which were stated by either side. Thus, for instance, the EU criticises poor reporting and compilation of official documents, reflecting the processes of democratisation in Central Asian countries, as well as a slowdown of economic reforms, etc. In turn, the countries in the region have criticised the EU for the lack of a clear strategy, ignoring regional and local conditions, and availability of double-standard approach. Since the establishment of official relations between Uzbekistan and Central Asia, the EU held regular political contacts at various levels. President of Uzbekistan Islam Karimov in January 2011 paid a visit to Brussels, where he had a meeting with President of the EU Commission Jose Manuel Barroso, European Commissioner for Energy Gunther Oettinger, and the NATO Secretary General Anders Fogh Rasmussen. During the talks, the parties exchanged useful and open views on the current state and prospects of developing relations between Uzbekistan and the EU. Undoubtedly, the firm partnership between the EU and Uzbekistan is very important for bilateral and multilateral cooperation in Central Asia. In the context of INOGATE and TRACECA, the EU plans to promote the development and expansion of regional infrastructure in the sphere of transport, energy, and trade in order to make better use of the economic potential of Central Asia and of regional cooperation. Being an important trade corridor between the East and South Asia and Europe, Central Asia will be able to benefit from the increase in trade turnover.[11]

Germany is Europe's principle industrial power. It is the main partner and EU's driving force in the development of cooperation with Central Asia. Germany is the main trading partner of Uzbekistan in Europe, and Uzbekistan is the second largest partner of Berlin in the region. If in 2007 the trade volume between the two countries amounted to about US$ 300 million, in 2011 it topped over US$ 560 million. Together with the leading companies of Germany, investment projects totaling over one billion euros were implemented in Uzbekistan. Cooperation is maintained in many areas, ranging from light industry and transport services to the production of medical products and pharmaceuticals, and agricultural products processing. Germany uses the airport in Termez in order to participate in activities of the organisation of the International Security Assistance Force (ISAF) in Afghanistan.

In the context of geopolitical changes in Central Asia we see the active involvement of India, Korea and Japan in the region with regard to bilateral and multilateral approaches in the beginning of the 21st century. In twenty years since the establishment of diplomatic relations between Central Asia countries and India there have been periodic exchanges of high-level visits, inter-governmental commissions, foreign office consultations, working groups and other institutional mechanisms to systemically work towards further developing and strengthening bilateral relations. It could be noted that in Soviet times Central Asian republics especially Uzbekistan had strong links with India. At present, the Central Asian countries are one of the largest beneficiaries under the Indian Technical and Economic Cooperation (ITEC) programmes, which offer human resource development training to about 300 candidates annually from this region, including 125 from Uzbekistan, who undergo training in India in such disciplines as IT, banking, textile industry, business management, English courses, hotel management, and others.[12] Additionally, around 30 students undergo long-term training programmes in India based on Indian Government scholarships.

Trade volume between India and Uzbekistan increased from US$ 73.5 million in 2007 to US$ 151.10 million in 2010. There are more than 60 companies in Uzbekistan with Indian capital. Close trade co-operation is established in such areas as pharmaceutics, aviation, textile and mining industry, IT and power sector. Uzbekistan supports Indian companies to expand investment co-operation in areas where they have leading technological potential. For instance, 'Spentex Industries' invested more than US$ 88 million in Uzbekistan, and it is one of the largest investors in the textile sector of Uzbekistan; a number of projects on processing raw cotton is being implemented jointly with it. In April 2006, Indian Prime Minister Manmohan Singh visited Tashkent and seven agreements including three agreements in energy and mineral sectors were signed between India and Uzbekistan.[13] Also during visit India-Uzbekistan IT Centre named after Jawaharlal Nehru was started in Tashkent with the main purpose and tasks to form an Institute for the study and development of software, assist in improvement of knowledge of specialists and students of Uzbekistan on IT, and formation of programmers of a world class. There is also an Indian Cultural Centre, which is actively functioning in Uzbekistan.

In 2011, President of Uzbekistan Islam Karimov paid a visit to the Republic of India and several agreements were signed, including economic packet over US$ 2.2 billion. The parties discussed also the evolving situation in neighbouring Afghanistan and reaffirmed the grave necessity of establishment of peace and stability in that country, for which one that would need to open up wider opportunities for regional co-operation and help institute and advance cost-effective routes reducing the distance between the markets of India and Central Asia. In this regard, as the two sides noted, prospects emerging from setting up Central Asia-Persian Gulf land transport corridor as well as Trans-Afghan access strip have been important. Uzbekistan has consistently supported India's candidacy to a permanent membership of the UN Security Council.

Bilateral relations between Central Asian countries and another highly developed nation Japan were established within a short time period. They gradually developed multilateral cooperation and there are different levels and trends in their contacts. One of the important areas of cooperation between Uzbekistan and Japan is the Japan's ODA programme for major investment and social programmes in the country. Over the last years, soft loans and commercial credits were allotted totaling more than US$ 2 billion, which were aimed at projects for the development of telecommunication networks, for renovation of the repair-and-construction plant in Tashkent, for the modernisation of airports in Samarkand, Bukhara, Urgench, as well as for projected railway Tashguzar-Baisun–Kumkurgan.[14] Japanese organisations, including the Japanese International Cooperation Agency, Japan Foundations, and others, are actively supporting the workers of culture, science, and education, coming to Japan on exchange programmes. Strong scientific cooperation between universities and research institutes has been established. In accordance with the official point of view, Japan and Uzbekistan maintain a regular dialogue on various issues and on partnership within the framework of international organisations, including the UN. Uzbekistan supports Japan's intention to become a permanent member of the UN Security Council and Japan fully supports the peace initiatives undertaken by Uzbekistan and other Central Asian countries to transform Central Asia into a zone free of nuclear weapons.

For two decades, Russia, China, the US and other countries have declared their decision to provide all-round support in establishing peace and stability in Central Asia and promotion of regional cooperation. Their declaration is certainly welcomed in Central Asian countries. However, among the major non-regional actors there exist some contradictions in assessment, strategies, and approaches to the region. From the perspective of Central Asian countries, the constructive dialogue and cooperation in the region, based on bilateral and multilateral relations should be optimal and effective for the US, Russia, China, and other leading countries.

Partnership with International and Regional Organisation

Relations between Uzbekistan and other countries in the region with major international organisations are an important priority for multilateral diplomacy. Of great importance for the success of economic and political reforms in the country is Uzbekistan's cooperation with the United Nations and its specialised agencies. Under the auspices of the UN Uzbekistan is actively involved in discussing and resolving international and regional issues. In particular, in his speeches at the 48th (September 1993), 50th (October 1995) 55th Session (September 2000), at the UN summit 'Development Goals of the Millennium' (2010), and UN General Assembly sessions President Islam Karimov focused on such topical issues in Central Asia, such as safety and environmental crises. The UN adopted a series of resolutions aimed at peaceful resolution of security issues in Afghanistan and Central Asia. The Republic of Uzbekistan takes an active part in the activities of various specialised agencies and committees of the UN and its humanitarian operations in Afghanistan. The UN Secretary General Kofi Annan visited Tashkent in October 2002, and the current UN Secretary General Ban Ki Moon was in Tashkent in 2010, during which they discussed such issues as efficient use of water resources, democratic reforms, as well as questions of UN reforming.

Uzbekistan and the UN through the activities of various agencies, including, above all, the UNESCO, develop partnerships in the field of culture, education, and preservation of cultural heritage in Uzbekistan. Significant events of cooperation have become the jubilees of great thinkers and encyclopedists, and public figures, celebration of which was widely held not only in our country but also in the UNESCO representation office in Paris. In addition, the anniversary dates of such ancient cities as Bukhara, Khiva, Margilan, Shahrisabz, Karshi, Samarkand, and Tashkent were also celebrated. A number of cities and cultural values of the republic have been included in the UNESCO List of World Cultural Values. Humanitarian cooperation is an important aspect of national, regional, and global sustainable development in the complex processes of globalisation. Alongside with that, in the end of the 20th-early 21st century, the UN faced many challenges and difficulties associated with low efficiency in addressing global and regional problems. As a result, academic and political circles of various countries, including Uzbekistan, discussed the need for substantial reform of the Organisation and enhancing its effectiveness in international and regional processes.

The partnership between Central Asian countries and the UN, EU, and NATO is important to ensure regional stability and security in the region and achieve their sustainable economic development. However, the high priority tasks are also stabilisation and economic reconstruction of Afghanistan. In view of the different approaches and understanding of the situation, there are many problems in the relationship between various states and organisations, including the UN, NATO, EU, and OSCE. At the same time, analysis of the UN, EU, OSCE, and other international organisations in Central Asia has shown that the activity of these structures needs to be improved. With the collapse of the bipolar world, the largest international organisations should take into account the interests of their members, rather than the interests of just one country or group of countries. It seems that international organisations need to develop a clear and long-term strategy in Central Asia, covering the issues of security and sustainable development.

The SCO has passed a number of interesting stages in its institutional and political development. In our view, there are two main periods in the process of formation and development of the organisation. The first stage begins in 1996, when the principles were formed as well as structural mechanisms of development of multilateral relations of member countries. This period is characterised by normalisation of relations in a number of key issues of security, prevention of any possible conflicts between the participating countries, overcoming the mutual distrust, etc. Transformation of the 'Shanghai Forum' in the SCO took place in June 2001 at the meeting of leaders of Russia, China, Kazakhstan, Kyrgyzstan, Tajikistan and Uzbekistan in Shanghai (China), where Uzbekistan joined the organisation as a new member-country. The year 2001 is regarded as the beginning of the second period in the development of the organisation. There has been significant institutional establishment of the organisation, the organisation's charter was adopted, the secretariat was formed in China, the anti-terrorist center was opened in Tashkent, etc. At present, the SCO is an international instrument to coordinate the areas of multilateral cooperation.

The results of our survey and interviews with experts from the countries of Central Asia and Russia carried out in 2006-07 have shown that the majority of experts (90 per cent) consider the SCO as the most successful organisation in Eurasia. At the same time, certain shortcomings were marked in development of the SCO, in particular, most of the projects of the organisation are mainly funded by Chinese investments, while other member countries could also wage more active investment policies. Apparently, it is necessary to take into account that the organisation is relatively new, and the shortcomings can be removed in the near future. Further development of cooperation is also necessary between the SCO and the EU, NATO, and other international organisations, which in turn should not consider the SCO only in geopolitical terms. It is advisable to recognize its contribution to regional security and development,[15] it is necessary to study the experience of integration processes in other parts of the world, in particular, the experience of the EU, NAFTA, ASEAN, etc. By all means, co-operation between the EU, NATO, OSCE, and the SCO will contribute to enhancing regional integration, economic development and security in Central Asia. With the growth of co-operation in the region between Russia, China and other countries, as well as extended cooperation in a broader sense, including observer countries (Mongolia, India, Iran, Afghanistan, Pakistan), the partnership is important with such leading actors as the EU, the US, Japan, Korea and other countries and international organisations.

Uzbekistan, along with other countries of the former Soviet Union, was a cofounder of the Commonwealth of Independent States (CIS), the Central Asian Cooperation Organisation (CACO) and other regional organisations aimed at strengthening economic, military, political, and cultural cooperation among member countries. CIS has been in existence for 20 years and, despite all the shortcomings, it remains the best form of multilateral cooperation in the interests of those countries, which it unites. However, it became clear long ago that this was a lengthy and complex process, the parameters of which are determined by the degree of interest in participating in one or another form of interaction. According to Uzbekistan, the CIS can and must play a coordinating role, becoming a platform for regulating business processes to maximise the socioeconomic benefits for all member states.[16] Undoubtedly, the Commonwealth can add to its credit that the dissociation of former Soviet republics was orderly and did not cause profound geopolitical upheavals. Providing institutional and legal conditions for equal dialogue and co-operation in complex issues, it has performed an important historical mission of promoting sovereign, independent states, allowing them to choose their own foreign policy, the model of economic reform and nation-building. In 2008, a concept of CIS development and the Plan for its implementation were accepted, where all states of the Commonwealth confirmed the priorities of the CIS. Some of the problems were discussed at summits of the CIS Council of Heads of State in Kishinev (October 09, 2009) and Moscow (December 10, 2010), but the critical decisions were not provided. Meanwhile, there is good reason to hope that in the future the CIS and other organisations will open new opportunities for deepening economic and humanitarian cooperation, and strengthening security across the region and around the world.

In 1992, the independent Central Asian countries—Kazakhstan, Kyrgyzstan, Uzbekistan, Tajikistan, and Turkmenistan—established an interstate structure, Central Asian Regional Cooperation (CARC), whose main objective was economic union by creating a common economic space and a single regional market.[17] In February 2002, at a meeting of the presidents of Uzbekistan, Kazakhstan, Kyrgyzstan, and Tajikistan, the Organisation of Central Asian Cooperation (OCAC) was officially established. There were a number of problems in the OCAC; in particular, for many years the heads of Central Asian countries signed more than 200 documents within the framework of integration. However, many of them remained unrealised, in particular, the Agreement On the Single Economic Zone (1994); On Establishing a Strategic Economic Development Programme up to 2005 (2000). A unified approach to the use of water resources in Central Asia has not been developed. The tendency of Tajikistan and Kyrgyzstan to address only their interests in the water and energy resources of the Syr Darya and Amu Darya rivers creates difficulties for Kazakhstan, Turkmenistan, and Uzbekistan.

At the summit of the Organisation of Central Asian Co-operation in St. Petersburg (October 07, 2005), it was decided to integrate the Organisation into the EurAsEC. During the meeting, Uzbekistan decided to join the EurAsEC. The amalgamation of the Organisation of Central Asian Cooperation and Eurasian Economic Community might contribute to further economic development of Central Asia, but this process has never ended. No doubt, the geopolitical situation in Eurasia should be taken into account in the analysis of the regional co-operation process. The SCO, CIS, EurAsEC, and other organisations will be provided with new opportunities for economic cooperation and integration among member countries, including the promotion of security in Central Asia. For more successful implementation of the integration processes of interstate cooperation in Central Asia, it is necessary to accomplish large-scale and long-term regional projects in various areas of economic, communication, and humanitarian cooperation that will allow for the development of cooperation with various regions of the world, and certainly for strengthening the security of Central Asia.

An interesting format for multilateral relations is the 'Central Asia plus Japan' established in 2004 in Astana, the capital of Kazakhstan. The main concepts of the interregional cooperation 'Central Asia plus Japan' were proclaimed as (1) respect for different viewpoints and opinions, (2) coordination and consistency of acts, and (3) cooperation on a transparent basis. Proposed by Japan and supported by countries in the region 'Central Asia plus Japan' represents a new format for regional and interregional cooperation. However, active implementation of the agreements and decisions, as well as expanding the range of cooperation of the participating countries will be necessary. Representatives of Central Asian countries believe that cooperation with Japan is strategically important and will contribute to closer trade ties, economic and investment relations between Eurasia, the Middle East, and Asian-Pacific region.

Today's independent Central Asian states have become active participants in various projects, revival of the Great Silk Road that promote economic and political cooperation of the young states of Central Asia among themselves and the developed nations in Europe and Asia-Pacific region. At present, Central Asian republics of Kazakhstan, Kyrgyzstan, Tajikistan, Turkmenistan, and Uzbekistan, as well as China, Iran, Pakistan, and countries of the Caucasus—Georgia and Azerbaijan—are involved in the process of organisation and coordination of transportation arteries and communications to connect Europe and Asia, East and West. Inclusion into the well-known transport corridor Europe-Asia (TRACECA) received a strong support of the European Union in the construction and modernisation of highways and rail lines. However, for the complete realisation of this idea, there are certain difficulties in formulating a common policy of the states through which the route passes, and the positions of various countries, including the US and Russia.

In the context of development of transport and communication system, we should note the geopolitical and geo-economic importance of transportation of hydrocarbon material from Central Asia and the Caspian region to international markets. In 2009, the construction of another gas pipeline Central Asia-China (passing through the territory of Turkmenistan, Uzbekistan and Kazakhstan) was completed, which allowed a stable transit corridor to be formed for natural gas as well as the direction for diversified hydrocarbon exports from Central Asia. In December 2010 in Ashgabat, there was also signed an intergovernmental agreement on construction of the pipeline TAPI (Turkmenistan-Afghanistan-Pakistan-India).[18] In addition, during the official visit of President of Uzbekistan Islam Karimov to Ashgabat in October 2010 the questions concerning the opening of the transport corridor Uzbekistan-Turkmenistan-Iran-Oman-Qatar and other Persian Gulf countries were discussed. By the spring of 2011, the leaders of five countries agreed on the technical details of this corridor and at the end of April 2011 in Ashgabat, the Foreign Ministers of Turkmenistan, Uzbekistan, Iran, Oman, and Qatar signed an agreement on establishing a new international transport corridor to connect Central Asia with the ports of the Persian Gulf. Given the extremely complex geopolitical and geo-economic position of Central Asia, the countries need to advocate diversification of routes and directions for resource development of the energy-rich region. Perspective plans for new transportation projects will depend on how optimal the balance of global, regional, interregional, and national interests will be in the implementation of projects. There is no doubt that the future of strong regional and interregional co-operation will contribute to stability and economic progress in Central Asia, and will make a significant contribution to the establishment of international stability at large.

During the last two decades, Uzbekistan tried to develop its bilateral and multilateral foreign policy, however, it was faced with numerous difficulties and challenges in the international arena. In the early years, there were also some problems related to financial and organisational matters. Analytical agencies and mass media seemed very weak in coverage and development of problematic aspects of foreign policy of the republic and the region as a whole. Uzbekistan has repeatedly expressed its interest in developing mutually beneficial relations with Russia, China, Germany, the US, Japan, India, Korea and other countries. Uzbekistan's co-operation with the leading states, international and regional organisations could strengthen stability and security in Central Asia, which would be important for global security.

Notes

1. *Molodyozh Uzbekistana*. 20 August 1991.
2. E. Abdullaev, "Ustoychivoe neravnovesie v otnosheniyah s Rossiey v politike Uzbekistana" *Mezhdunarodnye protsessy.* – (Moskva, 2006. – № 3.) – pp. 119-126; V. Bushkov, I. Majarov, A. Sobyanin *Rossiya v Tsentralnoy Azii: kak preodolet negativnye tendentsii* (http://www.cis.ng.ru/); A. Kurtov, A. Perepelkin, " Mezhdunarodno-pravovaya baza dvuhstoronnego sotrudnichestva Rossiyskoy Federatsii i Respubliki Uzbekistan" *Uzbekistan: obretenie novogo oblika.* V 2-x Tomakh / Pod red. E. Kojokina, Institut Strategicheskikh Issledovaniy, 1998. T. 2, pp. 7-170; V. Paramonov , A. Strokov, O. Stolbovskiy, *Rossiya i Kitay v Tsentralnoy Azii: politika, ekonomika, bezopastnost.* – (Bishkek, 2008) – Spr. 155.
3. V. Paramonov, A.Strokov, O. Stolbovskiy, *Rossiya i Kitay v Tsentralnoy Azii: politika, ekonomika, bezopastnost.* – (Bishkek, 2008), pp. 29-30.
4. Data provided by the Statistics Committee of Uzbekistan,Tashkent, 2007.
5. "Cooperation Built on Long-Term Interest", *Uzbekistan Today*, 2011, Number 24.
6. Data provided by the Statistics Committee of Uzbekistan, Tashkent, 2010.
7. I. Bao *Kitay: Strategicheskie v Tsentralnoy Azii i Sotrudnichestvo so Stranami Regiona* // Tsentralnaya Aziya i Kavkaz, 2001. № 1, p. 117.
8. *Washington Post* (Staff writer) 2002, March 12, p. 23A.
9. R. Seidelmann "Globalization, Regionalization and the Nations state and their effect on EU – Asian relations", *EU-Asian relations: state of affairs, problems, and perspectives* NESCA series: MACAU, 2005, Number 1, p. 80.
10. "The EU and Central Asia: Strategy for a New partnership" http://register.consilium.europa.eu/pdf/en/; Schmitz A. Interessen, "Instrumente, Einflussgrenzen. Die Europдische Union und Zentralasien, *Osteuropa. Machtmosaik Zentralasien. Traditionen. Restriktionen, Aspiration.* (Berlin. 2007), p 329-332.
11. "The EU and Central Asia: Strategy for a New Partnership" The Permanent

Representatives Committee,31 May 2007, p. 10.

12. Author was among who participated at *ITEC* program in 2002.
13. Ramakant Dwivedi, "An Appraisal of the Indian Prime Minister's Visit to Uzbekistan" <www.idsa.in/publications/stratcomments/RamakantDwivedi280406.htm>(July 15 2006).
14. Information received from the *JICA* office in Tokyo, in April 2010.
15. O. Antonenko, "The EU should not ignore the Shanghai Cooperation Organization" Center for European Reform, *Policy Brief.* - London, 2007, p. 6; Prajakti Kalra *and* Siddharth S Saxena, "*The Shanghai Cooperation Organisation has raised fears of an anti-Western bloc forming in Central Asia*" Shanghai or Bust, Delhi 27th April 2007, p. 2.
16. www.mfa.uz. (website of the Ministry of Foreign Affairs of Uzbekistan). Information on cooperation with the CIS. 2010, 10 August.
17. G. Rahmatulina *Dinamika Razvitiya Integratsionnyk Protsessov v Gosudartstvah SNG i Perspectivy Formirovaniya Yedinogo Ekonomicheskogo Prostranstva.* (Almaty 2004), p. 92.
18. M. K. Bhadrakumar "Pipeline project a new Silk Road," *Asia Times*, Hongkong, December 16, 2010.

11. Turkmenistan's Foreign Policy: A Comparison of the Niyazov and the Post-Niyazov Regimes

Lopamudra Bandyopadhyay

Turkmenistan's stance with regard to its foreign policy has been an amalgamation of strategic crests and troughs, accentuating an otherwise smooth change of domestic regime from that of the old order to the new. The dynamics of Turkmenistan's foreign policy had for long hinged upon the twin aspects of isolationism and neutrality. However, with the winds of change, this quaint Central Asian state has opened up not only its foreign policy, but also its attitude towards the world outside.

Turkmenistan's erstwhile head of the state, President Saparmurat Niyazov pursued a foreign policy of neutrality, which was associated with an economic policy of increased national self-reliance and autonomy using the country's natural gas revenues. However, ineffective economic management increased Turkmenistan's dependence on gas exports, primarily with regard to Russia as the controller of the major gas pipelines. Turkmenbashi became increasingly isolationist in his foreign policy. However, an exception to this isolation was a 2006 trip to Beijing and agreement on gas exports to China. Niyazov's successor, President Gurbanguly Berdimuhamedov has, during the course of his regime, made an effective transition towards a diplomatically active foreign policy and has been aware of the costs of economic mismanagement. The current regime has effectively tried to mend its relations not only with its immediate neighbours, but also with the major powers involved in the region.[1]

The paper endeavours to make a comparison between the foreign policy pursued by President Niyazov and that of his successor, in an attempt to understand the shift in the course of policy making with regard to foreign affairs. It also tries to comprehend the future of Turkmenistan's foreign policy taking into consideration the geopolitical importance of the country vis-a-vis Central Asia.

The Concept of Positive Neutrality in Turkmenistan's Foreign Policy

Turkmenistan, throughout the Niyazov era consistently fashioned its foreign policy in retrospect of Russia and the influence the latter continued to have within the region. Turkmenistan did not hold a particularly strong position with regard to the US, although formal relations had been established by early 1993. Washington was initially more interested in resolving the legacy of nuclear weapons left by the erstwhile Soviet Union in the region. Beleaguered with domestic economic concerns, limited military capabilities, and fragile neighbouring states, Turkmenistan decided to base its foreign policy on an unusual principle described as 'positive neutrality'.[2]

Very soon after its independence, Turkmenistan acquired membership in various international organisations, such as the Asian Development Bank (ADB), the Economic Cooperation Organization (ECO), the International Monetary Fund (IMF), and others, but this orientation toward multilateral relations was quickly diluted, and Niyazov abandoned multilateral approaches with bilateral relations articulated through the concept of 'Positive Neutrality'. The ascension of 'Positive Neutrality' eclipsed multilateralism for the remainder of Niyazov's rule; the consequence was the effective disengagement from international affairs and organisations that might have provided some benefit to Turkmenistan's development. Further, on December 12, 1995, the United Nations General Assembly unanimously adopted resolution A/50/80, recognising, and supporting the permanent neutrality of Turkmenistan.[3]

Positive Neutrality has always lacked lucidity; the rhetorical ambiguity complicated rather than enhanced Turkmenistan's international relations.[4] It is more likely, however, that the policy was not designed to improve external relations as much as it was designed to consolidate and increase domestic political control. The concept further, claiming that it provided the best means for mutual respect in its foreign relations, that it increased domestic and foreign security interests for the republic, and that it enhanced its internal growth. The purpose, in all probability, according to Turkmen officials, was to incorporate the republic into the world's economic system while liberating it from external pressures.[5]

Moreover, although enshrined in the republic's constitution, in practice Turkmenistan has been one of the worst violators of basic human rights in the world. Positive Neutrality inherently demanded that international partners respect the internal affairs of the republic and that Turkmenistan would not interfere in the affairs of others. With regard to this aspect, Turkmenistan abolished the death penalty in 2000, but did little to eradicate its repressive policies that limited employment, travel, or freedom of speech, press, or religion. At its nucleus, this policy was designed to promote cordial relations with all states while avoiding multilateral agreements that might offend its partners.[6]

Turkmenistan's Foreign Policy During the Niyazov Regime

Rapid changes ensued with the sudden disintegration of the Soviet Union. Following its dissolution, in December 1991, Turkmenistan became a member of the successor organisation, the Commonwealth of Independent States (CIS). In 1992, Turkmenistan also joined the United Nations, the International Monetary Fund (IMF), the World Bank, the European Bank for Reconstruction and Development (EBRD), and the Economic Cooperation Organization (ECO). However, President Niyazov was careful to ensure that none of these affiliations restricted his policy space. Relations with the IMF, World Bank and EBRD were extremely limited. The preferred multilateral institution was the UN, which usually made no attempt to influence domestic policy.[7]

Turkmenistan's participation in regional organisations and initiatives has been practically nonexistent. The only regional organisation where Turkmenistan's participation has been a real issue is the CIS. Turkmenistan, however, was not among the six CIS members, which signed the Collective Security Treaty in May 1992. When in the second half of the 1990s CIS members split into two competing groups (the Russian-led Union of Five and the GUUAM coalition), Turkmenistan simply adopted a neutral stand. In August 2005, Turkmenistan changed its CIS standing to associate member, citing considerations of consistency with its UN-recognised international neutrality status, and effectively withdrawing from the organisation.[8]

During the course of this time, Turkmenistan took certain steps in the realm of foreign policy that were in contradiction with its stand on neutrality, although they were in nature of minor significance. In 1997, a gas pipeline and a railway line were built between Turkmenistan and Iran. Also in 1996-97, a pipeline through Afghanistan was pursued initially with an Argentinean company Bridas, and then with the US company Unocal. The US support was, however, withdrawn in 1997 as domestic US opposition to working with the Taliban mounted. The rail line, as the only rail connection running south from Central Asia, could be a major transport corridor. In 2000, Turkmenistan joined the Asian Development Bank, but as with the World Bank and EBRD relations have been limited, and has also participated in the EU's BOMCA program, primarily as the recipient of materials for reconstructing a border crossing point with Uzbekistan.[9]

With the advent of the new century, President Niyazov travelled less and relations with his neighbours deteriorated even further. In the South Caspian, demarcation disputes led to shooting incidents between Turkmenistan and Azerbaijan. There were numerous frontier incidents with Uzbekistan, and in November 2002, President Niyazov accused Uzbekistan's President Karimov of involvement in an assassination plot.[10] In late 2004, Niyazov met former Canadian Prime Minister Jean Chrétien to discuss an oil contract in Turkmenistan for a Canadian corporation. In 2005, Niyazov announced that his country would downgrade its links with the Commonwealth of Independent States; he, further promised free and fair elections by 2010. An immense exception to this pattern was the President's 2006 trip to Beijing, which was followed by a high-level Chinese visit to Ashgabat. This was a sign of the extent to which foreign policy had become related to economic imperatives, notwithstanding Turkmenbashi's cherished neutrality.[11]

Turkmenistan's Foreign Policy During the Post-Niyazov Period

It may be stated that the foreign policy of Gurbanguly M. Berdimuhamedov might have been primarily influenced by two main forces: the preservation of external circumstances conducive to the maintenance of domestic political control as well as the reduction of international isolation. In simple words, post-Niyazov foreign policy had to achieve insulation without increasing Turkmenistan's isolation.[12]

At the very inception, post-Niyazov domestic politics remained strongly authoritarian. Further, Turkmenistani foreign policy has remained, since the end of the Niyazov era, essentially domestically oriented. It may be noted that a substantial change in the foreign policy strategies implemented by the new regime has not been complemented by a radical revision of the core aim of foreign policy.[13] It should be noted that Berdimuhamedov's foreign policy has continued to pursue essentially domestic targets through a relatively new strategy, built upon the establishment of 'more constructive relations with other members of the international community'.[14] A major factor in the emergence of this new scenario has been represented by the evolution of the energy security priorities of the EU and of the US. Central Asia in general and Turkmenistan in particular, have been assigned key functions in the new energy security paradigms conceptualised by Brussels[15] and Washington.[16]

It would be prudent now to delve into the relations that Turkmenistan shares with the major external players in the Central Asian region. They may be classified into:

1. Russia and China (powers, who have been quite active in the regional sphere)
2. The West, namely the EU and the US (powers interested in further involvement in the region)

Russia and China

Russia

Russia-Turkmenistan bilateralism remained, in the post-Niyazov era, the keystone of Turkmenistan's system of international relations. Since

2007, the two leaderships have continued to hold regular bilateral summits, as President Berdimuhamedov has met rather frequently with both Vladimir Putin and Dmitri Medvedev. Further, the volume of trade exchanged between Turkmenistan and Russia has remained significant,[17] and, conceivably most importantly, the Kremlin has continued to extend crucial international support to the Turkmenistan government. In other words, the relationship between Moscow and Ashgabat has preserved its extraordinary relationship even after the death of Niyazov.

At the apex of Niyazov's isolationism, Russia represented the central element of foreign policy formulation and implementation, as other bilateral relations and multilateral diplomacy more generally did not hold much relevance in the external strategies designed by the regime. However, at present, a significant segment of Turkmenistan's foreign policy is no longer exclusively oriented towards Moscow.[18]

The regime recently multiplied its efforts to diversify gas export options through a two-pronged strategy, which involved a series of agreements with China and Iran, and regular negotiations with state and non-state energy actors located in the West. To these ends, Berdimuhamedov has managed to place Turkmenistan at the epicentre of international gas politics. That is not to say that the post-Niyazov energy cooperation between Russia and Turkmenistan has developed smoothly, as confirmed by the gas crisis that unfolded in 2009-10. On April 09, 2009, the immediate interruption of gas delivery between Russia and Turkmenistan was provoked by the explosion of a branch of the Central Asia-Centre Pipeline located in the proximity of the Turkmenistan-Uzbek border.[19] While the Turkmenistan government promptly accused Gazprom of sabotage, Russian officials responded by underlining the 'purely technical' nature of the explosion.[20] A few days later, gas traffic between Turkmenistan and Russia was reduced by 90 per cent. The dispute between the two parties continued for nine months, in which Turkmenistan experienced a record GDP loss of 25 per cent. The underlying issue behind the dispute was Turkmenistan's pressure for a renegotiation of the export price Gazprom agreed to pay according to the gas deal of January 2009. Speculation in this regard was granted further weight by the terms of the gas deal finalised on December 22, 2009, in which Russia agreed to buy 30 bcm of gas from Turkmenistan at the price, considered more in line with European standards, of about US$ 250 per tcm.[21] Normal gas traffic between Turkmenistan and Russia resumed on January 10 2010.

After the conclusion of the 2009-10 gas disputes, Russo-Turkmenistan relations underwent a rapid process of normalisation. In the aftermath of a summit with Russian Foreign Minister Sergei Lavrov in March 2010, Berdimuhamedov reportedly stated that 'Turkmenistan will always have enough gas for Russia'.[22] As Russia's political support for any Turkmenistani regime is traditionally dependent on the intensity of the bilateral gas trade, Berdimuhamedov will carefully avoid energy policies that could significantly damage Russian energy interests. In other words, Moscow's political support is inseparable from Turkmenistan's participation in the Russian monopoly over the Eurasian gas trade.

China

In the post-Niyazov era, energy cooperation between China and Turkmenistan was primarily regulated by a landmark gas deal signed in 2007,[23] which determined the role of the China National Petroleum Company in the development of a number of gas fields in the Lebap velayat (eastern Turkmenistan) and in the construction works of a major pipeline. The provisions included in this agreement came to fruition with the inauguration of the Central Asia-China pipeline on December 14, 2009.[24]

During the Niyazov era, the completion of virtually all pipeline projects involving Turkmenistan proved difficult and in a number of cases, extremely unlikely.[25] In contrast, the Central Asia-China pipeline reached completion in a rather short period. The pipeline was inaugurated in a historic ceremony held in Saman-Depe, and was attended by the leaders of China, Kazakhstan, Turkmenistan and Uzbekistan—the project's major stakeholders.[26] This new pipeline, marked for the first time in more than a decade, the biggest-ever effort to export Central Asian gas without using Russian routes.[27]

Prior to 2009, economic cooperation between the two parties was rather insignificant, as the total value of Chinese direct investments in Turkmenistan for 2002 was only US$ 300,000, and in 2005 total imports from China accounted for less than 1 per cent of Turkmenistan's total imports.[28] These inadequate figures are now part of history, as massive amounts of Chinese investments are flowing into Turkmenistan. While a loan of US$ 4 billion represented Beijing's contribution to the China-Central Asia pipeline project, another loan of US$ 3 billion was granted to the government of Turkmenistan in order to develop the giant gas field of South Yolotan in June 2009.[29]

While China-Turkmenistan military cooperation developed quite substantially under Niyazov, the Berdimuhamedov era witnessed the emergence of an embryonic political cooperation between the two countries.[30] In this field, the key document has been represented by the 'Joint Declaration between the People's Republic of China and Turkmenistan', signed during Berdimuhamedov's official visit to China in September 2008. In the 13-point declaration, China expressed its appreciation for 'the remarkable progress made by Turkmenistan in nation-building and social and economic development', while the Turkmenistani government 'applauded the outstanding achievements China has made after 30 years of reform and opening-up'.[31]

While in the Niyazov era cooperation between China and Turkmenistan was essentially limited to minor energy projects, the Berdimuhamedov era witnessed an increase in the significance of energy cooperation between the two parties, as well as the emergence of a more political tone in the relationship. In other words, China has been acquiring more and more centrality in Turkmenistan's foreign policy system.

The EU and the US

The formulation of the EU Strategy for a New Partnership with Central Asia and, to a lesser degree, the appointment of Barack Obama as President of the US offered new opportunities in the development of the relationships between Turkmenistan and the West. Interestingly, both the EU and the US have considered the strengthening of their energy cooperation with Central Asia as an adequate response to a specific challenge, namely the diversification of their import options and the ensuing dilution of energy dependency on Russia or the Persian Gulf.[32]

When it came to approaching the Central Asian states to develop bilateral energy cooperation, the EU and the US had to negotiate their pragmatic interests in Central Asia with the promotion of good governance in the region. This problem acquired particular relevance in the context of the relationships established with Turkmenistan, on the basis of (1) the significant potential of Turkmenistan's energy reserves, (2) the authoritarian essence of the regime, and (3) the traditional reluctance with which the political elite has responded to external pressures for political liberalisation.

The conditionalities imposed so far from different EU organs have complicated the normalisation of the EU-Turkmenistan relationship, particularly with regard to the ratification of the Partnership and Cooperation Agreement (PCA) between the EU and Turkmenistan. Although the European Parliament is yet to ratify the PCA, on the basis of its concerns for the abysmal human rights record of Turkmenistan's government,[33] the approval (April 22, 2009) of an Interim Trade Agreement (ITA) between the parties appears a positive development in the establishment of fully-fledged relations between Brussels and Ashgabat. Similar measures are also included in the new strategy for Turkmenistan approved in April 2010 by the Board of Directors of the European Bank for Reconstruction and Development (EBRD). Criticisms expressed by member states or European nongovernmental actors are in evident contradiction with a number of EU official declarations on Turkmenistan, which have instead offered positive evaluations of Berdimuhamedov's reformist input.[34]

The tones and contents of these statements suggest that the EU perception of Turkmenistan's authoritarianism is rapidly shifting, as is also indicated by declining EU criticism of the country's authoritarianism.[35] Similar traits have also come to the fore in the context of US official assessment of Turkmenistan's domestic politics. In the 2009 meeting between Hilary Clinton, the US Secretary of State, and

President Berdimuhamedov, the issue of human rights was not raised by the US Administration. The absence of the human dimension from the US-Turkmenistani bilateral agenda was motivated by time constraints and, rather strikingly, its allegedly scarce relevance for Turkmenistan's political landscape. For Berdimuhamedov and his associates, this development became equivalent to regime consolidation. A substantial increase in energy cooperation with Turkmenistan is viewed by the Obama Administration as an essential tool to strengthen Washington's influence over decision-making circles in Ashgabat, to ultimately achieve an objective that successive US Administrations have failed to attain. As for the EU, it is in relation to the energy dimension that EU interests vis-a-vis Turkmenistan has been traditionally formulated: the energy sector accounts for approximately 90 per cent of EU imports from Turkmenistan.[36] While Turkmenistan's energy security has been associated traditionally with the ability to ensure a regular flow of revenues from the exploration, processing and, ultimately, export of gas resources, the EU has more recently identified the establishment of a 'Southern Gas Corridor for supply from Caspian and Middle Eastern sources'[37] as an essential step to increase its energy security. Turkmenistan's focus on diversification of energy exports seems also to be consistent with current US policies, which are focused on 'encouraging multiple pipelines out of the Central Asian region'.[38]

A number of decisive steps to consolidate the EU-Turkmenistan energy partnership were made in 2008. Following gas talks with EU officials in 2008, President Berdimuhamedov announced that an annual gas delivery of 10 bcm per year would reach the EU from 2009 onwards. This unprecedented move—which is nevertheless yet to translate into practical action—was soon followed in May 2008, by the finalisation of a more comprehensive 'Memorandum of Understanding and Cooperation in the field of Energy',[39] which essentially provided a reference framework for the development of the bilateral energy relationship. As we have seen, EU decision-makers have placed energy cooperation with Turkmenistan in a wider context: the development of the Southern Gas Corridor. Three pipelines projects will form the key arteries for the corridor—White

Stream; Nabucco—connecting Erzurum (Turkey) with Baumgarten an der March (Austria) via Bulgaria, Romania, and Hungary—and the ITGI (Turkey-Greece-Italy Interconnector Pipeline). The total capacity of the latter two pipelines is expected to reach approximately 40 bcm per year in 2020, 64 whereas White Stream's planned capacity is to exceed 30 bcm per year.[40]

The EU is particularly keen to involve Turkmenistan in the Nabucco project—a 3,300 km long pipeline, whose construction costs will exceed US$11 billion. Turkmenistan's participation is regarded as highly critical to the overall success of Nabucco, as the EU is eager to finalise a comprehensive supply deal with the Turkmenistani government. Interestingly, the US has also expressed a strong commitment to the Nabucco project, insofar as it contributes to the strengthening of the energy security of the EU.

The Emerging Geopolitical Importance of Turkmenistan as Illustrated by Recent Events

The arrival of Austrian President Heinz Fischer in Turkmenistan in October 2011 on an official visit has been significant with regard to diplomatic exchanges between the world leaders and the Central Asian nation. The main purpose of the visit was to explore further bilateral economic cooperation, likely focusing on Turkmenistan's vast gas reserves. President Fischer appealed to Turkmenistan President Gurbanguly Berdimuhamedov to contribute and support the creation of the Nabucco pipeline, a gas pipeline that is to run 3,300 kilometers from Turkey to Austria with gas from Iraq as well as other Central Asian nations, such as Turkmenistan. The pipeline would give a gas supply to the EU from a source other than Russia, something that has long been in the interest of many EU nations.[41]

Fischer's visit to Turkmenistan follows a series of other visits and bilateral dialogues between Turkmenistan and other nations. China recently held high-level meetings with the country in an effort to strengthen economic and diplomatic ties with Ashgabat. The US also held official talks with the Turkmenistan Government earlier this year in order to discuss 'the full spectrum of its bilateral relationships'.[42] Those two nations are only a few of the long list to have engaged in discussions with the Berdimuhamedov administration, with dignitaries from India, Pakistan, Russia and the EU having visited Ashgabat over the last year. The majority of these visits have been undertaken in order to secure deals to obtain Turkmenistan's gas supplies, which are among the largest in the world.[43]

Such visits and meetings are indicative of two things. Firstly, it helps reinforce the fact energy security is a top global priority and, more importantly in the context of this piece, that Turkmenistan continues to be one of the countries at the forefront of addressing energy security needs.[44] This has helped to make the country attractive to those nations with increasing energy security needs, such as the rising economies of the Global South and the developed world, who continue to face increased competition from the former for global energy supplies.[45]

Turkmenistan's appeal to the world because of its energy supplies is nothing new. It was a major reason why former President Sapamurat Niyazov was able to autocratically rule the country until his death in December 2006. The fall of the Soviet Union saw a development of the domestic oil and gas industry, which allowed it to be a reliable energy supplier in the post-Soviet era. However, Turkmenistan has found a recent greater appeal with other countries for two main reasons; its location and relative domestic stability, especially compared to other global energy suppliers now.

Being situated slightly west of China means that it could transport energy supplies from Turkmenistan without a need for shipping, which eliminates potential sea-based problems such as privacy. This is a similar case for India, who can also import Turkmen energy via land. For the EU, importing Turkmen (and other Central Asian) gas supplies to Europe via a pipeline lessen its reliability on Russia for its gas supplies, a reliability it has long sought to do away with. Turkmenistan has also remained relatively stable under the leadership of President Berdimuhamedov. This is significant in regards to energy security due to the instability that had plagued nations such as Bahrain (situated in the Persian Gulf) as well as Yemen, Somalia and Egypt, which are located along shipping lines between the Persian Gulf and Europe and the US.[46]

As previously mentioned, China has been that has engaged in high-level discussions with Turkmenistan this year in an attempt to address its energy interests. In August 2010, Chinese Foreign Minister Yang Jiechi met the Turkmen President and Foreign Minister for bilateral talks. That followed an agreement in March in which Turkmenistan agreed to increase natural gas supply to China by 20 billion cubic meters a year to a total of 30 billion cu m.[47] This is evidence not only of China's continually growing energy needs, but also of its preference to have Turkmenistan as a key partner in helping it address its energy security requirements.

India has also recently attempted to strengthen its relations with Turkmenistan as part of its own increasing energy security needs. In a rare sign of unity and agreement, India and its regional arch rival Pakistan signed an intergovernmental agreement on the Turkmenistan-Afghanistan-Pakistan-India (TAPI) gas pipeline with Turkmenistan in December 2010. India also held talks last week with a delegations headed by Turkmen Petroleum and Mineral Resources Minister Bairamgeldy Nedirov which centred on securing a contract to sell gas to India.[48] Like China, India too has been focusing on Turkmenistan to help in addressing its energy security requirements, so much so that it has been willing to work with Pakistan in order to secure Turkmen gas.

The US Assistant Secretary of State for South and Central Asian Affairs Robert Blake Jr visited the country, as well as Uzbekistan in February 2011, where a review of the Annual Bilateral Consultations, a US initiative to discuss bilateral issues with Central Asian nations, was conducted. Other traditional sources of energy imports, such as the Persian Gulf, remain of prime importance to the US. However, the current instability in nations such as Bahrain and Iraq along with its constant rivalry with Iran, has led it to place a greater significance on Turkmenistan and Central Asia in general for its energy needs.

Further, the EU Ambassador to Turkmenistan, Norbert Jousten, held talks with the Turkmen Government in September 2011, in order to discuss bilateral cooperation in the energy sector. This followed a visit to Turkmenistan by European Commission President Jose Manuel Barroso in January 2011, where energy issues were widely discussed between both Presidents.[49] Turkmenistan's vast gas resources and relative proximity to Europe has increased its appeal as an alternative gas supplier to the EU.

Conclusion

At a recent government meeting in January 2012, Turkmen President Gurbanguly Berdimuhamedov outlined the tasks for the ministry of foreign affairs for the year. Under the terms of the Programme of Action 2012, Turkmenistan will host in the second half of this year a seminar on security in Central Asia and the Caspian region with broad participation of relevant delegations.

"Turkmenistan considers it essential to ensure strategic stability and peace and to fully adhere to the Charter of the United Nations. Our country will continue to rigorously and consistently pursuing a policy of good neighbourliness and peace-making, actively promoting the work to achieve harmony and sustainable development," the Turkmen Head said. He added that Turkmenistan reject the use of military force as an instrument of foreign policy and international relations.[50] Berdimuhamedov or Arkadag, which is Turkmen for protector, was elected for his second term as President in February 2012.

Thus, it may be concluded that although the foreign policy initiatives adopted by President Niyazov both maintained as well as safeguarded the essential domestic structure of Turkmenistan. On the other hand, his successor, President Berdimuhamedov diversified the multi-vector policy of the country to include effective returns with regard to gas revenues. The present foreign policy of Turkmenistan hinges not only upon the energy security perspective, but also incorporates transnational policy initiatives with not only regional, but also global powers. Hence, it remains to be seen how far this tiny Central Asian country is able to emerge not only as a regional power, but also as an effective global player.

Notes

1. Richard Pomfret, 'Turkmenistan's Foreign Policy,' *China and Eurasia Forum Quarterly 6 (4)*, November/December 2008, p. 19.
2. Steven Sabol, "Turkmenistan: Permanent Transition or Elusive Stability?" *China and Eurasia Forum Quarterly 8 (3)*, September/October 2010, p. 17.
3. "Fifteen Years of Turkmenistan's Permanent Neutrality Brought Steady Realization of Nation's Aspiration to Become Force for Progress, says Secretary-General, The United Nations, Department of Public Information, News and Media Division," at http://www.un.org/News/Press/docs/2010/sgsm13316.doc.htm (Accessed on April 30, 2012).
4. For a detailed study of Positive Neutrality, refer to Boris O. Shikhmudarov, "Positive Neutrality as the Basis of the Foreign Policy of Turkmenistan," at http://sam.gov.tr/wp-content/uploads/2012/01/BORIS-O.-SHIKHMURADOV.pdf (Accessed on April 22, 2012).
5. Sabol, "Turkmenistan: Permanent Transition or Elusive Stability?" *China and Eurasia Forum Quarterly 8 (3)*, September/October 2010, p. 18.
6. Sabol.
7. Pomfret, 'Turkmenistan's Foreign Policy,' *China and Eurasia Forum Quarterly 6 (4)*, November/December 2008, pp. 20-22.
8. Pomfret.
9. Pomfret.
10. Pomfret, p. 22.
11. Pomfret.
12. Luca Anceschi, "External Conditionality, Domestic Insulation and Energy Security: The International Politics of Post-Niyazov Turkmenistan," *China and Eurasia Forum Quarterly 8(3)*, September/October 2010, pp. 95-96.
13. Luca Anceschi, *Turkmenistan's foreign policy - Positive Neutrality and the consolidation of the Turkmen regime,* (Abingdon-New York: Routledge, 2008), p. 140.
14. Slavomír Horák and Jan Šír, *Dismantling totalitarianism? Turkmenistan under Berdimuhamedov* (Washington, D.C.: The Central Asia-Caucasus Institute, Silk Road Monograph, March 2009), p. 67, at www.isdp.eu/files/publications/srp/09/js09turkmenistanunder.pdf (Accessed on April 10, 2012).
15. The general guidelines for the EU energy strategy in Central Asia are outlined in: Council of the EU, *The EU and Central Asia: Strategy for a new partnership* (Brussels: European Communities, 2007).
16. According to the US Department of State, the Obama Administration sees Turkmenistan as a 'leader in terms of energy security and energy supply.' "Remarks of Assistant Secretary Robert O. Blake, Turkmenistan's bilateral meeting," September 21, 2009, at http://www.state.gov/p/sca/rls/rmks/2009/129450.htm (Accessed on April 11, 2012).

17. The Russian Federal Customs Service reported that, in November 2009, the total trade exchanged between Russia and Turkmenistan amounted to US$ 980.6 million. The annual growth rate of trade between the parties was 11.97 per cent. See: Federal Customs Service, *Russian Federation: External trade with selected countries*, January-November 2009, at http://www.customs.ru/ru/stats/arhiv-stats-new/popup.php (Accessed on April 10, 2012).
18. Anceschi *op. cit*, "External Conditionality, Domestic Insulation and Energy Security: The International Politics of Post-Niyazov Turkmenistan," p. 99.
19. Bruce Pannier, "Pipeline Explosion Raises Tensions between Turkmenistan, Russia," *RFE/RL Feature Article*, April 13, 2009, at http://www.rferl.org/content/Pipeline_Explosion_Stokes_Tensions_Between_Turkmenistan_Russia/1608633.html (Accessed on April 15, 2012).
20. Pannier.
21. "On the Outcomes of the Visit of Gazprom Delegation to Turkmenistan," Gazprom website, at http://www.gazprom.ru/press/news/2009/december/article73466/ (Accessed on April 20, 2012).
22. "Transcript of the declaration of the Minister of Foreign Affairs of the Russian Federation S.V. Lavrov on the outcome of the meeting with the vice-president of the Cabinet of Minister of Turkmenistan, and Minister of Foreign Affairs of Turkmenistan R.O Meredov," Russian ministry of Foreign Affairs, at http://www.mid.ru/brp_4.nsf/0/EC4DC9EE5F7E161FC32576E8005C2A77 (Accessed on April 10, 2012).
23. The 2007 contract followed from a major Sino-Turkmenistani energy deal signed by Niyazov in April 2006.
24. Luca Anceschi, "Analyzing Turkmen Foreign Policy in the Berdimuhamedov Era," *China & Eurasia Forum Quarterly* 6, 4 (2008), p. 45.
25. Anceschi, *Turkmenistan's Foreign Policy*, p. 93.
26. The Central Asia-China pipeline - whose total length is of approximately 1,833 kilometres - starts at Saman-Depe, in the proximity of the Turkmenistani-Uzbek border, and then runs through Uzbekistan and Kazakhstan to end at Horgos (north-western Xinjiang).
27. For other accounts of the pipeline's inauguration, see also "China President Opens Turkmenistan Gas Pipeline," *BBC News*, December 14, 2009; "Cross-border Pipeline Pulls Region Closer," *The China Daily*, December 15, 2009.
28. Anceschi, *Turkmenistan's Foreign Policy*, p. 80.
29. Anceschi, *Turkmenistan's Foreign Policy.*
30. For background information on past developments and future prospects in the Sino-Turkmenistani military cooperation, see: Sébastien Peyrouse, "Military Cooperation between China and Central Asia: Breakthrough, Limits, and Prospects," *China Brief*, 10, 5 (March 05, 2010), pp. 10-14 at http://www.jamestown.org/uploads/media/

cb_010_25.pdf (Accessed on April 14, 2012).

31. "Joint Declaration between the People's Republic of China and Turkmenistan," at http://www.fmprc.gov.cn/eng/wjdt/2649/t511329.htm (Accessed on April 14, 2012).
32. Anceschi, *Turkmenistan's Foreign Policy.*
33. Anceschi.
34. Anceschi.
35. "EU-Turkmenistan Human Rights Dialogue," at http://www.consilium.europa.eu/Newsroom (Accessed on April 20, 2012).
36. Bureau of European and Eurasian Affairs, "Foreign Operations Appropriated Assistance: Turkmenistan Fact Sheet, January 20, 2009," at http://www.state.gov/p/eur/rls/fs/103639.htm (Accessed on April 20, 2012).
37. European Commission, Directorate General for Energy and Trade, "Memo - EU Energy Security and Solidarity Action Plan: 2nd Strategic Energy Review," at http://ec.europa.eu/energy/strategies/2008/doc/2008_11_ser2/strategic_energy_review_memo.pdf (Accessed on April 17, 2012).
38. See the remarks of US Deputy Assistant Secretary of State George Krol at the International Gas Conference held in Ashgabat on April 23-24, 2009 in Jim Nichol, *Turkmenistan: Recent Developments and US Interests,* CRS Report for Congress 7-5700, September 10, 2009, p. 9.
39. For the full draft, see: "Memorandum of Understanding and Cooperation in the Field of Energy between the EU and Turkmenistan," at http://ec.europa.eu/energy/international/international_cooperation/doc/mou_turkmeni stan.pdf (Accessed on April 17, 2012).
40. Michael Denison, *The EU and Central Asia: Commercialising the Energy Relationship,* EUCAM Working Papers no. 2, July 2009, at http://aei.pitt.edu/11477/1/1883.pdf (Accessed on April 29, 2012), p. 6.
41. Catherine A. Fitzpatrick, "Turkmenistan Weekly Roundup," *Eurasianet.org,* at http://www.eurasianet.org/node/64357, (Accessed on April 18, 2012).
42. "U.S.US envoy to visit Turkmenistan, Uzbekistan," *Xinhua, People's Daily Online,* at http://english.peopledaily.com.cn/90001/90777/90852/7286558.html, (Accessed on April 20, 2012).
43. Bruno de Paiva, "Turkmenistan at Forefront of Global Energy Security Needs – Analysis," *Eurasiareview,* at http://www.eurasiareview.com/16102011-turkmenistan-at-forefront-of-global-energy-security-needs-analysis/, (Accessed on May 12, 2012).
44. Paiva.
45. Jim Nichol, Central Asia: Regional Developments and Implications for US Interests, Congressional Research Service, January 03, 2012, at http://www.fas.org/sgp/crs/row/RL33458.pdf, pp. 51-53, (Accessed on April 28, 2012).
46. Paiva, "Turkmenistan at Forefront of Global Energy Security Needs – Analysis".
47. 'Turkmenistan Agrees to Raise Natural Gas Supply to China,' at http://www.china.

org.cn/world/2011-03/02/content_22039238.htm (Accessed on May 01, 2012).

48. Paiva, "Turkmenistan at Forefront of Global Energy Security Needs – Analysis."
49. "EU Commission President Barroso visits Turkmenistan," at http://www.europahouse-tm.eu/files/EU%20Commission%20President%20Barroso%20visits%20Turkmenistan_Europa%20House_TK_%20ENG_January_2011.pdf , (Accessed on May 01, 2012).
50. For a detailed discussion of Central Asian Security, refer to K. Santhanam (ed.), *Eurasian Security Matters*, India-Central Asian Foundation, (New Delhi: Allied Publishers, 2010), pp. 3-137.

12. Turkmenistan's Foreign Policy after Niyazov: Looking beyond 'Positive Neutrality'?

Angira Sen Sarma

The sheer abundance of hydrocarbon reserves and its location have made Turkmenistan a significant country in the Central Asian region, which have attracted international attention since its independence in 1991. Seating on 24.3 trillion cubic metres of gas[1], the country has the largest gas reserves in the region. It accounts for about 11.7 per cent[2] of the world's share of natural gas. It is also rich in oil reserves and its borders with Iran, Afghanistan and the Caspian Sea make the country geo-strategically significant.

Since its independence, Turkmenistan like other Central Asian Republics (CARs) embarked on a new path. Among other issues, charting out a foreign policy was one of the challenging tasks for the newly independent country. Turkmenistan evolved a 'distinctive foreign policy'[3] under the former President, Saparmurat Niyazov, which made it stand out in the region. On December 12, 1995, the UN General Assembly approved resolution No A/50/80, which recognised Turkmenistan's neutral status. President Niyazov termed Turkmenistan's neutral status as 'positive neutrality', which he described as not practicing 'self-isolation' but taking a 'positive' and a 'constructive position'.[4] December 12 is celebrated as a national holiday in the country to commemorate its neutral status. Under the concept of 'positive neutrality' as envisaged by President Niyazov, the foreign policy objectives of the Republic are:[5]

- Maintain the national sovereignty of Turkmenistan, enhance its role and relevance in international relations
- Create the best-possible external environment for the country's domestic growth

- Pursue Turkmen national interests through the use of all forms of international diplomacy
- Provide for the security of Turkmenistan through political and diplomatic means
- Develop constructive and mutually beneficial cooperative ties with all international partners on the grounds of parity and mutual respects
- Assure that Turkmenistan's foreign policy moves are fully in line with the international law and the UN Charter

Although the country announced its 'neutral status', it did join a few multilateral institutions but participation in these bodies was limited. Turkmenistan joined several multilateral institutions like International Monetary Fund (IMF), the World Bank, the European Bank for Reconstruction and Development (EBRD), Asian Development Bank (ADB), United Nations (UN), etc. The only multilateral institution that the country is closely working with is the UN—its association with organizations like EBRD, IMF and the World Bank is 'extremely limited'.[6]

Turkmenistan has kept out of most of the regional groupings. Turkmenistan joined the CIS after independence but did not sign the Collective Security Treaty of 1992. From 2005, Turkmenistan is only an associate member of the CIS. The country is not a member of the SCO, CSTO, EurAsEc, and CAREC programmes. Of late, Turkmenistan is participating in the SCO summit meetings as a guest.

President Niyazov has been criticised for his authoritarian style of running the country. Some of his domestic policies had negative impact on the country's foreign policy. The human rights' record in the country became a stumbling block for developing closer cooperation with the West. It has often been argued that Niyazov used the policy of 'neutrality' to shield the country's domestic policies, which has been criticised for its repressive measures. Economic imperatives made it essential to maintain close relations with some countries like Russia and Iran. But otherwise, the country became insulated from the outside world, especially regarding security issues and its engagement with multilateral institutions.

After Niyazov's death in December 2006, Gurbanguly

Berdimuhamedov became the new President in January 2007. Amidst a lot of criticism, the country saw a transition of power after Niyazov, who had been the President since the country's independence till his death. Berdimuhamedov, after assuming power introduced a few policy changes, which is also reflected in the foreign policy domain. Few changes were evident in domestic policies like reversing Niyazov's policies on education, pensions and exchange rate systems, removing the golden statue of Niyazov and using the conventional names of months—all which raised hopes about a 'new' foreign policy.[7] The international community expected to see Turkmenistan coming out of its isolation and engaging with the outside world, which is however, not the case, as exceptions are made only on a selective basis. The 2008 Constitution of the country mentions that 'permanent neutrality' continues to be the country's central foreign policy principle.

The paper examines whether there has been any substantial change in the country's foreign policy orientation after Niyazov. Turkmenistan, in the past few years is cooperating with foreign partners, especially to diversify its energy markets. Is Turkmenistan's initiative in recent years about engagement with the outside world only limited to the sphere of energy? The paper will also study Turkmenistan's relationship with the neighbouring countries, which has not always been smooth, at least with a few of them. Turkmenistan's growing role in regional stability needs also to be explored given its geographic proximity to Afghanistan. With such emergent trends, India also needs to tap the new opportunities available today and revitalise its relations with Turkmenistan.

Energy—The Driving Force Behind Turkmenistan's Relations with the Outside World

The economy of Turkmenistan has always been primarily dependent on gas exports. Energy issues have thus always been the driving factor in determining Turkmenistan's relations with the outside world. Even during Niyazov's time, the country's neutral status has been questioned by many experts because of Turkmenistan's dependence on Russia to export gas to international markets. Since Soviet times, the pipelines connecting

Turkmenistan to international markets traverse through Russia, giving Russia a stronger bargaining position. Gazprom, the Russian Company is the main buyer of Turkmen gas, which is then re-exported to Europe. In 2011, Russia imported 10.1 billion cu m of gas from Turkmenistan.[8] But since its independence, Turkmenistan has been keen on reducing its dependence on Russia for export of its gas supplies. Although Berdimuhamedov immediately after becoming President visited Russia (April 2007), the bilateral relations have not always been smooth. Russia-Turkmenistan relations reached a low point in 2009 when the main pipeline transporting Turkmen gas to Russia exploded. Turkmenistan suspected Russian hand behind the explosion. Russia stopped purchasing gas from the Republic, which had costs the Turkmen exchequer about US$ 1 billion per month.[9] After nine months of stalemate, Turkmenistan resumed gas supply to Russia.

Post Niyazov, Turkmenistan has been keen on cooperating with other countries that have a strong interest in the rich hydrocarbon resources of the country. The Republic has 'emerged over the past two years as a major priority for the great powers with stakes in Central Asia'.[10] The energy factor has been one of the determining factors of Turkmenistan's relations with other big players in the region, namely China and the US.

The China connection was strongly felt in Niyazov's regime. Niyazov's visit to China in 2006, and later, the visit of a high level Chinese delegation to Turkmenistan indicate the important role energy factor played in Turkmenistan's relations with the outside world even during Niyazov's time. The primary objective of this visit was to explore the possibilities to deliver Turkmen gas to China, thus diversifying Turkmenistan's energy basket. Niyazov's trip to China became more significant as Niyazov during this time rarely made foreign trips.[11]

In 2007, CNPC signed a production sharing agreement with Turkmenistan to explore and develop gas fields on the right bank of the Amu Darya River and for Turkmenistan to supply 30 billion cubic metres of natural gas to China for a period of thirty years through the pipeline.[12] Turkmenistan's desire to expand its engagement with China is evident from the November 2011 visit by Berdimuhamedov to China. During this visit, both sides noted the need to 'deepen energy cooperation and establish a long-term and stable strategic energy partnership. Both sides should boost cooperation in non-resources sectors such as transportation, telecommunications, chemicals, textile, agriculture, medical care, and high technology and jointly create a sound environment for cooperation'.[13] The completion of the Central Asia-China gas pipeline is a major development in the region, giving Turkmenistan and the region an alternative to Russian pipeline system.

The 1,833 km Central Asia-China gas pipeline originates from Gedaim at the Turkmenistan-Uzbekistan border crosses central Uzbekistan and southern Kazakhstan and finally reaches Horgos in the northwest region of Xinjiang.[14] Two lines (each 1,833 km) of the pipeline run parallel;[15] the first line became operational in December 2009. In 2011, China imported 14.3 billion cubic metres of gas from Turkmenistan.[16]

Post Niyazov, the US too got greater opportunity to engage with the Republic. Turkmenistan and the US today are cooperating in many areas like border and regional security programmes, educational exchanges and English language training. The country's energy resources and its proximity to Afghanistan and Iran are the main drivers influencing U.S. interests in Turkmenistan. According to Prof. Stephen Blank, "Central Asia and Turkmenistan are important because of their geographical location and major energy holdings".[17] Also, the US needs Turkmenistan's cooperation for the success of pipelines like Nabucco. The Nabucco pipeline would give Turkmenistan access to European markets bypassing Russia. The Republic in 2009 agreed to sell 10 billion cu m of gas annually to the Nabucco pipeline[18] but the pipeline is yet to be materialised.

Turkmenistan and Its Neighbours

Turkmenistan's relation with its immediate neighbours is also an important indicator of its foreign policy orientations, which has witnessed little change since Niyazov's time. Being a landlocked country, Turkmenistan is dependent on other countries for trade.[19] Even at the height of its adherence to the policy of 'positive neutrality', Turkmenistan was positively oriented towards countries that gave a channel to reach international markets. During Niyazov's time, because of economic interests, Turkmenistan had 'maintained good relations with Iran and Russia, while having troubled relations with other regional countries such as Azerbaijan and Uzbekistan'.[20] Post Niyazov, Turkmenistan's relations with its neighbours is still primarily dependent on economic considerations.

Uzbekistan and Kazakhstan

Among the five CARs, Turkmenistan shares border with two countries—Uzbekistan and Kazakhstan. Border conflicts and ethnic issues have often been the cause of tension between Uzbekistan and Turkmenistan. There are disputed regions between the two countries, which have created rift in the bilateral ties. A large number of ethnic Uzbeks and ethnic Turkmens reside in Turkmenistan and Uzbekistan, respectively. Often friction between ethnic groups erupted because of the 'nationalist policies towards their respective ethnic minorities'[21] followed by the two countries, which had a bearing on the bilateral relations. Cross-border smuggling is another issue building tensions between the two neighbours.

A major blow to the bilateral relations came in 2002 after a failed assassination attempt on President Niyazov. The allegation of Uzbekistan having masterminded the coup against Niyazov cost the Uzbek Ambassador his post.[22] Soon after the incident, Turkmenistan forcibly relocated ethnic Uzbeks from the border region,[23] which caused further damage to the bilateral relations. Despite the cracks in 2002, there were steps to normalise the relationship from both sides at a later period. The bilateral summit held in November 2004 was a sign of mutual interest in improving bilateral ties. There were domestic and external compulsions contributing to the change of attitude on both sides. According to many analysts, both the countries were severely criticised by the international community for their poor human rights' records and unstable relationship with the neighbouring countries.

President Karimov's visit to Turkmenistan in 2010 is a positive development in the bilateral relationship. The setting up of Turkmen-Uzbek joint venture to distribute and maintain vehicles manufactured in Uzbekistan was one significant development reflecting growing ties between the two countries.[24] Improving the bilateral relation was also essential for the successful implementation of the Central Asia-China pipeline, which passes through Uzbekistan-Kazakhstan before reaching China.

Turkmenistan's another important Central Asian neighbour is Kazakhstan, which is also an energy rich country in the region. The delimitation of the border between Turkmenistan and Kazakhstan was done during Niyazov's time. In 2001, both sides signed the Treaty on Delimitation and Demarcation of border, which however did not include the delimitation of the national sectors in the Caspian Sea. Bilateral relations with Kazakhstan were restricted during Niyazov's regime. Today, that picture is changing. There have been exchange visits on both sides after Berdimuhamedov took over as President. Economic cooperation, especially energy ties is an important component of the bilateral relationship. On May 12, 2007, a trilateral summit was held at Turkmenbashi in Turkmenistan among Kazakhstan, Russia, and Turkmenistan. The summit cut a deal on construction of a gas pipeline around the Caspian Sea and modernising the existing Soviet period pipelines in the region. The pipeline is expected to transport Turkmen gas from western Turkmenistan via Kazakhstan to Russia and onward to Europe.

The Turkmenistan-China gas pipeline also transits through Kazakhstan, which has given further impetus for the improvement of bilateral ties. Again, on May 28-29, 2007 when Berdimuhamedov visited Kazakhstan, both sides signed 'a long-term agreement on expanding cooperation in trade, economy, science and culture'.[25] In September 2007, when President Nazarbayev visited Turkmenistan, cooperation in energy and trade were prioritised. Another important development indicating the growing proximity between the two countries is the project to construct the Uzen-Gyzylgaya-Bereket-Etrek-Gorgan railway line. This railway connection is a part of the International North-South Transport Corridor, which is a multi-modal transportation corridor connecting India Ocean and Persian Gulf to the Caspian Sea via Iran and further connecting to St. Petersburg and North Europe through Russia.

The recent visit to Turkmenistan by the Kazakh Foreign Minister, Yerzhan Kazykhanov in May 2012 reflects the mutual interest in building stronger economic relations. The Kazakh Minister stated, "We have a great interest in expanding contacts in the energy sector. Our countries are both extracting mineral resources, we have similar position on transportation and delivery of energy resources to foreign markets and we can work closely in this area."[26] In 2010, the bilateral trade was US$ 143 million.[27] It is reported that in 2011, the bilateral trade reached US$ 183 million.[28] Both sides have acknowledged the important role the joint Turkmen-Kazakh Intergovernmental Commission play in deepening the bilateral ties, which have been regularly holding its annual meetings.

Azerbaijan

The common history, language and ethnic affinity failed to develop strong bilateral ties between Turkmenistan and Azerbaijan after their independence following the breakup of the Soviet Union. The bilateral relations had a difficult period during Niyazov's time. Personal animosities and a number of political issues had damaged the bilateral relationship.[29] One thorny issue has been the demarcation of the southern Caspian Sea. The dispute even today is a bone of contention between the two countries. The dispute is over an oil field in southern Caspian Sea, which is called Kyapaz in Azeri and Serdar in Turkmen. Both the countries claim the oil field as their own. During Niyazov's time, the relations between the two countries were damaged to the extent that Turkmenistan closed its embassy in Azerbaijan in 2001.

Since Berdimuhamedov's assumption of Presidency, there were specific efforts to improve the relations. In 2007, Turkmenistan reopened its Embassy in Azerbaijan. Berdimuhamedov paid his first visit to Azerbaijan in May 2008. Few other developments that made some difference in diplomatic relations are: setting up a Joint Cabinet Ministers' Commission, Azerbaijan's Foreign Minister's visit to Turkmenistan and an agreement on Azerbaijan's debt dispute with Turkmenistan.[30] These initiatives marked a change in policy on both sides.

Another effort was the proposal for the joint exploration of the disputed oil field.[31] However, this issue is hardly resolved till date, and is still creating tension between the two countries. Back in 1997, Niyazov was hardly inclined towards Azerbaijan's proposal for joint development of the field. [32] Recently, tensions again erupted between the two countries after Turkmenistan started exploratory work on the field, which seems to violate the agreement signed between the two countries in 2008, whereby, both sides had decided that neither country will undertake any exploration or production work in the field till all issues regarding the division of the sea bed are resolved.[33] Azerbaijan immediately protested against Turkmenistan's action, with counter-arguments from Turkmenistan that its patrolling boats, which were undertaking 'scientific' work in different part of the Caspian, were stopped by Azerbaijan.[34] The incident deteriorated the relationship between the two countries.

Resolution of the Caspian dispute would, in the future, help in materialising the Trans-Caspian pipeline, supported by the west. The pipeline would reduce both these countries reliance on Russian pipeline system to reach the international market. Russia has time and again protested against the pipeline project. The existing dispute between Azerbaijan and Turkmenistan has somewhat spoilt the pipeline prospects.

Afghanistan and Iran

The on-going crisis in Afghanistan is a concern for Turkmenistan, which shares about 744 km border with Afghanistan. Being an immediate neighbour, Turkmenistan faces the brunt of the deteriorating situation in Afghanistan and therefore making it an important stakeholder in Afghan stability. Earlier during the Taliban regime, Turkmenistan had established economic ties with Afghanistan and had sold hydrocarbon to Afghanistan.[35] In his address at the 65th session of the UN General Assembly, Berdimuhamedov suggested five measures for resolution of the Afghan imbroglio[36]—(1) as a neutral country, Turkmenistan under UN would host a high-level international meeting on Confidence Building Measures in Afghanistan and development of efficient institutions of state power, (2) Turkmenistan would assist training of personnel in management structures in various sectors under UN supervision and programmes, (3) assist Afghanistan in developing transport infrastructure, (4) substantially activate efforts to step up construction of Turkmenistan-Afghanistan-Pakistan-India (TAPI) pipeline, and (5) the Republic is ready to consider increasing electric power supply to Afghanistan and expanding Turkmenistan's energy infrastructure for installing and networking on the Afghan territory. The Afghanistan factor could be one key issue encouraging greater cooperation between Turkmenistan and other CARs. Turkmenistan's initiative to cooperate to resolve the Afghan crisis is evident from the fact that the country has allowed 'blanket over-flight' and refuelling rights to aircrafts carrying humanitarian aids to Afghanistan.

Iran is an important neighbour of Turkmenistan, with which the country has shared friendly ties. During Niyazov's presidency, Turkmenistan-Iran bilateral relationship had been strong. Berdimuhamedov also continued with the earlier policy of friendly bilateral relations. Iran is an important trade partner of Turkmenistan. The bilateral trade in 2010 was US$ 412.4 million.[37] Hydrocarbon is an important item of bilateral economic cooperation. Iran's primary export to Turkmenistan consists of foodstuffs, healthcare equipment, automobiles and advanced technological good.[38] There are about 146 Iranian companies engaged in several industrial and constructional projects in Turkmenistan.[39]

A delegation from Iran, led by Deputy Foreign Minister for Consular Affairs Hassan Qashqavi, visited Turkmenistan in June 2012. Both sides noted the 'productiveness of bilateral cooperation in energy, transport, and communication sectors'.[40] At the side-line of the SCO June 2012 summit meeting, Berdimuhamedov met Iranian President Mahmoud Ahmadinejad. Both sides discussed several bilateral and regional issues. A number of joint projects, which have qualitatively strengthened the bilateral relationship, are the construction of the 'Dostluk' reservoir, Tejan-Sarakhs-Mashad railroad, inter-state pipelines and power lines. Efforts to further cement the ties are evident from the willingness to build the railway project connecting Iran-Turkmenistan and Kazakhstan. The construction of the Iran-Turkmenistan section has already began, which is expected to be completed by end of 2012. The project would connect Central Asia with the countries of the Persian Gulf.

Turkmenistan has been selling gas to Iran since Niyazov's period. By an agreement between the two sides, Turkmenistan agreed to supply gas to Iran for 25 years.[41] Korpeje-Kurt Kui pipeline, which was opened in 1997, has been the only pipeline till 2010 transporting Turkmen gas to Iran. In 2010, the second gas pipeline between Iran and Turkmenistan was inaugurated. The pipeline, Dauletabad-Sarakhs-Khangiran connects Dauletabad gas field in Turkmenistan to Iran, which increased Turkmenistan's gas supply to Iran. President Ahmadinejad while inaugurating the pipeline said, "This pipeline will be a good stimulus for energy cooperation between Turkmenistan and Iran, as well as for delivery of Turkmen gas to the Persian Gulf and the world market."[42] The pipeline has given Turkmenistan an alternative market, and has helped Iran to supply gas to its northern parts. In 2011, Iran imported 10.2 billion cu m of gas from Turkmenistan.[43]

India and Turkmenistan

India needs to tap every opportunity in view of Turkmenistan's growing interest in bilateral engagements. Deepening ties with the country through exchange visits are of economic and strategic significance for India. Berdimuhamedov's visit to India in May 2010 indicated the Republic's interest to engage with India. From the Indian side, Vice-President Hamid Ansari visited Turkmenistan in 2008 and Foreign Minister S.M. Krishna visited in 2009. There is mutual interest in deepening bilateral relationship, which needs to be nurtured for a strong meaningful bilateral relationship.

Given the vast hydrocarbon reserves in Turkmenistan, India could strive for meaningful energy partnership. As Turkmenistan is also looking for alternative markets for its gas exports, deepening bilateral ties in the sector is mutually beneficial. If the TAPI pipeline project finally sees the light of the day, it would be a major impetus to the bilateral relationship. For the first time, it would give India direct access to the region's hydrocarbon reserves. Of late, there has been progress in the TAPI project, raising optimism about the pipeline. There is greater political willingness among all the member countries. However, the security of the pipeline, which passes through Pakistan and Afghanistan remain one of the major bottlenecks.

Both countries held the first Joint Working group on Energy at Ashgabat in October 2006.[44] India's participation in the country's energy sector include: Profit Sharing Agreements (PSA) in Caspian blocks, service contracts for onshore projects (PSA is not allowed for onshore activities) and TAPI pipeline.[45]

Turkmenistan's border-sharing with Afghanistan makes the country strategically important for India. The deteriorating security situation in Afghanistan is a major security concern for India too. For India, the country is an important partner because of its 'proximity to Afghanistan and its ability to deal with Taliban'.[46]

One of our weakest links is our abysmally poor bilateral trade figures. In general, India's trade with Turkmenistan is very low, probably the lowest among all the five Central Asian republics. Today, Turkmenistan is taking initiatives to build more infrastructures in the country like industrial plants, government buildings, hotels, sports facilities, housing, schools, universities, libraries and transport.[47] These efforts by the Turkmen government provide opportunities for the Indian business community to explore possibilities of economic engagement with the independent republic.[48]

Conclusion

Since Berdimuhamedov became President, there has been very little change in Turkmenistan's foreign policy orientation over the last five years. Turkmenistan continued with its policy of 'positive neutrality'. The initial optimism that the country would break free from the earlier policy seems to have waned. Not much has changed in the country, except a few small changes. Berdimuhamedov has 'led to greater openness in principle towards international cooperation, Turkmenistan remains mostly isolationist in its foreign policy, using its neutrality as a shield to avoid unwanted international entanglements'.[49] Berdimuhamedov's willingness to continue with the policy of 'positive neutrality' was evident even when he was the interim president. In the campaign for the 2007 presidential election, the only foreign policy issue placed before the people was Berdimuhamedov's 'intention to reinforce its commitment to Positive Neutrality'.[50] Turkmenistan is practicing a 'more pro-active foreign policy strategy',[51] if not introducing any substantial changes. This strategy is seen by some scholars as an attempt by the President to gain legitimacy for his regime.[52]

The Berdimuhamedov government will continue to make small adjustments in selective cases. The developments in the past few years indicate that the country is becoming 'diplomatically active'.[53] Berdimuhamedov's frequent visits to foreign countries are setting a trend of active diplomacy. In the first year of his presidency, Berdimuhamedov visited the US, Belgium, Russia, and Iran.[54] The country is following 'selective engagement', mainly in the economic sphere to cooperate with other countries.[55] So far, Turkmenistan's effort to engage with the outside world is more targeted towards diversifying its energy markets and bilateral economic cooperation with countries. Even during Niyazov's time, energy and economic cooperation determined Turkmenistan's relations with other countries. Today, Turkmenistan is cooperating with Turkey, France, and Russia in constructing facilities and infrastructure in the country.[56] The country has leased its sectors in the Caspian Sea for exploration to a number of countries like the UAE, the US, Russia, China and Germany and it has welcomed countries to build pipelines in the country.[57]

With the neighbouring countries, efforts are taken to improve ties, especially to boost economic cooperation. Turkmenistan is taking keen interest and is cooperating with the international community to stabilise Afghanistan, which is essential for its border security. The country's foreign policy will remain unchanged and the country will prefer to remain insulated from the outside world in several areas, only if such a policy serves its domestic interests.

Notes

1. B. P. Statistical Review of World Energy, June 2012, at www.bp.com/statisticalreview (Accessed on July 02, 2012).
2. B. P. Statistical Review of World Energy.
3. Luca Anceschi, *Turkmenistan's Foreign Policy: Positive Neutrality and the Consolidation of the Turkmen Regime*, (London-New York: Routledge, 2009), p. 1.
4. Anceschi, p. 28.
5. Anceschi.
6. Richard Pomfret, "Turkmenistan's Foreign Policy", *China and Eurasia Forum Quarterly*, vol. 6, no. 4 , 2008, p. 20.
7. Pomfret, p. 27.
8. B. P. Statistical Review of World Energy.
9. Leland R. Miller, "Courting Turkmenistan", August 28, 2009, at http://www.foreignpolicy.com/articles/2009/08/28/courting_turkmenistan (Accessed on January 05, 2012).
10. Miller, "Courting Turkmenistan".
11. Pomfret, "Turkmenistan's Foreign Policy", p. 22.
12. "Central Asia-China Gas Pipeline", at http://www.cnpc.com.cn/en/aboutcnpc/ourbusinesses/naturalgaspipelines/Central_Asia%EF%BC%8DChina_Gas_Pipeline_2.htm, (Accessed on January 12, 2011).
13. "Hu Jintao Holds Talks with Turkmen President Berdymuhamedow", November 23, 2011, at http://www.fmprc.gov.cn/eng/wjb/zzjg/dozys/xwlb/t881804.htm (Accessed on July 02, 2012).
14. Central Asia-China Gas Pipeline.
15. Central Asia-China Gas Pipeline.
16. B. P. Statistical Review of World Energy.
17. Stephen J. Blank, "Turkmenistan and Central Asia after Niyazov", Strategic Studies Institute, September 2007, at http://www.strategicstudiesinstitute.army.mil/pdffiles/pub791.pdf (Accessed on October 11, 2011)
18. Miller, "Courting Turkmenistan".
19. Hooman Peimani, "Turkmenistan Reconsiders Relations with Uzbekistan", June 04, 2003, at http:www.cacianalyst.org/?q=node/1204/ (Accessed on July 07, 2012)
20. Peimani.
21. Peimani.
22. Peimani.
23. Peimani.
24. "Uzbekistan-Turkmenistan: A New Phase of Cooperation", October 21, 2010, Press Service of the President of the Republic of Uzbekistan at http://www.press-service.uz/en/news/show/main/novyiye_etap_sotrudnichestva/ (Accessed on April 10, 2012).

25. Chemen Durdiyeva, "Turkmenistan and Kazakhstan Intensify Strategic partnership", October 03, 2007, at http://cacianalyst.org/?q=node/4710 (Accessed on May 12, 2012).
26. Kazakhstan and Turkmenistan Ready for Increased Cooperation, May 14, 2012, at http://kazworld.info/?p=21394 (Accessed on July 07, 2012).
27. Asian Development Bank, "Key Indicators for Asia and Pacific", 2011, at http://www.adb.org/key-indicators/2011/country-tables (Accessed on June 12, 2012).
28. Kazakhstan and Turkmenistan Ready for Increased Cooperation.
29. Pomfret, "Turkmenistan's Foreign Policy", p. 31.
30. Azer Karimov, "Turkmen President to Pay Historic Visit to Baku", at http://www.cacianalyst.org/?q=node/4863 (Accessed on July 12, 2012).
31. Pomfret, "Turkmenistan's Foreign Policy", p. 31.
32. Fariz Ismalizade, "Political Changes in Turkmenistan Open New Opportunities for Azerbaijan", Eurasia Daily Monitor, vol. 4, issue 9 at http://www.jamestown.org/single/?no_cache=1&tx_ttnews%5Btt_news%5D=32389 (Accessed on July 09, 2012).
33. Anar Valiyev, "Azerbaijan-Turkmenistan Relations: Shattered Brotherhood", June 27, 2012, *Jamestown Foundation Eurasia Daily Monitor* 9, issue: 122 at http://www.jamestown.org/programs/edm/single/?tx_ttnews%5Btt_news%5D=39548&cHash=6a125c6590a825caa7aeac2f8b821080 (Accessed on July 07, 2012).
34. Shahin Abbasov, "Azerbaijan &Turkmenistan: Renewing Caspian Sea Energy Dispute", July 11, 2012, at http://www.eurasianet.org/print/65646 (Accessed on July 12, 2012).
35. Meena Singh Roy, "Strategic importance of Turkmenistan for India", *Strategic Analysis,* vol. 35, no. 4, July 2011, p. 673.
36. Address by His Excellency Mr. Gurbanguly Berdimuhamedov, President of Turkmenistan at the 65th Session of the UN General Assembly, at http://www.turkmenistanembassy.org/turkmen/news/President-speech-65UN-English.pdf (Accessed on February 12, 2012).
37. Asian Development Bank, "Key Indicators for Asia and Pacific".
38. Ariel Ferrar-Wellman, Robert Frasco, "Turkmenistan-Iran Foreign Relations", July 08, 2010, at http://www.irantracker.org/foreign-relations/turkmenistan-iran-foreign-relations (Accessed on June 02, 2012).
39. "Tehran, Ashgabat seek to boost trade", at http://www.tehrantimes.com/economy-and-business/99669-tehran-ashgabat-seek-to-boost-trade (Accessed on July 12, 2012).
40. Foreign Minister of Turkmenistan receives delegation of Iran, at http://www.turkmenistan.ru/en/articles/16347.html (Accessed on July 12, 2012).
41. "Turkmen Gas Company Increases Gas Exports to Iran", February 2012, at http://www.presstv.ir/detail/229127.html (Accessed on July 07, 2012).

42. "Turkmenistan Opens New Iran Gas Pipeline", January 06, 2010, at http://news.bbc.co.uk/2/hi/asia-pacific/8443787.stm (Accessed on July 12, 2012).
43. B. P. Statistical Review of World Energy.
44. Embassy of India in Ashgabat, at http://www.indianembassy-tm.org/bilateral.html (Accessed on June 02, 2012).
45. Embassy of India in Ashgabat.
46. Roy, "Strategic importance of Turkmenistan for India", p. 675.
47. Roy, p. 679.
48. Roy.
49. Dmitry Gorenburg, "Turkmenistan's Isolationist Strategy Eases, to a Point", March 21, 2011, at http://russiamil.wordpress.com/2011/03/21/turkmenistans-isolationist-strategy-eases-to-a-point/ (Accessed on July 07, 2012).
50. Anceschi, *Turkmenistan's Foreign Policy: Positive Neutrality and the Consolidation of the Turkmen Regime*, p. 141.
51. Anceschi, p. 145.
52. Anceschi, p. 145.
53. Pomfret, "Turkmenistan's Foreign Policy", p. 19.
54. Pomfret, "Turkmenistan's Foreign Policy", p. 29.
55. Gorenburg, "Turkmenistan's Isolationist Strategy Eases, to a Point".
56. Gorenburg.
57. Gorenburg.

13. Zhanaozen and Beyond

P. L. Dash

Never since December 1986—when Almaty erupted into violence in Perestroika years protesting the appointment of Gennady Kolbin as the communist party boss of Kazakhstan—did the country witness such violent upsurge as it did at the fag end of 2011. From Almaty to Zhanaozen[1]—between Perestroika of 1986 and two decades of independence in 2011—much water has flowed under the bridge. Kazakhstan was largely peaceful; prosperity visited it visibly due to its oil and gas endowments. The country and its leadership had gathered numerous accolades on many fronts. In the backdrop its overall development, Kazakhstan was scheduled to celebrate its 20th anniversary of independence and its capital, Astana in north of the country, was unveiling the replica of 'Arc de Triompe' to mark this anniversary. Something seemingly went wrong in another part of the country, where oil workers were striking since May 2011. Their 7-month old strike was enough to trigger this violence. During this period, the authorities were lackadaisical; they did not attach due importance to the strikers' grievances, used more sticks than carrot during negotiations, tried to divide and rule, doled out lollypops to those who stood by the official approach and punished those who aired the extant grievances of the workers and their plight in the villages. Enough was enough for the residence of Zhanaozen, who decided to stage a march of protest against the authorities and in support of their colleagues. This paper focuses on the ferment in society around Zhanaozen, why the violence flared, and the modus operandi of dealing with a crisis like Zhanaozen by authorities, who seem democratic, but behave in an autocratic manner, taking shelter under the facade of good, democratic governance.

Winter of Discontent

The people knew exactly what they were doing, but the authorities did not. People knew that they were going on a peaceful march en masse to the city square; authorities did not know how to deal with such a peace march. The people were unarmed; the authorities had force at their disposal, both police and the army. People did not expect the authorities to fire at them; authorities did not expect the crowd to swell. They panicked and decided to use force to disperse the crowd. When their efforts at crowd dispersal failed, they fired teargas cells, water canons, and blank shots in the air. That did not deter the people simply because they were nonviolent and least expecting violence from the side of the administration. The authorities never came out with details as to how the protest turned into violence; what they depicted was the post-violence days and how they were diligently dealing with the incident and that law and order had been restored and maintained since Zhanaozen happened and life had limped back to normalcy.

The real causes of the uprising are many—first, it is oomph and opulence on the one hand and poverty and privation on the other that had caused an irreversible social friction, uncompromising enough to tell on the real state of affairs. Second, in rural Kazakhstan, particularly in newly industrialised oil zones, there is a yawning gap between the urban and rural settings. In this divide, some people live far too well and others have nothing. The real reason however boils down to unequal distribution of the profit of the oil industry—and they are huge—but not to the benefit of the society. Third, is how the rulers live and how the ruled just survive. The ideas of liberty of the Soviet era may have truncated effect, but the ideas of equality and fraternity, leading to justice has not died down. It still kindles a flicker of hope among the deprived people to obtain justice in Kazakh society, but that was not to happen in the post-Soviet two decades under Nazarbayev, despite the country registering commendable economic growth in last two decades.

Innumerable twitter messages said, "Look at how Alia Nazarbayeva lives, how much the president spends on her birthday, and in contrast, how people in villages live with no money to buy bread." This shows the divide more glaringly than anything else does. Since the oil workers strikes started in May 2011, hundreds of workers have been rendered jobless. In some cases both bread earners of the family have been sacked, rendering the family to suffer and the children more deprived. This fermented the discontent of the dismissed workers and drove them to streets to air their grievances, and they were met with batons and bullets.

President Nazarbayev indeed asked the regional authorities to deal with the delicate situation brewing in and around Aktau after the May strike had begun; his injunctions were not heeded. The locals knew about what he had instructed and what the town authorities did. The gap between promises of the government, and practice by the implementing agencies was too shoddy an affair to be disclosed. Apparently, there was a communication gap between the regional/provincial bosses on the one hand and the central authorities on the other. This was a potential point of discord among the lay Kazakh workers, who were laid off and people who witnessed their plight after they were sacked. As winter descended, the problems became acute. Supplies were less, availability of goods was still less and money in the hands of villagers was a scare commodity. All these taken together brew a cocktail of conflict for the people to take cudgels with the rulers. Seven months were enough for the authorities to act but they dilly dallied with the situation that finally flared up in December 2011.

Course of Events

It all began on December 16, 2011 when the country was gearing up to celebrating two decades of independence and awaiting the New Year to arrive, the 1000 odd fired workers in Zhanaozen had a different agenda. They planned a protest march to the town square, demanding reinstatement on their jobs. All those oil workers, who considered their wage low, joined them demanding wage hike and all those oilmen, who did not get their danger pay for months extended support too and came out to the street. Thus, three clear groups of disenchanted oilmen came on the streets—the laid down workers, the higher wage demanders, and those who demanded on time payment of arrears of their danger pay. An insidious conflict bubbled on the surface and snowballed into street fight between the authorities and the protesters.

As the crowd swelled unbelievably, the local police and security apparatus were nonplussed. They called in 1,500 more troops from nearby Mangyshtau to deal with the situation. By the time these forces arrived, protestors had already torched government buildings and busses. In the city square mob-cop clashes took place and bricks, bottles and Molotov cocktails from the unarmed public flew freely, attacking and injuring the security forces; some of them brutally beaten. The police retaliation came swiftly, killing 16 people.[2] Unverified reports from western sources put the figure of those killed at 50 and Russian news agency ITAR-TASS put it at 70. The government claimed that the protestors had looted some ATMs and ransacked the office of KazMunayGas and other government buildings. Their action was shocking and incredible; the situation took the form of riots and was slipping out of hands. The local authorities did not know how to handle the situation; central guidance was not forthcoming for crowd control. It came far too late for instituting commission to go into what caused the riots followed by a visit by Nazarbayev.

The moment they knew that some policemen have been beaten and another 3 killed, the local law enforcement authorities clamped down heavily, closed roads to Aktau and other nearby city centres, blacked out the internet access for the public, making it difficult for information to percolate. As a result, there emerged contradictory reports about the development of events, the actual numbers killed, and the state of affairs in the township. In the second stage of the protest march, on December 17, 2011 the riots spread to a nearby village, Shetpe. The villagers in Shetpe marched to the railway track and blocked a train coming from Aktau. The police fired on the blockading protestors, and as a result, one person was killed. Now, the authorities learned the crowd control method; it was firing on the crowd and suppressing them—a method that may have given instant relief, but ultimate cure lies in redressing the grievances of the people. What the authorities claimed, the villagers disclaimed and what the authorities counterclaimed, the protestors branded as lies.

Thereafter Astana immediately swung into action and imposed a 3-week emergency up to January 05, 2012, which was further extended till January 31, 2012 by President Nazarbayev. If the situation was not tense, what was the need to extend the emergency? The government claimed everything normal and life running smoothly, but it was hard to believe in the absence of credible information coming from government sources and contradictory claims coming from various other sources. In an effort to control the damage to its international prestige, the Kazakh ambassador to the US, Irdishov had been giving regular press statements on the developments in Zhanaozen, but these statements did not tally with other sources that vastly differed with the ambassador.

Another source that adduced a different argument, albeit not so credible to believe, was the stage- managed nature of the Zhanaozen conflict. This group argued that the entire episode had been stage managed by pro Kulibayev supporters to favour Nazarbayev's son-in-law, Timur Kulibayev, who is not in the parliament now. The January 15 parliamentary elections would perhaps take him to the parliament and he is Nazarbayev's choice as his successor. The argument was flawed; hence hard to believe because nobody would like to have a riot stage managed, more so Nazarbayev, and that too on the eve of parliamentary elections, risking the lives of hundreds of people. At least, there are no buyers for this argument neither in Kazakhstan nor in elsewhere.

Nazarbayev Takes Stock

President Nazarbayev visited Zhanaozen on December 22, 2011, five days after the riots took place. What he saw was burned vehicles lying on road sides, charred hotels and office buildings standing mute testimony to the fatal riots, empty corridors of looted banks, which was once bustling with transacting crowd, overturned safe vaults, piles of ashes and debris everywhere, deserted streets, shocked officials with a pal of gloom written on their faces. He could not believe his eyes. For a moment, this 72 year old, matured, and astute Soviet era politician had paused. Stunned and speechless, he stepped in glum mood to action. His visit was not publicised; very few details were available on the visit. As Khabar TV channel reported later, the president candidly admitted that he wanted to visit the striking workers in June 2011, but was assured that steps were taken to deal with the strike. Once again in September 2011, he expressed his desire to visit Zhanaozen but was again dissuaded by the local administration that everything was all right, and a visit was not necessary. Apparently, he was misinformed and misled and the result was what had led to Zhanaozen in December 2011.

The President had attributed two causes to the riot: neglecting the cause of the strikers and using high-handed administrative methods to deal with a delicate situation like strike, demanding wage hikes and payment of unpaid danger pay. These demands were legitimate and workers had a genuine grievance, which was not addressed. The administration instead sacked 2000 workers whose livelihood was at stake because each striker was a bread earner of his family. They were workers from the oil and gas companies of KazMunayGas, KarazhanbasMunayGas, and its branches Argymak Transservice and Tulpar Munai service. When the strike was slowly spreading, the president was misinformed and misguided by the local administration. The situation was more dangerous because large chunk of the share of KazMunayGas, where the protestors worked, was held by Samruk-Kazyna sovereign welfare fund headed by President's son-in law, Timur Kulibayev. Nazarbayev had immediately announced the sacking of Kulibayev and resolved to restore normalcy for the sake of residence of Zhanaozen, its capital Aktau 150 kilometers away and the province Mangyshtaú. The president, who had announced an Aktau development project in 2007 to expand this only Caspian port city of Kazakhstan, was sure after visiting the ravaged Zhanaozen that the peaceful Nazarbayev legacy for Kazakhstan was at stake.

The President was appraised about the loss. 17 people died—16 in Zhanaozen and 1 in Shepte—more than hundred were injured including 17 law enforcement officers, and over 40 commercial and administrative buildings were damaged. The loss was colossal and to the tune of 2 billion Tenge (US$ 13.6 million).[3] The President, however, defended the police action and stunned the public when he revealed that each rioter was paid 20,000 Tenge or US$ 135 to intrude into the crowd, who assembled for celebrating the Independence Day. The miscreants were drunk and armed and prepared to do anything. This was why the colossal loss of lives and property. It was a well organised riot to tarnish the image of Kazakhstan;

the President promised to bring to book all those responsible for the ugly incident and ordered the prosecutor general to impartially investigate the entire episode and book those found guilty. He also revealed that some of the miscreants had vanished, and were untraceable. He, however, promised relief, and said that Zhanaozen will be rebuilt and sacked workers would get back their jobs; if not in the same place, elsewhere in Kazakhstan. The government will bear the responsibility of providing transportation and accommodation and ensure safety of workers. As of January 04, 2012, employment applications from 918 workers have been submitted to the 'OzenMunayGas' company and 390 applications to 'KarazhanbasMunayGas'. Overall, 1308 people have applied for new jobs.[4]

Most public facilities and all government offices were functioning normally, including local shops, the central market, drug stores, as well as the election commission. Educational institutions were no exception. Zhanaozen was home to 22 secondary schools, 15 public and 13 private pre-school educational organisations and 4 pre-school mini centres. Zhanaozen's more than 22,000 students had returned to classrooms as normal. Law enforcement investigations were ongoing. As of January 05, 2012, five criminal cases had been opened and 29 suspects were detained with the permission of the court. Overall, 287 suspects had been held administratively liable for disturbing the public order in Zhanaozen.

Meanwhile, the President has sacked a number of officials he considered responsible for misguiding him and delaying a solution to the oil workers strikes. On January 04, 2012, he had also extended the emergency in Zhanaozen. The presidential website said, "I resolve to extend the state of emergency in the town of Zhanaozen in Mangyshtau region until 7 am on January 31, 2012."[5] In view of the countrywide parliamentary elections scheduled for January 15, 2012, it was rumoured that Zhanaozen will not go to elections and instead nominate members. The Constitutional Council also announced that 50,000 voters in a town of 1,10,000 people did matter little and the government controlled media adduced all sorts of arguments not to conduct elections in the town when the state of emergency was in vogue. However, President

Nazarbayev vetoed this decision of the Constitutional Council, which meant Zhanaozen went to elections along with other constituencies in Kazakhstan on January 15, 2012.[6] The political astuteness of President Nazarbayev was evident in this decision to carry Zhanaozen along with others to the Majilis (Parliamentary) and Maslikhals (local representative bodies) elections and not exclude Zhanaozen simply because a state of emergency had temporarily prevailed there. The veto power of the president once again showed how he vastly differed from the local administration in his approach to Zhanaozen problem, and sometimes even disagreeing with them on crucial issues of conflict management and problem solutions. As a result, he commanded the respect of the locals, while the local administration was denigrated and disrespected by the people. The elections were held on January 15, 2012 and the emergency ceased on January 31, 2012 but the shadow of the riot lingered on in public memory as one of the most shocking episodes of independent Kazakhstan.

Stake Holders

The Zhanaozen riots, occurring on the very day of the 20th anniversary of Kazakh independence implied how people valued democracy. Similarly, its brutal consequences revealed how democracy could be butchered by autocratic authoritarianism, in this case exercised not by the president but by local administration. A cost benefit analysis of the December event in Zhanaozen told the tale of a great stakeholder—democracy and the election process in Kazakhstan. The riots had died down, but they had made clear two things—first, six months of democratic protest through oilmen's strike did not cut any ice with the authorities, and second, the authorities were intolerant of expression of public anger. What followed was the damage control exercises dictated from Astana, and certainly not from the goodwill of those, who controlled the local affairs.

The initial decision about postponement of scheduled elections from January 15 to an unspecified date by the Constitutional Council was making democracy a victim. December 16 was the final day for withdrawal of nominations, and nominations were already afield in Zhanaozen. Once again, Astana and the president prevailed. Come whatever, it was decided by the president to conduct elections as scheduled. The leadership was apparently scared of the flaring fire of popular sentiments spreading elsewhere in the country, particularly to the copper mining town of Karaganda.

The second stakeholder was the Nazarbayev legacy for Kazakhstan. Twenty years of impeccable record of governing the largest and richest country of Central Asia was tarnished by a single incident—Zhanaozen—in mid-December 2011. A family controlled affair went berserk and one of the most important townships burst into flames was indicative of the loose grip of Nazarbayev family on the affairs of UzenMunayGas. The important lessons from here were (1) look beyond the family and do not amass property of the state in your hands at the expenses of workers' welfare, and (2) do not be greedy; the needy in the country need your help. Nazarbayev had to look beyond the family to ensure participatory democracy at the regional level in Kazakhstan. He has miles to go in this path.

The third stakeholders were those officials who dissuaded the president not to visit Zhanaozen and Aktau, who assured him that everything was in place and drew a rosy picture of settling the workers strike by firing 2,000 workers, without heeding to their plights. Some of them have lost their jobs, others reshuffled and would be under scanner for their activities, still others—the more cunning ones of the administration—are gingerly relating themselves to the strike, riots and its aftermath. This group has to reorient their attitude to conflict management because Zhanaozen was a case in point that awfully went awry. These middle level bureaucrats were collecting pieces of threads for their survival. For some of them Zhanaozen turned to be the last straw of their career when the enquiry committee submitted its report three months later.

Finally, the stakeholder here was the economy of Zhanaozen. It was a typical township based on management of a single economy—the oil economy and the politics and the wealth surrounding it. What lay ahead was how to diversify such singular economies to a more modern base of infrastructure, industry and service sector mix so that no single sector suffered the loss as did the oil township of Zhanaozen. Zhanaozen was part of history, but its imprints were evident in many spheres of politics and economy of Kazakhstan, likely to cast shadows on the governance methods and style in future that Nazarbayev or no Nazarbayev could ignore.

Power Pyramid

Zhanaozen had shaken the power pyramid in Kazakhstan assiduously built by Nazarbayev for years as a model of democracy in Central Asia. Some strong popular resentment that centred around the controversy of shifting the capital from Almaty to a more freezing city of Astana was surmounted by the administration. Whatever accolades you gather abroad cannot earn you popular eulogy at home. Moreover, here for everything autocratic, a power pyramid is responsible.

In the power pyramid drawn below, the President and the first family occupy the top slots. As commander in Chief of the armed forces, the President enjoys absolute power in every aspect of life. The family follows him. Everyone knows how powerful Nazarbayev's daughter and son-in-law are. Moreover, everyone is loyal to them. The ministers are cronies of the President, and in turn, their advisers are cronies of the ministers. A coterie forms around the Presidential administration where everyone knows everyone, and it is they, who are the rulers. The top bureaucracy is not selected through any national competitive examination, and instead, handpicked by the administration. As a result, hundred percent loyalty is ensured and dissent is ruled out. They form around each other a concentric circle of rulers supplementing and complementing their interest at every level. They are the managers of state affairs, controllers of its treasury, distributors of its wealth and resources, and finally the dispenser of the destiny of the country. Their subordination to the top hierarchy is symbolic of the strength of the President. They represent the President at every level and are the ears and eyes of the intelligence services of the country. Expansively, they pervade countrywide, and opposition to them attracts harsh punishment.

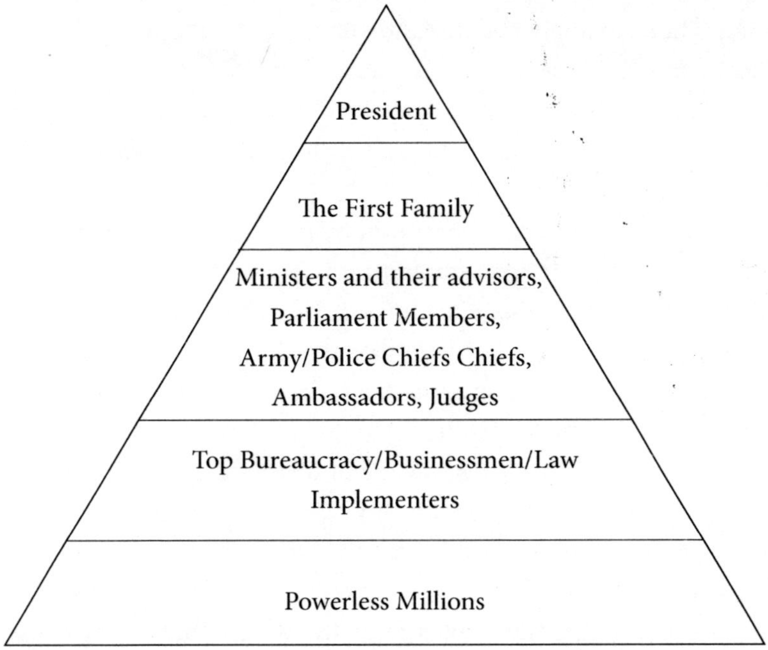

The teeming millions are ruled. They do not have direct access to their rulers enumerated above because they are all big people. They do not walk on the streets, and do not visit bazaars and hospitals. They do not stand in the queue. For them everything is done out of turn. In case of obtaining any favour from them, people have to search for a via media of tangible contacts. The gap between the rulers and the ruled is yawing and too big to be perceived. If Nazarbayev is the God, his ministers are demigods. They are away from people. While the elite and top echelon of the rulers contact their counterpart cronies in different ministries to get their work done or dole out favours to whosoever they like, in their everyday contact, people meet petty police officers in the streets, drivers and conductors in the buses, school and college teachers in educational institutes and clerks in offices—the door to the boss is almost always closed.

Millions of workers who are busy in their day-to-day life, unconcerned about the affairs of the state, often cannot digest the high handedness of the elite and their apathetic attitude to the plight of workers. This is precisely what had happened in Zhanaozen—an apathetic top dissuading the President to visit the striking workers and glossing over the problem as solved. However, the roots of apathy on the one hand and antipathy of the public on the other have generated disillusionment and disenchantment hard to suppress for long.

They are the people and the so-called democracy is by them, for them and of them. They go and vote mutely for the candidate nominated by the ruling party without a murmur. In post riot Zhanaozen they too have done so with the hope that a better day may come in future. Nazarbayev commands indisputable respect as the tallest leader in Kazakhstan and there is no practical political alternative to Nur Otan—the political party he heads. Opposition parties have been muted in the past; those allowed are pro-establishment. People know how practically all potential political leaders have been sidestepped by the stringent election procedures that the regime promulgated to pave a smooth way for it to power. These people also know that their votes carry the weight, but they themselves do not. They could be browbeaten to be ruled the way rulers wish them to be, and in case of Zhanaozen, this wish went awry and the authorities were acutely aware of this lapse. Dissent like Zhanaozen must not repeat. That is not good for the state, good for the people, or for the leadership of Nazarbayev.

Let Past Not Repeat

Two decades of independent political history in Kazakhstan is not without blemish. On the contours of long years of political placidity, there are blanks spots to be filled, unwritten saga to be unveiled and many political rivalries to stud the pages, when historian will undertake an impartial evaluation of history and politics under Nazarbayev. Such a scenario would emerge after the exit of Nazarbayev from power. Four major political eliminations will definitely find a place in impartial history writing. The desire to sustain in power has driven Nazarbayev covertly and his supporters overtly to eliminate potential political opposition in the country, which is virtually non-extant in Kazakhstan. Intolerant political leaders, incapable of understanding the essence of democracy, endeavour to perpetuate their rule by any means. In the process of exercising their power, they eliminate a number of people, who even raise legitimate issues for resolution, which seem inconvenient to the rulers. The Kazakh episode is quite interesting.

In 2006, Altynbek Shershenbayev was a potential opposition leader in Kazakhstan. His popularity gradually grew. He raised pertinent issues of democracy concerning freedom of expression. In the process, he incurred the wrath of Timur Kulibayev, then the Kazakh Intelligence Chief, who happened to be the son-in-law of President Nazarbayev. Kulibayev ordered detailed investigation to the activities of Altynbek Shershenbayev. Following the orders, Kulibayev left for Austria and Shershenbayev was reportedly killed. For Nazarbayev, a major roadblock is removed; for the country, a great political talent was lost. One wonders whether the President knows about this!

Similarly, Nunkadilov Zaminbek was a Kazakh politician, who was mayor of Almaty. He knew the goings on at the top echelon of the administration and around the president pretty too well. He sought an appointment with the president to brief him about some real issues of business and businessmen in Kazakhstan in general, and Almaty in particular. He could not meet the President, but a few days later, he was found dead, apparently killed, in his own house. The police termed this political elimination a suicide and the case was closed. His family, however, has different tales to tell.

Narmakhan Tyakboi was the former Procurator General of Kazakhstan. By virtue of his position, he was close to Nazarbayev and a member of his command. Tyakboi floated his own political party that was never allowed to be registered. With his immense popularity in the country and among politicians for his clean image, he decided to harness it and joined hands with businessman cum political aspirant, Bulat Abylov to run for president in 2011 on behalf of 'Azat'. Both Tyakboi and Abylov were sidestepped and their dream never materialised. Abylov is considered the Khodorkovsky of Kazakhstan.

An identical fate waited for Zhobtis, who was the Chief of Kazakh Human rights Bureau. He waged a relentless struggle for ensuring human rights in Kazakhstan. On the flimsy ground of breaking traffic rules, he was once arrested for causing an automobile accident. The court gave him eight years in prison for his crime. "So, tow my line, or else I will tow you first to a dead end, then to jail or to the infinity, where no one can meet you." These are few of the famous cases of inconvenient political oppositions to Nazarbayev. Many small incidences in the provinces go unnoticed. Zhanaozen has opened up a chapter of democracy in Kazakh history and the President must open his eyes to see what has been happening elsewhere.

Beyond the Polls

On January 15, 2012, Kazakhstan went to polls. 900 polling booths across the country witnessed voting commencing at 7 am in the morning. The election passed through the eyes of 7,000 poll observers and 120 foreign journalists—the biggest political event in the country. Now that the Parliamentary elections to Majilis and Mastaliks in Kazakhstan were over, giving Nur Otan, the Nazarbayev led party an absolute majority of 81 per cent votes to rule, further stocktaking has to take place. The President has been doing that through the electronic and print media, often magnifying the voices of the people. He has the legitimate right to do so because he has commanded the legitimacy of a leader of 9.2 million voters in Central Asia's richest country. The president had rescheduled the elections from August 2010, when they were due to January 15, 2012 when they were held. For the first time opposition has had a voice in the parliament. Representatives of the Ak Zhol and KNPK, who had crossed the threshold of 7 per cent and gathered 7.3 per cent of the mandate, do have their representation now.[7]

Three conclusive lessons the administration must draw—(1) not to repeat a new Zhanaozen, (2) fill the gap in communication between the local and central administration, and (3) pay urgent attention to the fact that reform measures benefit the grass roots. Zhanaozen is passé, but its impact is not so. The fact that there are reports of similar discontent brewing in other mining areas is a sad reminder to the administration that such repetition may occur with variance elsewhere in Kazakhstan.

This is happening because workers are living a miserable life, while the bureaucracy is fattening. Nazarbayev has to pay adequate attention to streamlining the local administration and curbing high handedness of those dealing with everyday affairs. Precisely, he had to ensure that administrative personnel at the grass roots level become more responsive to the need of their constituencies than to harass people.

Secondly, what Zhanaozen had shown was a glaring gap between how the local administration talked and how the central administration commanded. What the locals wished to preserve was what the centre desired to protect. Yet, there was a potential clash of reading the correct situation. The local administration naively thought that alone stick would be enough to deal with striking oil workers and paid little attention to palliative measures that could have addressed the workers' grievances. The flash point occurred when both sides lost trust, misunderstood each other, and talked in different languages. The tinderbox was ready, the explosion was awaited about which the centre knew vaguely, and the local administration knew little. This was the result of incompetent reading of a combustible situation ripened with workers' protests. Such situation ought not arise and repeat.

Thirdly, in the aftermath of the fatal riots, many financial allocations have been announced for rebuilding Zhanaozen. Workers have been promised jobs, pay hikes and other benefits. Locals have been assured of rebuilding of the schools and hospitals in their township. Nazarbayev must ensure that there is no gap between the promise and practice. The people of Zhanaozen have gone with the mainstream of national polls with the hopes of a better future in Mangyshtau region. Their hopes need not be belied. These three pillars are the ones on which the Nazarbayev legacy in future will continue to yield rich dividends to Kazakhstan and its people.

Notes

1. Zhanaozen is the new name of Soviet-era township called *Novyi Uzen*. It acquired the new name in 1992 after Kazakhstan became independent. The township is located in south-west of Kazakhstan. Similarly, capital Aktau carried between 1964 and 1992 the name of Soviet era city Shevchenko. Taras Shevchenko, the noted Ukrainian poet

was exiled to this town. It is the only port of Kazakhstan on the Caspian coast in the Mangystau peninsula.

2. Ruby Russell and T. Umaraliev, "Violent Unrest Clouds Kazakhstan's Political Future", *The Washington Times,* December 23, 2011.
3. News Bulletin of the Embassy of the Republic of Kazakhstan in the US, *Zhanaozen Special Issue,* no. 3, January 07, 2012.
4. Ibid. *Special Issue,* no. 2, January 05, 2012.
5. www.akorda.kz
6. News Bulletin of the Embassy of the Republic of Kazakhstan in the US, *Zhanaozen Special Issue,* no. 5, January 11, 2012.
7. These figures are taken from the website of *Kazakhstan Today* on January 16, 2012.

14. Coping with Religiosity and Extremism in Central Asia: The Case of Kazakhstan

Debidatta Aurobinda Mahapatra

This article analyses the rising menace of religious extremism and terrorism in Central Asia with special focus on Kazakhstan, which was till recently considered an island of stability in the Eurasian landscape. Developments of past one year indicate that Kazakhstan has been a new initiate into the whirlpool of religious extremism and terrorism with the rise of extremist organisations like 'Jundallah al-Khilafat' (JaK-soldiers of the Caliphate). Interestingly, this organisation, which emerged in the country last year, could be found to have links with extremist organisations in Afghanistan-Pakistan region, with ideological sustenance from the North Caucasian extremists. The making of new law by Kazakh Parliament in 2011 regulating extremism and pronouncements by the Kazakh authorities including President Nazarbayev indicate that extremism and terrorism are the raging issues, which cannot be tackled by ad hoc mechanisms. The article focuses on these intricate and interlinked factors in the Kazakhstan, while analysing the underlying factors that led to the rise of religious extremism and terrorism in this Central Asian state.

Central Asian Polity, Society, and Challenges

Central Asia is the region that spreads from the Caspian Sea in the west to central China in the east, and from southern Russia in the north to Afghanistan in the south. In this study, Central Asia consists of the five former Soviet republics of Kazakhstan, Kyrgyzstan, Tajikistan, Turkmenistan, and Uzbekistan. Some scholars add Afghanistan and Mongolia in the geographical definition of the region, in addition to Chinese province of Xinjiang and Tibet. In terms of geography, Kazakhstan is the largest country in the region. Covering an area of 2.7 million sq km, it has vast resources and enormous economic potential. Its varied landscape stretches from mountainous, heavily populated regions of the east to the sparsely populated energy-rich lowlands in the west, and from the industrialised north, with its Siberian climate and terrain, through the arid, empty steppes of the centre, to the fertile south. Kazakhstan has a population of 16 million, with the Kazakhs making up over half the population, the Russians comprising just over a quarter, and Ukrainians, Germans, Chechens, Kurds, Koreans, etc. accounting for the rest. Major languages spoken are Kazakh and Russian, and majority of people profess Islam and Christianity. After its independence, Kazakhstan came to limelight due to its rich energy resources, which has witnessed massive foreign investment. The major oil pipeline in Kazakhstan links the Tengiz oil field in the west to the Russian Black Sea port of Novorossiysk that opened in 2001. The per capita income in Kazakhstan is US$ 2,483 (December 2010). Since the independence of the country, Nursultan Nazarbayev is the President. In 2005 presidential elections, he was elected for another 7-year term.

All Central Asian states are to varying degrees multi-ethnic, with the share of the majority population ranging from less than 50 per cent in Kazakhstan to 80 per cent in Uzbekistan. Central Asian states have ethnic linkages to each other—Kazakhstan, Kyrgyzstan, Uzbekistan, and Turkmenistan are all Turkic-speaking nations; only Tajikistan differs due to its Persian ethnic and cultural roots. In addition, the political borders between these states correspond poorly to ethnic settlement patterns. Most blatant is the case of southern Uzbekistan and northern Tajikistan, which are both highly multi-ethnic and populated in comparable numbers by both ethnic groups. Such cross-border ethnic ties also, significantly, exist with Central Asia's southern neighbours. Afghanistan's role as a bridge between Central and South Asia is illustrated most clearly in its ethnic divisions. Roughly, half its population consists of Pashtuns; nevertheless, more Pashtuns reside in Pakistan than in Afghanistan; likewise, Baluchs live on the territory of Pakistan, Iran, and Afghanistan. On the other hand, over a quarter of Afghanistan's population is composed of Tajiks, Uzbeks, and Turkmens, residing in the North of the country, on its border with Central Asia. As for China, its northwestern Xinjiang province is the home of the Uighurs, Turkic people of close to 10 million people speaking a language almost identical to Uzbek. Interestingly, Kazakh, Kyrgyz, and Uzbek communities also exist in Xinjiang.

These ethnic links have a considerable impact on the security of the concerned states. Especially in an age of increased global ethnic awareness, ethnicity has become one of the principal challenges to the security of multi-ethnic states to an extent that requires no illustration. In the last few decades, China has seen the rise of Uighur separatist movement encouraged by the achievement of independence by their kin in Central Asia. Pakistan's erstwhile relations with Afghanistan were deeply coloured by its fear of Kabul fanning the flames of separatist movements among Pashtuns and Baluchs.[1] In the last few years, the war in Afghanistan has taken on an increasingly ethnic character. Hence, Taliban are, despite their religious garb, widely understood as a Pashtun movement; the Uzbeks were rallied around the warlord Abdul Rashid Dostum before his defeat at the hands of the Taliban; and Northern Alliance leader Ahmed Shah Masoud's main constituency is the Tajik community. The ethnic milieu of Afghanistan, Pakistan and the countries of the region is increasingly affected by the cross-border ethnic linkages. These linkages are at times further strengthened by geopolitical and economic interests of stakeholders and actors in the region. Thus, ethnicity is unlikely to lose its political relevance in the near future. As discussed in later pages, ethnic dimension of Afghan conflict coupled with it religious dimension has its reverberating impacts in Central Asian countries including Kazakhstan.

According to Thomas Barfield, the concept of ethnic nationalism in Central Asia did not emerge from the bottom up; instead, it was imposed from the top down by the Soviet government in the areas under its control. This was done by dividing Central Asia's three geographically based multiethnic khanates (Khiva, Bukhara and Kokand) into five arbitrary ethnic republics (Turkmenistan, Uzbekistan, Tajikistan, Kyrgyzstan, and Kazakhstan).[2] He argues that the new ethnic republics were an attempt to both destroy the old khanate identities that had deep historical roots, and to preempt the nascent political movements that had earlier proclaimed the unity of Central Asia in terms of either pan-Turkism or the greater Islamic community.[3] After their emergence as independent states in post-Soviet period, these countries found it difficult to instill an ethnic national identity except among the Turkmen and Kyrgyz who already had a common identity. While Uzbekistan was able to define its diverse population as primarily 'Uzbek' by finding in 15th century conqueror Timur their national historical founder, the Kazakhs faced a dilemma of giving ethnicity priority in a state where Slavs constituted about half of the population. While Tajikistan found it relatively easy to apply a common Tajik ethnicity among its majority Iranian language speakers, it found it impossible to get them to think of themselves as a national unit, a situation that led to a vicious civil war in the initial years of the Soviet collapse.

Stability and development in Central Asia are inextricably linked with the stability and development of neighbouring countries. Afghanistan shares border of more than 2,000 km with three countries of the region—Tajikistan, Uzbekistan, and Turkmenistan. Hence, the developments in Afghanistan have their impacts in these countries as well as the whole Central Eurasia. In this context, one of the serious issues that the Central Asian states have to confront is the issue of religious extremism and drug trafficking. The erstwhile Soviet Union and its control over borders with Afghanistan had precluded the possibility of spread of drug trafficking into its regions, including Soviet Central Asia. After the Soviet collapse, especially after the Russian withdrawal from Tajik border with Afghanistan in 2005 the issue of drug trafficking along with religious fundamentalism has become a major concern for the region. The simultaneous tightening of borders by Iran and Turkey has provided the trafficker the only option to use the porous border with Central Asia through the famous Silk Road to Russia and Europe. According to an estimate, in 2006 the opium cultivation increased 59 percent over 2005 placing Afghanistan in the situation of the world's leader in opium poppy production with an estimated share of 92 per cent of the global production.[4]

Aftermath of the Soviet collapse, the suppressed religious identities, and related aspirations burst forth. Significant sections of Central Asian people developed interests to study Islam through the education process. However, this process in many cases gave way to radical Islamic movements. According to Boris Petric, who used extensive firsthand ethnographic data since 1992, the peaceful educational process of reclaiming Islamic knowledge, practices, and institutions during the early 1990s was transformed into the rise of radical Muslim militant movements.[5] In this context, an analysis of the Islamic Movement of Uzbekistan (IMU) appears necessary. The organisation founded in 1998 by Juma Namangani and Tohir Yuldeshev declared its goal to overthrow the Government of Uzbekistan and to replace it with an Islamic state. In 2000, the US State Department declared it as a Foreign Terrorist Organisation. The IMU in 1999 and in 2000 carried out two principal military campaigns operating from Tajikistan. The war in Afghanistan destroyed numerous IMU operational bases and reportedly killed its leader Namangani at Mazar-i-Sharif. However, there are reports of reorganisation of the movement in Afghanistan and Tajikistan under the command of a new leader, Gulbuddin Hekmatyar, an Afghan Pashtun who opposes Karzai's government in Kabul. The Uzbek police forces hold the IMU responsible for the kamikaze attacks of 2004 on the US and Israeli Embassies in Tashkent and the revolt that inflamed Andijan in 2005. The IMU has also found itself in a particularly favourable situation to control the drug trafficking from Afghanistan to Central Asia. Islamic Renaissance Party in Tajikistan perhaps is another Islamic-oriented organisation in Central Asia. As mentioned earlier, after the collapse of the Soviet Union, Islam has started to play a role in the region and in areas such as the Ferghana or the Batken region, grievances are increasing and the Islamic movements act as spokespersons for the discontent, organising protests and rallies.

An interesting point is that the Central Asian states have not declared constitutionally to be Islamic states, though the majority of population belongs to the Sunni Islam religion. Perhaps to the exception of some Islamic movements like IMU and stray government policies, none of the countries of the region has adopted or supported any religious fundamentalist organisation or agenda. The impact of the atheist communist ideology on these states might have influenced these countries in developing a secular politics and governance. Besides, the influence of ancient nomadic traditions has also affected the everyday practice of the religion. In Central Asia, it is interesting to note that the two identities—clan and religion—have played roles in shaping the society. The clan identity inherited from ancient nomadic traditions has shaped much of the politics there.

Some scholars, however, argue state regulation over religion should be curtailed to the minimum. "Islam should be saved from political sterilisation," argues Kamoludin Abdullaev. He argues that Islamists should be given a role to play in contemporary Central Asian politics. He found that the states in Central Asia have adopted three different approaches to an Islamic challenge: to combat and control (such as in Uzbekistan), to control strictly (as in Turkmenistan), and to control but with some cooperation with emerging Islamic political activists (as in Tajikistan).[6] The main crux of the argument is that drawing the Islamists into the political sphere is profitable rather than harmful and forceful imposition of any model of governance with the support of 'secular and democratic' under the guise of uprooting terrorism may not bode well for the future of the region. Despite this interesting argument, there is a need to differentiate between radical and moderate version of the Islam. For the Central Asian region, closer to terrorism-infested Afghanistan, which has recently witnessed resurgence of Taliban forces, the analysis needs to go deeper to find whether the current political situation can afford to provide a ground to Islamist forces.

Transnational organised crime is another factor that plays havoc in Central Asia. According to Alessandra Ceccarelli, in Central Asia there is an inherent connection between the leading tribal families, political elites and organised crime. This connection has helped in proliferation of criminal networks in politics and society.[7] The economies of the region have progressively become dominated by criminal activity with smuggling, trafficking, and other activities linked to transnational organised crime as the major source of income. Central Asia's strategic location makes these developments issues of global concern. According to the official statistics of the United Nations Office on Drugs and Crime in 2011, 92 per cent of the world's heroin is produced in Afghanistan.[8] Of this, around 65 per cent is smuggled into Europe and America along the Silk Road, through the Central Asian Republics and Russia.

After the collapse of the Soviet Union, the newly emerged republics of Central Asia experienced the breakdown of central planning and inter-republican trade under the Soviet auspices, highly monopolistic market structures, and high inflation coupled with declining output. Besides, all these states suffered from the nation-building travails. The system is rampant in corruption, clan-rivalries, favouritism, nepotism, and lack of efficient management. Freedom House, an independent organisation in the US, has characterised the countries of the region as fully corrupt, and called them not free. The corruption rating in these countries has surpassed the Transparency International Standard of corruption rate. Despite two decades of freedom, the countries have remained volatile, susceptible to wide range of power politics, and religious chauvinism and extremism. The decade of the 1990s was a decade of decline for Central Asia. In his work, Eric Sievers uses the idea of 'comprehensive capital', in order to find out the causes of decline. He argues that that sustainable development involves more than just preserving physical capital. It depends upon a virtuous cycle of increasing stocks of physical capital along with less tangible phenomena of health, education, institutions, and trust. Central Asia with their poor economy and infrastructure and due to lack of transparent government failed in achieving these objectives thus further contributing to the decline.[9]

Other factor that has impacted the Central Asian politics is the issue of migration. Furthermore, its linkage with extremism and terrorism has created obstacles on the path of stability and growth. Whether it is migration issues in Eurasia and its linkage with menace of extremism and terrorism, or discovery of same linkage in Western Europe, or South Asia, or North America, or other parts of the world, the increasing realisation that these issues cannot be treated separately but to be seen in a comprehensive framework, has gained currency in recent months. Whether it is the 9/11 that brought out the menace of terrorism to the world stage ensuing the contested 'global war against terrorism', or rise of far right in parts of world and its extreme manifestation as reflected in the 2011 Norwegian shoot out case, these are some of the crucial issues which will likely be precarious and threatening in coming months and years. Some of the developments such as Kazakh President Nursultan Nazarbayev's call for making law regulating migration and extremism or the pronouncements at the 20th anniversary of Commonwealth of Independent States (CIS) in Dushanbe in September 2011 in context of extremism and terrorism indicate that these are some of the raging issues, which cannot be tackled in Central Asia by ad hoc mechanisms; rather there is a need to evolve an international agenda to tackle these issues and challenges thrown by them.

President Nazarbayev raised this issue in the first of week of September 2011 in parliament and strongly argued for enacting a law regulating migration and religion as he could find a link between illegal immigration and Islamic extremism in his country. To quote him, "The parliament has to consider adopting a law on religious activity … It is about protecting the state from religious extremism."[10] He further observed, "Whoever wants may come here, whoever wants may open a mosque and name it after his father. No one knows what these mosques are really doing, no one has approved (their opening) … But, as a state, we should put our home in order." Perhaps it does not come as a surprise from the leader of the biggest country in Central Asia, with majority Muslim population. The Central Asian leaders are concerned at the rate of illegal immigration to their countries and its linkage to extremism and terrorism. One can juxtapose the concerns of Nazarbayev to the concerns expressed by a former Central Asian leader Kurmanbek Bakiyev in 2009 at Shanghai Cooperation Organisation. In the context of illegal migration from Afghanistan towards Central Asia, Bakiyev observed, "If the conflict against the Taliban deepens further in Afghanistan, which direction will people head in? God help us, they will move toward Tajikistan, Kyrgyzstan, Uzbekistan, and beyond."[11] Russian Foreign Minister Sergei Lavrov, while participating in the meeting of CIS leaders at Dushanbe in September 2011, observed, "Cooperation within the Commonwealth of Independent States brings positive results in the economy, labour migration and the struggle against organised crime, drug trade, extremism, and terrorism."[12] In the era of globalisation and inter-connectedness with the proliferation and penetration of information technologies, it is difficult to fight the menaces of illegal migration, extremism, and terrorism by wherewithal of a single country, howsoever powerful it may be.

Extremism and Terrorism in Kazakhstan

The rise of religious extremism in Kazakhstan is a recent phenomenon. Past decades of the Soviet rule with its atheist ideology had contributed to the secular character of the country. The breakup of the Soviet Union generated interests in religion, but that in no way affected the secular character of the state. The proximity of the Western Kazakhstan to North Caucasus might have impacted the politics of the country, but that did not significantly altered the social discourse in the region which most veered around a secular, stable and developing economy with an authoritarian set up at the top. However, the rise of religious organisations and mosques in the post-Soviet period has caused concern in Kazakhstan. For instance, aftermath of the independence there were only 68 mosques in the country, which grew into 2,350 in 2011. Out of Kazakhstan's 16.5 million people, 72 per cent are formally considered followers of Islam and 25 per cent of the Russian Orthodoxy.

This section particularly focuses on underlying factors that spur religious extremism and terrorism in Kazakhstan. The author identifies four main factors—the Taliban factor, the North Caucasus factor, the poverty and underdevelopment factor, and the Arab factor—that have played crucial roles in the rise of religious extremism and terrorism in Kazakhstan. The Taliban is highly critical of the supportive role of Kazakhstan in the US activities in Afghanistan aftermath of terrorist attack of 2001. In May 2011, the Taliban criticised the Kazakh government of 'protecting American interests instead of taking into account the aspirations of their people and the regional interests'. It also appealed the

Kazakh people to 'stand against this wrong policy of their rulers'.[13] Hence, it is no surprise that JaK in Kazakhstan was born in the Afghanistan-Pakistan border areas in Waziristan, as the key figures of this organisation Rinat Habidulla, Orynbasar Munatov, and Damir Znaliev have their base in the border area of Afghanistan and Pakistan. They also took part in combat operations against NATO forces in Afghanistan from Khost province in coordination with the Haqqani group of Taliban militants.[14]

In case of Kazakhstan, the emergence of religious extremism and terrorism is a nascent phenomenon. While in case of other Central Asian countries such as Uzbekistan or Tajikistan, the religion-based violence can be traced to 1990s aftermath of the Soviet collapse; in case of Kazakhstan, 2011 appears quite crucial from this point of view. The authorities were initially hesitant or undecided as to what to term the violence that started rising in the second half of 2011. However, particularly after the terrorist attacks in Aktobe region in July 2011, President Nazarbayev expressed concerns over the threat of religious extremism and tasked the Agency for Religious Affairs with drafting a new law on religion. Nazarbayev told the Parliament in September, "There is a growing risk of interethnic and inter-religious conflict. The threat of a new onslaught of international terrorism remains high,"[15] and in the same speech, he urged the law making body to consider a new law on religious activities to bring order to our house.

The adoption of new religious law, signed by President Nazarbayev on October 13, 2011, appeared to provide another spur in rising extremist activities in Kazakhstan with active support of the Taliban, though it intended to curb the same. The new law defined Kazakhstan as a secular stated and banned adoption of any religion as state religion and declared all religions equal before the law. However, the strict registration requirements are likely to permit only two religious communities to operate nationwide—the Hanafi school of Islam and the Orthodox Christian Church—whose historical role 'in the development of the culture and spiritual life of the nation' is recognised in the preamble.[16] The new law banned prayer rooms in state buildings, required re-registration of all religious organisations and missionary activities, and made the building of new places of worship subject to state approval. Nazarbayev strongly supported law, which was passed by parliament and signed by him within a span of one month, as a 'necessary step' to protect the country from 'Islamic extremism'. The new law stipulated that in order to be registered with the Agency for Religious Affairs, local religious communities should have no less than 50 members, and for regional and national level religious communities the minimum number should be 500 and 2,500 respectively. Article 7 of the law banned believers from praying in government offices, as well as on the premises of educational and health service institutions. It also restricted prayer at railway stations and airports for believers to designated prayer rooms.[17]

The second half of 2011 witnessed a number of terrorist attacks in Kazakhstan in places like Aktobe and Atyrau (also called the oil capital of Kazakhstan), further corroborating the fears of rising extremism and the rising nexus between extremists in the Northern Caucasus and Kazakhstan. One of the well-known websites called Kavkaz Tsentr, propagating the ideas of the Caucasus radicals, published a message by JaK in December 2011, which claimed responsibility for the attacks in Kazakhstan. The Kazakh authorities also claimed that the investigations found the direct involvement of JaK in perpetrating the attack in Atyrau, a major energy hub in the country.[18] It also brought another dimension of extremism in Kazakhstan that JaK is not only interested to attack government establishments and intimidate it, but also interested to target its economic ties with other countries.[19]

The Chechen rebel fighters also use Atyrau region, which is close to Astrakhan region in Russia, as an easy access in spreading ideas of Jihad to Kazakhstan. Experts note the similarity of the methods and tactics of the Soldiers of the Caliphate in Kazakhstan to those used by Islamist militants in Dagestan, who target the police force and government structures.[20] However, the Chechen or Dagestan connection to religious extremism and violence in Kazakhstan is a recent phenomenon. The earlier case was that though Chechen fighters travelled to Kazakhstan, it was not for extremism purpose but for medical treatment in local hospitals. As revealed by Bolat Shaimanov, the head of the Mangistau regional department of the National Security Committee, some wounded Chechen fighters received medical treatment in local hospitals.[21] Their active support to Kazakh extremists came to focus in 2009 when Russian security services reported the killing of an unspecified number of terrorists who allegedly carried Kazakh passports. In February 2010, the Russian Federal Security Service announced that two residents of Aktobe, Albert Abdikarimov and Raimbek Yerzhanov, surrendered to Russian security forces when an apartment block was surrounded in Makhachkala, capital of Dagestan.[22] Atyrau is showing signs of growing extremism with 70 per cent of practicing Muslims between the ages of 13 and 30 influenced by Salafism, a radical variety of Islam in contrast to traditional Islam of Kazakhstan influenced by moderate versions such as Hanafism and Sufism. Perhaps, the most notable influence from the North Caucasus on the rise of extremism in Kazakhstan is the influence of Aleksandr Tikhomirov, a Russian born Christian who later converted into Islam and took a new name Said Buryatsky. Buryatsky was one of the main ideologues in North Caucasus propagating Jihad in terms of conducting a 'holy war' against the Russian soldiers in the region.[23] The Kazakh authorities also claim that the JaK cell in Kazakhstan was found under the influence of Buryatsky, who was killed in 2010 by the Russian forces.

Besides the Taliban and North Caucasus factors, the lack of mechanisms in Kazakhstan to address the grievances of the common people and the problems of poverty and unemployment too has aided religious extremism in the region. Marat Shibutov argues that terrorism in Kazakhstan is home-grown and attracts young 'social losers', who have come of age in the post-independence period, with few opportunities.[24] Poverty and unemployment as in case of other conflict situations, such as Kashmir or Chechnya too attracts the young to join the extremist movement to earn a livelihood. Junne and Verhoken strongly argue that economic reconstruction contributes positively to long-term political harmony,[25] which seems to be lacking in Kazakhstan. The influence of Wahabism from Arab world too has played a crucial role in fomenting religious extremism in Kazakhstan. While most Muslims in the country profess the moderate Hanafi school of Islam, the recent influence of radical varieties particularly Salafism and Wahabism are more prominent among the younger generation of Kazakhs.[26] Poverty and underdevelopment and radical Islam make a deadly combination in attracting the youth and giving them hopes of development and emancipation. As rightly pointed out by Margarita Assenova, lack of understanding of Islam too leads to misinterpretations of the religion. The Religious Affairs Agency in Kazakhstan claims that only seven percent of the Muslim clergy in 2,500 mosques is capable of correctly interpreting Islam.[27]

Conclusion

Religious extremism and terrorism in Central Asian countries including in Kazakhstan can be viewed through macro as well as micro prisms, owing to the framework one uses for analyses. Looking from a macro perspective the Central Asian state of Kazakhstan like other four 'stans' in the region has witnessed the churning caused by the collapse of the Soviet Union. The newly independent countries were faced with prospects of development and democracy as well as challenges of authoritarianism, religious extremism, and underdevelopment. That the states mantled a secular grab is no mean achievement, but the mantle seems to be wearing thin with the influences from abroad particularly from Af-Pak region and the Arab and from home particularly from underdevelopment and conflicting interpretation of religion. The Af-Pak borderlands supplied men for the rise of extremism and the Wahabism from Arab supplied the ideological content and funding to this extremism. Whether it is extremism and terrorism in Uzbekistan or Tajikistan, or inter-ethnic violence in the wider region, or the rise of nexus from North Caucasus to further south, all these developments cannot be totally viewed as disparate as they have linkages which are at times subtle and at time obvious.

However, looking from a particularistic, micro perspective the menace of religious extremism and terrorism in Kazakhstan is a nascent phenomenon. Once considered the island of stability and growth, the news of Kazakhstan seldom appeared as a playground of extremist forces as in some other countries of Central Asia; it was a stable country moving on the path of development. It is only in 2011 that Kazakhstan appeared in the map of religious extremism in the Eurasian landscape. The moot question then rises whether the country will further lapse into chaos and caught in the whirlpool of extremism, or will be strong enough to ward off this menace. As the new law on religion passed in October 2011 indicated, the leadership appeared to have adopted a tough posture to fight the extremism in the country. But the problem is a kind of double-edged razor as the open ban of religious activities such as public prayers in institutions may push the hardliners to underground, thus further widening the fault lines in the society. From this point of view, President Nazarbayev will have a tough task to perform in the coming days.

Notes

1. Selig S. Harrison, *In Afghanistan's Shadow: Baluch Nationalism and Soviet Temptations*, Carnegie Endowment for International Peace, Washington, DC, 1981.
2. Thomas Barfield, "Afghanistan is not the Balkans: Ethnicity and Its Political Consequences from a Central Eurasian Perspective," *Central Eurasian Studies Review*, 4 (1) 2005, p. 4.
3. Barfield, "Afghanistan is not the Balkans: Ethnicity and Its Political Consequences from a Central Eurasian Perspective".
4. Alessandra Ceccarelli, "Clans, Politics and Organized Crime in Central Asia," *Trends in Organized Crimes*, 10 (3) 2007, pp. 19-36.
5. *Central Eurasian Studies Review*, vol. 2, no. 3, Fall 2003.
6. Barfield, "Afghanistan is not the Balkans: Ethnicity and Its Political Consequences from a Central Eurasian Perspective".
7. *Central Eurasian Studies Review*, vol. 2, no. 3, Fall 2003.
8. For details see, http://www.unodc.org/documents/data-and-analysis/WDR2011/World_Drug_Report_2011_ebook.pdf
9. Eric W. Sievers, *The Post-Soviet Decline of Central Asia: Sustainable Development and Comprehensive Capital*, (London: Routledge, 2003).
10. James Kilner, "Kazakh President wants to monitor Muslims more closely after 18 arrested for terrorism," *The Telegraph*, September 01, 2011.
11. "SCO Summit: 'Beast of the East' Appears to Have Lost its Teeth," Radio Free Europe/Radio Liberty, May 16, 2009, http://www.rferl.org/content/SCO_Summit_Beast_Of_The_East_Appears_To_Have_Lost_Its_Teeth/1755390.html (Accessed on December 25, 2010).

12. "CIS successful cooperation vehicle - Lavrov," http://english.ruvr.ru/2011/09/02/55582072.html (Accessed on January 15, 2011).
13. *China Daily*, May 22, 2011.
14. Jacob Zenn, "'By the Hands of Men Who Don't Fear Death' – Jund al-Khilafa Launches Islamist Insurgency in Kazakhstan," *Terrorism Monitor*, 9 (43) 2011, http://www.jamestown.org/single/?no_cache=1&tx_ttnews%5Btt_news%5D=38701(Accessed on January 15, 2012).
15. Margarita Assenova, "Kazakhstan Adopts a Controversial Religious Law," *Eurasia Daily Monitor*, 8 (188) 2011. http://www.jamestown.org/single/?no_cache=1&tx_ttnews%5Btt_news%5D=38519 (Accessed on April 23, 2012).
16. Assenova, "Kazakhstan Adopts a Controversial Religious Law".
17. Farkhad Sharip, "Kazakhstan Imposes Tougher Measures to Stem the Rise of Religious Extremism," *Eurasia Daily Monitor*, 8 (194) 2011. http://www.jamestown.org/single/?no_cache=1&tx_ttnews%5Btt_news%5D=38559 (Accessed on April 23, 2012).
18. Jacob Zenn, "Network of Jund al-Khilafah in Kazakhstan Wider than Predicted," *Eurasia Daily Monitor*, 9 (12) 2012, http://www.jamestown.org/single/?no_cache=1&tx_ttnews%5Btt_news%5D=38895 (Accessed on March 20, 2012).
19. Jacob Zenn, n. 14.
20. Farkhad Sharip, "Militants Escalate Terrorist Attacks in Kazakhstan," *Eurasia Daily Monitor*, 8 (211) 2011. http://www.jamestown.org/programs/edm/single/?tx_ttnews%5Btt_news%5D=38672&cHash=8f065b922eef3966afc8c63b7b157da0 (Accessed on April 23, 2012).
21. Sharip, "Militants Escalate Terrorist Attacks in Kazakhstan".
22. Sharip, "Militants Escalate Terrorist Attacks in Kazakhstan".
23. Zenn, "Network of Jund al-Khilafah in Kazakhstan Wider than Predicted".
24. Birgit Brauer, "Is Kazakhstan Threatened By Islamic Terrorists?," *Eurasia Daily Monitor*, 8 (209) 2011, http://www.jamestown.org/single/?no_cache=1&tx_ttnews%5Btt_news%5D=38654 (Accessed on January 20, 2012).
25. Gerd Junne and Willemijn Verkoren, *Postconflict Development: Meeting New Challenges*, (London: Lynne Reiner, 2004).
26. Assenova, "Kazakhstan Adopts a Controversial Religious Law".
27. Assenova.

15. Moving beyond Nomadism: Emerging Equations in Kazakh-Mongol Relations

Sharad K. Soni

The end of the Cold War brought about changes in the world's geopolitical power structures giving way to the parallel changes in expectations and attitudes toward international relations—firstly, the collapse of the erstwhile Soviet Union left the existence of only one superpower, that is, the US; secondly, although turmoil and conflict continued, it was limited in scope and had geostrategic implications, and thirdly, more open borders allowed globalisation and regionalisation to prosper, with both positive and negative consequences.[1] Such a post-Cold War scenario with changes in bilateral, regional, and multilateral relations has been seen as a by-product of global geopolitical and regional geostrategic changes that redefined the whole gamut of international relations. One fine example of this scenario is the Kazakh-Mongol relationship which has been growing for quite sometimes now in the true spirit of cross-border cordial relations.

Both the Kazakhs and Mongols, who have similar nomadic identity, share a common Soviet legacy except that Mongolia has been an independent country since 1921, while Kazakhstan became independent in 1991. The relations between the two countries developed since the 13th century when Kazakhstan belonged to the domain of the Great Mongol Empire and remained in the sphere of the Mongol successor states until the beginning of the 16th century when parts of Kazakhstan were annexed by Tsarist Russia. By the 1860s, the territory belonging to what is now the Republic of Kazakhstan, were gradually absorbed into Russian Turkestan. Although there was a brief period of autonomy towards the end of Tsarist rule, the Kazakhs subsequently was assimilated into the Soviet setup. In 1920, the area of present-day Kazakhstan became an autonomous republic within Soviet Russia. However, it became a new political entity during the Soviet delimitation in the 1930s, becoming a Soviet republic in 1936 until it declared its sovereignty as a republic within the USSR in October 1990.

However, the turning point came soon after the Soviet collapse when Kazakhstan declared its independence on December 16, 1991. Intrinsically, not only Kazakhstan but also other Central Asian Republics in the post-Soviet period have emerged as new geopolitical entities thus becoming the centre of global attention. Kazakhstan's role as a regional leader in Central Asia and as an influential player in global geopolitics has increased so much that it attracted global attention including Mongolia for expansion of bilateral and multilateral ties. Having come out of almost 70 years of Soviet order, Mongolia was one of the first countries in the world to recognise the independence of Kazakhstan. Ever since the two sides established their diplomatic relations on January 22, 1992, there has been a steady growth in their ties in almost all areas of political, economic, and cultural realms. Moreover, globalisation and efforts towards establishment of peace and security in the Eurasian space have influenced the two countries alike, thus pushing them to adopt more or less the same concept of 'multi-vector' or 'multi-pillar' foreign policy and declaring their countries to be nuclear-weapon-free-zones.

Since bilateral relations between the two countries have not been restricted to their nomadic identities alone, the discussion here seeks to emphasise some key issues pointing to the emerging equations in the overall ambit of Kazakh-Mongol relations. While doing so, it delves into the common factors in the cross-border bilateral ties between the two sides in political, economic and cultural fields, apart from dealing with the magnitude of relationship on vital issues including those concerning with the ethnic Kazakh diaspora of Mongolia and their post-Soviet emigration to Kazakhstan, where they are known as *Oralmans*. In this context, it focuses on few facts revealed during a field study undertaken by this author in July-August 2011 at Khovd and Bayan Ölgii provinces of Mongolia in connection with a research project on 'Kazakh Diaspora in Mongolia'.

Kazakh-Mongol Cross-Border Ties: Common Factors

The importance of Kazakhstan's relationship with the outside world has been influenced by two factors—(1) is a large reserve of hydrocarbon resources located mostly in the country's western oblasts, and (2) its geostrategic location that has increased Kazakhstan's status in Central Asian and global affairs.[2] It's certain that Kazakhstan has become the most developed country in Central Asia over the past decade as a result of its rapid oil-driven growth and pragmatic foreign policy termed as 'multi-vector' foreign policy.[3] It has skillfully balanced the country's diverse range of interests and maintained a sensible equilibrium among Kazakhstan's three most significant international partners, that is, Russia, China and the US, whose interests compete in the region. Kazakh leadership often emphasises that Kazakhstan's continuing 'activist, multifaceted, and balanced foreign policy is to defend the country's independence and national interests'.[4] To that end, Kazakhstan places priority on relations with Russia, China, the US and the EU in that order, and reiterates its commitment to the SCO and the single EEC.

On the other side, like the Central Asian republics, Mongolia too is landlocked with the distinction of being the second largest landlocked country in the world after Kazakhstan. The geographical compulsion of being landlocked signifies the strategic importance of Mongolia, and therefore, geostrategic rather than geopolitics plays a significant role in this country. Once termed as one of the most isolated and remote countries of the world, today Mongolia is regarded as a developing country, which seeks to enhance its status on world map by strengthening its solidarity and cooperation with both the developed as well as developing countries. In the 1990s, Mongolia opted not only for socioeconomic changes but also for a new constitution and democratically elected governments.[5] As part of such changes, the seven decades' old unilateral foreign policy that was dictated by Moscow was rejected. Apart from the adoption of a new constitution, Mongolia also reformulated its national security and foreign policy, taking into account the ongoing international developments. As specified in the Foreign Policy Concept, Mongolia's foreign policy priority began focussing on 'safeguarding of its security and vital national interests by political and diplomatic means, and creating a favourable external environment for its economic, scientific and technological development'.[6]

It has been observed that by pursuing the 'multi-pillar' foreign policy Mongolia has not only been trying to maintain balanced relations with Russia and China but also forging mutually advantageous ties with other countries especially those considered as its 'third neighbours'. The United States and some democratic governments in the west as well as Asia-Pacific countries fall into the category of Mongolia's 'third neighbours'. It is anticipated that these 'third neighbours' may bring added value to Mongolia's acts of balancing Russia and China and the projection of Mongolia's place in the international arena with its 'new regional identity of a Northeast Asian country'.[7] Like Kazakhstan, Mongolia too has skillfully balanced the country's varied range of interests and maintained a sensible equilibrium among its three most significant international partners, that is, Russia, China and the US, whose interests compete in Mongolia. According to its foreign policy norms, Mongolia's endeavour is to build strong relations with Kazakhstan too. Bilateral relations between the two sides are showing signs of development based on equality and mutual benefit.

That the views of the two countries converge on several issues of common concern signifies that their foreign policies are based on pragmatic and non-ideological foundations and are motivated by the perceived interests of the regimes concerned. The fundamental factors that have governed bilateral relations between Kazakhstan and Mongolia are:

- Nomadic identity that Kazakhstan and Mongolia share in addition to ethnic Kazakhs that form the largest minority population of Mongolia
- Geographical proximity and economic complementarities make Kazakhstan and Mongolia natural partners for increased economic and trade ties
- Mongolia, like Kazakhstan, is a country that is rich in mineral assets and both have huge energy resources
- Both Mongolia and Kazakhstan have adopted 'multi-vector' or

'multi-pillar' foreign policy, which means a willingness to develop and improve strategic, diplomatic and economic ties with major geopolitical powers in the international arena, such as China, Russia, US, Europe, India and the Islamic world

- Kazakhstan-Mongolia relations have not developed in a vacuum, as the two nations already share a platform in the multilateral forums like the SCO
- Both Mongolia and Kazakhstan are nuclear-weapon-free-zones. Mongolia has declared itself a Nuclear-Weapon-Free Zone (NWFZ) in 1992 and the Central Asian states have endorsed the creation of a Central Asia Nuclear-Weapon-Free-Zone (CANWFZ) in the Almaty Declaration of 1997

Magnitude of Bilateral Relations

Notwithstanding the above mentioned common factors that have contributed much to the development of bilateral relations between Kazakhstan and Mongolia, one of the key issues in the growth of economic and trade ties is the need to develop interregional cooperation in such sectors as infrastructure and transport, banking, energy, air links, tourism, agriculture etc. In fact, the development of trade relations is hampered by the absence of a proper road connecting Kazakhstan and Mongolia, which the two sides are willing to build through Russian territory.[8] It may be pointed out that in terms of geography Kazakhstan can be considered the third neighbour of Mongolia after Russia and China, as the easternmost point of Kazakhstan is within 50 km or so of the westernmost tip of Mongolia. However, they do not share a border with each other directly—rather, the two countries are separated by a small part of Russia and China. The other crucial issue is related to Mongolia's ethnic Kazakh diaspora, and their migration to Kazakhstan. The following discussion deals with all these issues in order to highlight the magnitude of bilateral relations.

Following the establishment of diplomatic relations between the two states, Kazakh President Nursultan Nazarbayev visited Mongolia in October 1993, and concluded a Treaty of Friendly Relations and

Cooperation. The treaty determined the basic directions of Kazakhstan-Mongolia relations and laid the foundation of bilateral trade and economic cooperation. Several other agreements concerning commercial-economic and cultural cooperation and a protocol on cooperation between foreign policy departments and national banks of Kazakhstan and Mongolia were also signed. Further, the Mongolian President N. Bagabandi's visit to Kazakhstan in 1998 and the return visit of Kazakh President Nazarbayev to Mongolia in 1999 provided the much-needed motivation at that point of time for the development of mutual relations. Repeatedly high-level bilateral visits continued including that of the Mongolian Presidents N. Bagabandi, and subsequently, Nambaryn Enkhbayar in 2002 and 2006 respectively. The two sides signed more than 40 bilateral contracts and agreements until the next official visit of Kazakh President Nazarbayev to Mongolia took place in 2008.

Nazarbayev's discussion with his Mongolian counterpart Enkhbayar focused the ways of further enhancing the bilateral economic, trade, investment, and transport cooperation.[9] It was proposed that subsidiaries of Kazakh banks in Mongolia, through which Kazakh companies can make investments in Mongolia would be set up, besides constructing a road between the two countries for expansion of trade and economic relations. It was also decided that Kazakh-Mongolian Direct Investment Fund be established with the aim to finance profitable projects in such spheres as energy, transport and logistics, financial sector, telecommunications, tourism, light and food industry, ore-mining industry, production and processing of energy products on Mongolian territory. Both sides agreed to set up air links between the Kazakh city of Ust Kamenogorsk and western Mongolian city of Bayan-Ölgii. Besides, a number of bilateral agreements were signed, including the agreements on cooperation in education, programme for cooperation for the period 2009-12 between the ministries of foreign affairs, MoU on cooperation between the Kazakhstan Ministry of Labour and Social Protection and Ministry of Social Protection and Labour of Mongolia.

It is encouraging to note that currently over 25 categories of goods are being traded between the two sides. Kazakhstan mainly exports grain, mineral oil, tobacco machine tools, tyres, spare parts and petroleum products etc. and imports from Mongolia meat, wool, fluoric spares, carpets, wool, leather goods, consumer goods, and crude copper, which are processed in Kazakhstan. One of the priority directions of trade and economic cooperation between the two sides has been to develop cooperation between East Kazakhstan oblast of the Republic of Kazakhstan and western aimags (provinces) of Mongolia. Yet, trade turnover between the two countries for 2007 amounted only to US$ 36 million, which was less than what was recorded in 2006. Decrease in the trade turnover was due to absence of mutual borders, transport problems, lack of information at the two governments' disposal on tax system and trade possibilities of both countries. Therefore, while visiting Mongolia on August 06-07, 2008, Kazakh President Nazarbayev emphasised more on increasing the bilateral trade turnover; in order to do that, he felt the necessity of activating the work of inter-governmental commissions of both countries apart from stimulating activities of other mechanisms for development of trade relations. As a result, the inter-governmental Kazakh-Mongolian commission on trade and economic, scientific, technical, and cultural cooperation began to work with meetings taking place in both countries alternatively. However, ironically, not much improvement in trade relations has been seen in recent times. According to statistical data of Kazakhstan, in 2011 the bilateral trade turnover amounted to just US$ 36.8 million in which the share of exports was US$ 35.4 million, while imports remained much low at US$ 1.4 million.[10] What will be the trade figure in 2012 is yet to be seen, though for the period January-March 2012, it stands at US$ 10 million including exports—US$ 9.9 million and imports—US$ 100 thousand.

Despite a dismal picture in trade figures, steps have been taken towards cooperation in the sphere of investment and setting up of joint enterprises. In 2007, 34 joint enterprises with Kazakhstan's investments were registered in Mongolia. Some events that were organised in December 2007 by the Kazakhstan Fund of Sustainable Development 'Kazyna' further set the stage for the business circles of both countries to get to know each other with the objective of assessing possibilities of cooperation in the sphere of investment in mining and auto transport sector as well as creation of small enterprises for production of asphalt bitumen and signing of an agreement on cooperation in the tourism sector. In the agricultural sector, the two sides are willing to take joint projects on Kazakh import of drought-proof wheat seeds and their cultivation as well as exchange of experiences in the field of education and training of agricultural specialists, particularly the Mongolian veterinaries. A bilateral forum was already held in 2009 with the participation of scientists, representatives of business and civil servants of the two countries to discuss joint projects and farming problems. A few years back it was revealed that 17 Kazakh companies had invested some US$ 6,63,000 in Mongolia.[11]

Such a magnitude of relations underscores the interest the two sides are showing in cooperating each other in varied areas. In this regard, following points are self-explanatory which also help understand the emerging equations in the overall bilateral relations:[12]

- While Kazakhstan has been the main hub of foreign investment since 1991, attracting nearly US$ 40 billion, primarily in the energy sector, it has been modestly investing some of its surplus petroleum revenue in Mongolia since 2000. There are now about 7,700 Kazakh companies operating in Mongolia, the majority in the production, service, geology, and mining sectors. There is certainly room for improvement in bilateral cooperation on joint ventures and investments
- Mongolia has sought Kazakh assistance in developing its oil potential and energy sector. Topics already under discussion include Kazakh investment in constructing an electric power station to utilise Shivee Ovoo's coal deposits and a fifth thermo-electric power station in Ulan Bataar. It is to be noted that since 1991 Kazakhstan has become one of the world's rising petro-states
- Mongolia's bid for Kazakh assistance seems to be influenced by the fact that Astana is having the world's ninth-largest petroleum reserves, and there has lately been an indication that petroleum production will expand threefold over the next decade. It has been estimated that

if existing development plans are implemented, Kazakhstan's current 1.3 million barrels per day (BPD) output will rise to 2.7 million by 2020

- The Mongolian government is optimistic that if it is successful in attracting Kazakh and foreign investment in its hydrocarbon industries, the country could fulfill its domestic demands for oil products by 2015. Ulan Bataar's energy sector has already raised nearly US$ 640 million in foreign investment since 2007. Mongolia's energy sector's main attraction is its Tamsaga deposit, which contains an estimated 1.5 billion barrels of oil
- Mongolia and Kazakhstan are also looking to improve air links with flights from Astana to Ulan Bator and Bayan-Ölgii, the home to most of Mongolia's ethnic Kazakh diaspora. This is required given the fact that despite the proximity of Mongolia and Kazakhstan, their borders do not meet and road links are through Russia and China
- The running of motorable road between Ust Kamenogorsk and Bayan Ölgii has been one of the activities planned for the development of bilateral cooperation and the establishment of direct relations between the relevant sectors' organisations

On the issue of regional peace and security, there is a commonality of views between the two countries. Ulan Bataar has shown its support for the efforts of Astana in strengthening regional security through regular participation in multilateral regional forums in the capacity of an observer at the SCO and as a member of the CICA. Mongolia also took part in the OSCE Summit held in Astana on December 01-02, 2010 and other subsequent meetings. The OSCE is now considering Mongolia's application to become its member.

In other areas of cooperation like the cultural sphere, the two sides are carrying out regularly the days of Mongolia in Kazakhstan and days of Kazakhstan in Mongolia aimed at developing cultural relations between the two countries. In September 2012, while the Astana City Cultural Day will be held in Ulan Bataar, a Mongolian concert and an exhibition on Mongolia will simultaneously be organised in Astana and Almaty.

The two sides are also interested in joint researches of Turkic heritage situated on the territory of Mongolia. Currently, 230 representatives of the Mongolian youth study in Kazakhstan. Kazakhstan has agreed to continue these traditions as part of strengthening cultural and educational cooperation between the countries. There has been an agreement to receive in Kazakhstan 120 people of Bayan-Ölgii *aimag* annually to undertake study in construction, agricultural, farming, veterinary, and service sectors. According to the intergovernmental agreement in the sphere of education, there is an annual exchange of students between of higher education institutions of the two countries. As per the decision taken by the Ministries of Education of the Republic of Kazakhstan and Mongolia, a branch of the East Kazakhstan state university at Bayan Ölgii was opened in 2001, which in fact remains as the first branch of a Kazakh university abroad.

In 2003, the Kazakh Ministry of Education and Sciences delivered more than 9,600 textbooks and manuals for the children of the Kazakh Diaspora in Mongolia. In March 2006, the National Library of Kazakhstan sent books to the regional central library in the Bayan-Ölgii *aimag* within the frameworks of UNESCO international project on promotion of languages, cultural variety, and education in Mongolia. Every year the Ualikhanov Institute of History and Ethnology organises an ethno-archeological expeditions in Mongolia with the aim to identify Kazakh-ethnographic, ethno-sociological processes of the Kazak ethnic group in Mongolia as well as to carry out architectural-archeological research of ancient Turkish monuments in Mongolia.

The 'Oralman' Factor in Kazakh-Mongol Bilateral Ties

The word 'Oralman' meaning 'one who came back' or 'returnee' began to be used as an official term by the Kazakhstan authorities to describe ethnic Kazakhs who have immigrated or repatriated to Kazakhstan from across Asia and Europe. The oralmany from Mongolia are often called as Mongolian-Kazakhs who have a long history of coexistence with the Mongols. The background story of Mongolian-Kazakhs or the ethnic Kazakh diaspora in Mongolia reveals that Kazakh nomads have roamed the mountains and valleys of western Mongolia with their herds since the 19th century.[13] However, after the establishment of Mongolian statehood the country proclaimed itself as a People's Republic in 1924 after which many of the ethnic Kazakhs left their semi-nomadic lifestyle and began settling down in the western Mongolian plateaus. This western region also includes the Bayan-Ölgii aimag, which in 1940 was formed as a separate administrative unit for the Kazakh national minority.[14]

Having a population of 88,056 (2010 Census) with a territorial area of 45,800 sq km, the Bayan-Ölgii aimag comprises 2.9 per cent of the whole Mongolian territory with13 territorial administrative units.[15] Bayan-Ölgii aimag, alone accounts for more than 78.4 per cent of the Kazakh population, thus, apart from being the most numerous, the Kazakhs are the only minority in Mongolia forming the majority of one aimag. Moreover, 88.7 per cent of the total population of Bayan-Ölgii city is composed of Kazakhs. Besides, Kazakhs also comprise over 10 per cent of the population in neighbouring Khovd aimag. In this area, the Kazakhs are said to have started coming in the 1930s, partly from Xinjiang and partly from Bayan-Ölgii.[16] While the majority of Kazakhs continue to live in the traditional aimags to the extreme west, more recent migration eastward to the urban areas has resulted in significant growth in their numbers, especially in Mongolia's capital Ulan Bataar. Though a sizeable number of Mongolian-Kazakhs in the post-Soviet period migrated to Kazakhstan, they still form the largest ethnic minority group in Mongolia. As recorded by the 2010 Population and Housing Census of Mongolia, the total number of Kazakhs in the country today stands at 1,01,526.[17] Looking at the Census years, it has been found that the Kazakh population registered a constant increase from 4.3 per cent in 1956 to 4.7 per cent in 1963, 5.2 per cent in 1969, 5.3 per cent in 1979 and 5.9 per cent in 1989.[18] But in 2000, it got sharply reduced to 4.3 per cent to witness a further decline in 2010 when the figure came down to just 3.9 per cent.

The decline in the number of ethnic Kazakh population after 1989 ensued primarily due to their migration from Mongolia to Kazakhstan in the early 1990s. Basically, they were encouraged by the Kazakhstan government's call for return to their country of origin or what they call as their 'historic homeland' as described by Article 1 of the Kazakhstan's Law on Immigration adopted in June 1992. It appears that Kazakhs from Mongolia were among the first to respond to the call for repatriation as in 1991-92 alone a total of 60,000 Mongolian-Kazakhs migrated to Kazakhstan, which till date numbers approximately 87,000 as per record of the Deputy Governor's office of Bayan-Ölgii.[19] The motivation for Kazakhstan's policy of repatriation was a perceived need to increase the number of ethnic Kazakhs, and such motivation remained 'closely linked to the process of nation building, preservation of national identity and culture as well as internal stability'.[20] This became clear soon after the independence of Kazakhstan at the First World Kurultai (assembly) of Kazakh people held in 1992 when the authorities urged ethnic Kazakhs wherever they were to return to Kazakhstan and promised them a number of benefits with simplification in citizenship procedure. The Mongolian-Kazakhs who have migrated to Kazakhstan now fall under the category of Oralmans, and are a pertinent factor in the bilateral ties between the two countries.

Despite the fact that both the Mongolian and Kazakh governments are seriously involved in negotiating on the simplification of procedures for the settlement of citizenship issues and the visa regime for Mongolian-Kazakhs, the migration process is extremely slow as within Kazakhstan they are politically, socially, economically and even culturally marginalised, and hence their integration into the new society remains unrealized.[21] Interestingly, on June 21, 2000, President Nazarbayev issued a special decree granting Kazakh citizenship to 1882 Mongolian-Kazakhs who settled down in Kazakhstan after emigrating from Mongolia in the early 1990s.[22] On the other hand, the status of ethnic Kazakhs as a minority within the State of Mongolia appears to be free from any systematic discrimination. They enjoy equal rights with their Mongol brethren within the country, as was the case in the past. There has never been any instance of ethnic repression of Kazakhs by the Mongolian government. Moreover, this policy has been continuing with absolutely no sign of change, which also encourages Mongolia's Kazakh diaspora to have the benefits of dual citizenship, if Kazakhstan agrees to do so. Already on October 27-28, 2011, during the Fifth Mongolia-Kazakhstan Consular Consultative meeting the two sides agreed to initial an agreement on simplifying the process of providing citizenship to Oralmans from Mongolia in order to overcome the dual-citizenship-related difficulties.[23] In accordance with a mutual decision, a Mongolia-Kazakhstan working group is now expected to meet on agreed date to resolve the issues of dual citizenship.

Kazakh Government Policies/Programmes for Oralmans

As of 2005, an estimated five million ethnic Kazakhs lived outside Kazakhstan in more than 40 countries,[24] including those returned to their homeland until that time. However, what is worth to be noted here is that despite an allocation of each year quota for the number of Kazakhs eligible to return to Kazakhstan, the arrival figure far exceeds the quota. According to the International Organisation for Migration (IOM), in 2001 more than 10,000 families of Oralmans (ethnic Kazakh returnee) arrived in Kazakhstan as against permissible limit of 600 families or 3,000 people.[25] With the economic development taking place in Kazakhstan, the quota for Oralmans since 2009 has been increased to 20,000 families a year which has been continuing even now. All this has been done under various government policies/programmes. It was in 1997 that a Law 'on migration' and a branch programme for migration policy in 2001-10, aimed at sustainable socio-economic and demographic development, protection of migrants' rights, strengthening of the state security was adopted. This was followed by the adoption of 'conception of Republic of Kazakhstan's migration policy in 2007-15', aimed at improvement and development of new mechanisms regulating migration processes in the republic.

However, the most successful migration policy launched by the Kazakh government is the Nurly Kosh (Blessed Migration) programme, which was launched on January 01, 2009. It targeted three groups of migrants: the ethnic Kazakhs living abroad; skilled former citizens of Kazakhstan; and citizens living in depressed zones. The Nurly Kosh programme which ran until 2011 covered almost 3.5 to 4.5 million ethnic Kazakhs living outside Kazakhstan—some 1,00,000 of them in Mongolia—with incentives to move to specific areas identified by the government. East Kazakhstan, which is considered by many Kazakhs in western Mongolia as their ancestral homeland, is one of them. During the programme implementation period, Kazakhstan's officials visited western Mongolia to promote the benefits of Nurly Kosh, which included one-off subsidies, paid travel costs and low-interest mortgages. Approximately, 1,92,000 families or 7,60,000 Oralmans took advantage of the Nurly Kosh programme. In addition to reimbursement of relocation costs, and providing repatriates with money for housing and financial support, a few seats in the universities and other institutions of higher learning were kept reserved for the Oralmans.

Each migrating family numbered on an average of five people. Kazakhstan opened its doors to another 3,00,000 Kazakhs over the 3-year Nurly Kosh programme. The Kazakh government spent some US$ 130 million (19.4 billion KZT) on re-settlement benefits for the Oralmans, which included employment assistance, study of the Kazakh and Russian languages, education enrolment quotas, and welfare benefits, free healthcare and housing subsidies.[26] The Kazakh government is now considering launching a revised programme, that is, resettlement programme on the pattern of Nurly Kosh, which will regulate Oralmans' geographical distribution, employment, and the provision of housing. Already a new Migration Act has been passed in 2011, according to which Oralmans will no longer have to wait years for getting Kazakhstani citizenship; rather they may receive it after spending a year in the country. Such an issue of citizenship, which is also a major concern for the Oralmans from Mongolia, has always been prioritised by the two countries as more than 70,000 Kazakh people have moved to Kazakhstan from Mongolia with 60,000 becoming Kazakhstan citizens, including approximately 33,000 with dual citizenship.

In the past 20 years, Kazakhstan's Oralman policy has brought 8,60,000 ethnic Kazakhs back to the country; over 100,000 of them have resettled in the sparsely populated, but oil-rich Mangystau province, according to government statistics.[27] According to the 2009 census of Kazakhstan, the Kazakhs are the largest population accounting for 1,00,96,763 people or 63.1 per cent of the total population of over 16 million, which in 1999 census was calculated at 80,11,452 or 53.5 per cent of the country's then total population of nearly 15 million.[28] Between the two censuses, that is, during the entire period of 1999-2009, the overall Kazakh population grew by 20,85,311 or 26 per cent, a sharp increase that was mainly driven by inflows of Oralmans to the country. This shows that Oralmans are being encouraged to stay in their ethnic homeland and enjoy various benefits extended by the Kazakh government's migration policies and programmes. Nevertheless, there are also evidences of fraudulent cases of receiving repatriation benefits. According to a report released by Interfax-Kazakhstan on January 27, 2011, Kazakhstan's Prosecutor General's Office has identified numerous cases of Oralmans receiving repatriation benefits without ever crossing the Kazakh border.[29]

Conclusion

The above discussions indicate that ever since 1992, Kazakhstan and Mongolia have been engaged in cordial cross-border relations. There is commonality of views between the two countries on several bilateral, regional and multilateral issues as they have been pursuing the same concept of 'multi-vector' or 'multi-pillar' foreign policy. However, issues concerning bilateral economic and trade relations, cooperation in mining, oil and energy sectors, air and transport links as well as the situation of those ethnic Kazakhs living in Mongolia and those who became *oralmans* after migrating to Kazakhstan point to the emerging equations between the two countries. As regards the situation of ethnic Kazakh diaspora in Mongolia, what is being noticed is that within Mongolia there has been a peaceful co-existence between the Buddhist Mongols and Muslim Kazakhs for a long time now, and there has been no instance of any inter-ethnic tensions between the two communities. In the 1990s the economic situation in Mongolia was not conducive enough compared to Kazakhstan which is why migration to Kazakhstan was considered to be voluntary in nature. Today, there are few Mongolian-Kazakhs who are inclined to migrate to Kazakhstan. The main reason for this is Mongolia's development—i.e. Mongolia's economy in 2011 grew at a rate of over 17 per cent and is predicted to increase further in 2012 largely because of the mining boom. According to World Bank projections, the mining boom is likely to make Mongolia the fastest growing economy in the world by 2013 when the annual GDP growth rate is expected to be 22.9 per cent.

Nevertheless, no one knows what the future holds for local Mongolian-Kazakhs who speculate whether there might be better prospects for them across the border in Kazakhstan. While talking to this author, Tilek Bakhyt, a resident of Khovd sum in Mongolia said, "I have a job teaching English in my village school, but life is not easy in this underdeveloped rural area. Income is low. It's hard here, It's better in Kazakhstan, for sure."[30] Bakhyt is just the type of well-qualified migrant that Astana would like to attract, and that Mongolia can ill afford to lose. The outflow of ethnic Kazakhs has had an economic and cultural impact on the Kazakh diaspora in Mongolia that is difficult to assess given the fact that they believe in preserving and maintaining the traditional Kazakh culture even in this age of modernity. Expressing concerns over intellectual loss among the Mongolian-Kazakh community, Ospan Nabi, a journalist at Bayan-Olgii's broadcasting center says, "We have already experienced an outflow of several members of the intelligentsia and hence our intellectual potential has gone down. Now that Mongolia is becoming strong economically, we must give a serious thought on discouraging the migration of Mongolian-Kazakh minority."[31] Though Kazakhstan government has taken several Oralmans friendly policies and programmes, it is just the economic motive that was the reason of Mongolian-Kazakh migration in the past and will remain so in the future as well. On the diplomatic front, however, issues related to the dual citizenship for Mongolia's ethnic Kazakhs appears to be a crucial factor in the smooth sailing of friendly ties between Mongolia and Kazakhstan. Yet, the single common factor that will benefit both Mongols and Kazakhs is nomadic psyche despite the fact that globalisation cleared the way for them to move beyond nomadism and accept the reality of modernity, not in outlook but in action.

References and Notes

1. Saul Bernard Cohen, *Geopolitics of the World System*, (Lanham: Rowman & Littlefield, 2003), p. 87.
2. Reuel R. Hanks, "'Multi-vector politics' and Kazakhstan's Emerging Role as a Geo-strategic Player in Central Asia", *Journal of Balkan and Near Eastern Studies*, 11 (3), September 2009, pp. 257-258.
3. Daniel Wagner and Luca Costa, "Kazakhstan's Balancing Act", *Foreign Policy Journal*, June 15, 2011, at http://www.foreignpolicyjournal.com/2011/06/15/kazakhstans-balancing-act/ (Accessed on November 16, 2011).
4. Stephen Blank, "Kazakhstan's Foreign Policy in a Time of Turmoil", April 26, 2005, *Eurasianet*, at http://www.eurasianet.org/departments/insight/articles/eav042705.shtml (Accessed on December 17, 2008).
5. Ariunsanaa Tunjin,"Mongolia's National Security and Nuclear-Free Policy", *Korean Journal of Defense Analysis*, 15 (1), 2003, p. 102.
6. See "Concept of Mongolia's Foreign Policy", *Strategic Digest*, 26 (2), 1996, p. 188.
7. Sharad K. Soni, "China's Periphery Policy: Implications for Sino-Mongolian Relations", *India Quarterly* 65 (3), 2009, pp. 254-255.
8. "Discussions to take place to build Mongolia-Kazakhstan road", August 07, 2008, at http://www.mongolia-web.com/content/view/1930/40/ (Accessed on November 16, 2011).
9. "Kazakhstan-Mongolia Relations to Grow", at http://www.kazembassy.in/weekynew_arch/Archives/newsvol160.htm#2 (Accessed November 16, 2008).
10. Ministry of Foreign Affairs of the Republic of Kazakhstan, "Cooperation of the Republic of Kazakhstan with Mongolia", May 16, 2012, at http://portal.mfa.kz/portal/page/portal/mfa/en/content/policy/cooperation/asia_africa/06 (Accessed on July 20, 2012).
11. "Mongolia and Asia", at http://www.globalsecurity.org/military/world/mongolia/forrel-asia.htm (Accessed July on 18, 2012).
12. For more details, see John C. K. Daly, "Kazakhstan and Mongolia broaden Relations", *Eurasia Daily Monitor*, 5 (74), April 18, 2008, at http://www.jamestown.org/single/?no_cache=1&tx_ttnews%5Btt_news%5D=33562 (Accessed on November 16, 2011).

13. "The Muslim Kazakhs of Western Mongolia", at http://www.30-days.net/muslims/muslims-in/asia-east/mongolia/ (Accessed on September 28, 2011).
14. B. Shirendyb et al, *History of the Mongolian People's Republic*, Translated by William A. Brown and Urgunge Onon, (Cambridge, Massachusetts: Harvard University, 1976), p. 343.
15. *2010 Population and Housing Census of Mongolia: The Main Results*, National Statistical Office, Ulan Bataar, 2011, p. 20.
16. Peter Finke, "Common Property to Open Access: Changing Pastoral Land Tenure in Post-Socialist Mongolia", 2000, at http://dlc.dlib.indiana.edu/dlc/bitstream/handle/10535/658/finkep060700.pdf?sequence=1 (Accessed on December 18, 2011).
17. *2010 Population and Housing Census of Mongolia: The Main Results*, National Statistical Office, Ulan Bataar, 2011, p. 26.
18. For more detailed analyses, see Sharad K. Soni, "Post-Soviet Migration of Mongolian-Kazakhs to Kazakhstan", in Anita Sengupta and Suchandana Chatterjee (eds.), *Eurasian Perspectives: In Search of Alternatives*", (Delhi: Shipra, 2010), pp. 213-225.
19. This data was obtained by the author from the Deputy Governor's office in Bayan-Ölgii on August 06, 2011.
20. *Status of Oralmans in Kazakhstan: Overview*, UNDP Kazakhstan, Almaty, 2006, p. 8.
21. Alexander C. Diener, Kazakhstan's Kin State Diaspora: Settlement Planning and the *Oralman* Dilemma," *Europe-Asia Studies*, 57 (2), March 2005, p. 327.
22. Soni (2010), p. 223.
23. "Mongolia-Kazakhstan Consultative Meeting Held", October 31, 2011, at http://www.mad-mongolia.com/news/mongolia-news/mongolia-kazakhstan-consultative-meeting-held-7381/ (Accessed on January 16, 2012).
24. President Nazarbayev's Speech at Third World *Kurultai* of Kazakhs held in Astana on September 25, 2005.
25. See Alfred Kueppers, "Ethnic Kazakhs Find Titular Homeland to be Economic Haven", April 22, 2003, at http://www.eurasianet.org/departments/culture/articles/eav042203.shtml (Accessed on March 19, 2012).
26. Gulmira Kamziyeva, "Astana develops new Oralman repatriation programme", November 02, 2011, at http://centralasiaonline.com/en_GB/articles/caii/features/main/2011/11/02/feature-01(Accessed on March 19, 2012).
27. Nate Schenkkan, "Kazakhstan: Concern Rising over Ethnic Kazakh Returnees", February 29, 2012, at http://www.eurasianet.org/node/65064 (Accessed on June 27, 2012).
28. *Results of the 2009 National Population Census of the Republic of Kazakhstan: Analytical Report*, The Agency on Statistics of the Republic of Kazakhstan, (Astana, 2011), pp. 19-20.
29. "Kazakhstan in Focus", *Interfax-Kazakhstan*, January 27, 2011, at http://www.

interfax.kz/?lang=eng&int_id=in_focus&news_id=466 (Accessed on March 19, 2011).

30. Author's Interview with Tilek Bakhyt, a Mongolian-Kazakh who teaches English Language at a school in Khovd Sum, August 03, 2011.
31. Author's Interview with Ospan Nabi, a Mongolian-Kazakh journalist at Bayan-Olgii's broadcasting center, August 06, 2011.

16. Cinematic Imaginings of the Nation: Spotlight on Kazakhstan

Rashmi Doraiswamy

Much has changed in Central Asian cinema in the last twenty years of Independence. The industries have moved on, carrying much from the Soviet times. Cinema played an important role in nation building in the Central Asian region during the Soviet times, and continues to do so now. Over the last two decades, the amateur cinema and popular cinema of the Soviet times has mutated to handle different themes and styles. Of all the Central Asian countries, Kazakhstan has the most vibrant film industry. Part of the reason for this could well be the fact that it was witnessing a surge in filmmaking with several young talents from Sergei Solovyov's workshop in VGIK in Moscow who formed the Kazakh New Wave at the end of the eighties, continued to make films even after the collapse of the Soviet Union. Although both Uzbek and Kazakh governments took interest in the film industry after attaining independence, the Kazakh industry has developed rapidly over the last twenty years in terms of infrastructure. This is because Kazakhstan has had political and economic stability over the past two decades and has seen steady development. According to Gulnara Abikeeva, Kazakh cinema occupies this pride of place in the Central Asian region due to four reasons: "… the continued financing of cinema by the state, the Kazakh New Wave's role in drawing international attention to this cinema, the high creative potential of the people working in this industry and the contribution of foreign producers in the development of cinema in Kazakhstan."[1]

Kazakh Film Studios is the biggest in the region with three blocks, two pavilions, and a lab for colour developing, editing, and sound labs. The sound studio is one of the ten Dolby approved in the world. Shinarbaev and Narymbetov have rooms here. There are several private studios in Kazakhstan as well. Among the more important are Aktan Sataev's studio, Sataifilm and Aldangar Productions, which produced Rustam Abdrashev's *Gift to Stalin* (2008). The 'Almatinsky Gosudarstvenny Khudozhestvenny Teatralnyi Institut imeni Zhurgenev' has Faculties of Film, Choreography, Art, Animation, where teaching and research in the performative arts is done. Kazakhstan has been regularly organising the Eurasia Film Festival in Almaty. This festival has recently begun to focus on films from the Turkic World ('Tyursky Mir'), that includes films from Central Asia, Azerbaijan and Turkey. Tajikistan has also started organising a film festival 'Didori Dushanbe', with a competition section of films from Turkey, Russia, Afghanistan, Iran, and Mongolia. Kyrgyzstan too organises two film festivals on a smaller scale. The fact that the organisation of festivals continues despite the fact that many of the countries of the region are economically challenged shows the importance of the space that culture occupies in this region, as well as the way the festivals insert themselves into the geopolitics of the region. Russia, for instance, where production of films in the post-Soviet period has gained in momentum, styles, and genres, aims to focus on its own production. The Sochi festival has turned into a focus on films from the Russian Federation. Kazakhstan, on the other hand, which is trying to position itself as a 'leader' in the region, taps on the 'Turkic World' affinities (even if this is a short-lived focus). Tajikistan, on the other hand, taps films from Iran, due to its language and cultural links with this neighbour, as well as from other countries in its neighbourhood that have a very modest film production.

This article analyses two post-Soviet films from Kazakhstan (in detail) in an attempt to understand cultural discourses on the nation, to examine how discourses in the cultural field dovetail with or diverge from political discourses. *Nomad* (*Kochevnik*, 2006) and Satybaldy Narymbetov's *Mustafa Chokai* (2008) were both supported by the government, made by Kazakhfilm, the state-owned studio, and were intended to imagine a Kazakh identity. The President, Nursultan Nazarbayev, took a personal interest in both the films. Akim Tarazi, one of the writers of *Mustafa Chokai* states:

"I am one of the authors of the film on *Chokai*—a film, which whose idea was born, in many ways due to our President. Nursultan Abishevich literally was the source of the creation of the image of Chokai. In April 2000, exactly ten years ago, Nursultan Abishevich asked me "Why, Akim, don't you get involved with the work on Ablai-Khan?" I replied that there were enough were enough creative people working on this project. Then the president said: "So why then don't you work on Mustafa Chokai?" I agreed that the tragic figure of Chokai, his fate, his life, required a creative conception. But a lot of resources were needed for that. The President said, "Let that not worry you." And exactly a year later, the phone rang. .... He asked me how much time was needed for a script on Chokai. I said a year. He asked me whether it was impossible to do it in three months.[2]

President Nazarbayev is not the only head of state to take a political interest in cinema. According to Power and Crompton, "In October and November 2001 Pentagon officials began a series of meetings with Hollywood directors, screenwriters, scenarists and specialists in disaster movies to 'solicit the help of Hollywood in the war against terrorism and imagine possible future scenarios and responses to them. White House advisors also met with Hollywood executives to discuss the role of Hollywood in 'getting the right ideological message across not only to Americans, but also to the Hollywood public around the globe.'"[3] Cinema, particularly, Hollywood, works as what Power and Crompton call a 'celluloid fund of geopolitical knowledges'. These are popular knowledges as against the formal knowledge of academic discourse. The propagation of these knowledges is important for ideological purposes.

Nomad

One of the directors of *Nomad* was Sergei Bodrov who subsequently directed the historical epic *Mongol* (2007) on Chingiz Khan. The other two directors were the Czech émigré to the US—Ivan Passer, and Talgat Temenov from Kazakhstan. Ivan Passer gave up on the film half way through and Sergei Bodrov finished the film. Talgat Temenov made the Kazakh version. The film begins and ends with a statement by President Nazarbayev. It makes no pretense that it is not a film made to order by the government and by order of the President himself. Rustam Ibragimbekov, known in the US as the scriptwriter of Nikita Mikhalkov's *Burnt by the Sun* (which won the Oscar for Best Foreign Film) and the Soviet Eastern, *White Sun of the Desert* (Vladimir Motyl, 1969), has written the script.

Nomad is cast in the genre of an action film that is also a historical spectacle film. It draws on the genre of the 'Soviet Eastern' and attempts to make it national and global at the same time. It tells the tale of a Kazakh tribe that fights the Dzungars, a tribe from Mongolia. The child, Mansur, is saved by a master warrior Erali during an attack by the Dzungars on the mother and the group, while they were travelling. Erali brings up Mansur along with other children and trains them in fighting skills that will enable them to overthrow the Dzungars. The Kazakh President allotted US$ 32 million for the film from the state budget. Made at a cost of US$ 40 million, *Nomad* is the most expensive Kazakh film ever. The film, however, is reported to have recovered only US$ 79,123 in the US.[4] The sets of the 18th century Turkestan were created by the set director of *Gladia*tor, the Pole Krek Klyakovich, who has worked on almost all of Emir Kusturica's films and the art direction for the film was by the Italian Franco Fumogali, who has won twelve Oscars. Part of the shooting was by Ulrich Steiger, who has shot *Godzilla*. Documentary filmmaker and writer Asiya Baigozhina in her article 'Cinema in Central Asia Today' explains the link between politics and cinema in the 'need' to assemble such an international crew: "Kazakhstan, according to experts, is the leader among Central Asian countries. In all its initiatives, it aims at multi-vector cooperation. Cinema is no exception. Collaboration with foreign partners became the 'done' thing after *Nomad*, in which Americans, Europeans, and Russians worked together."[5] This impressive set of film professionals who worked on the film could not ensure its success. But then, films made on historical personages such as *Amir Timur* (Uzbekistan), *Dzhambul*, *Abai* (Kazakhstan), too were not really appreciated by audiences outside the post-Soviet space.

In Kazakhstan, reactions were mixed. The film was conceived as a 'blockbuster from above' with the President and State pumping in funds and using the services of some of the best known professionals in the field from all over the world to create an image of Kazakhstan. ('Blockbuster from above' is a paradoxical phrase, for blockbusters are only created by the audiences who flock to see a film, with the cash ringing at the box office). The lay responses to the film, as well as the more restrained academic viewpoints, point to different assessments of the film. While some opinions on internet discussions did reflect a positive appraisal, very pointed questions were asked by others. The weak plot, the unconvincing acting, the action scenes that lack punch, the fact that American actors play the main roles, the huge budget… all this and more come up for discussion. "What is expected of a pseudo historical film?... What is expected is: beautiful landscapes, historical settings, beautiful girls, good horse riders, battle scenes, some kind of moral values in the end and at least some kind of a plot," says Tagir. He goes on to state that while the first part of the film is satisfying, the ending disappoints since it does not have a fitting finale.[6] Status states, "I became interested in the film, not because of its *suzhet*, which is as banal as any epic about the heroism of one nation, but because I wanted to see how it looked."[7] Mukhtar has a more angry response: "It is shameful that Kazakhstan, having announced itself an independent state in the world arena, is promoting talentless American actors, with Kazakh money from oil and gas. This money had it been used to save children and old people who needed it from death would have helped the image of Kazakhstan more."[8] Another writer says, "What the actors from across the ocean—Jay Hernandez, Kuno Bekker, Mark Dacascos, and Jason Scott Lee—are doing in a historical film about Kazakhs is a rhetorical question. Hollywood Globalisation (Chinese play Japanese, Swedes play Russians and so on) has suffocated independent Kazakhstan …. People's heroes speak in English, and look like second-rate actors of Mexican descent."[9] These 'lay' opinions on the internet reflect the disappointment with the film that does not satisfy either at the level of narrative, or spectacle or even a sense of rudimentary nationhood, where people would like to see actors from their own country play the lead roles, since the film is about their past.

The artistic director of the Eurasia Film Festival and film scholar, Gulnara Abikeeva, states, "The film was made like a myth, like a fairy tale, a legend, and has almost no relation to the genre of historical. Yes, the action in the film covers the time of the war between Kazakhs and Dzungars and has known historical figures, but in reality, this is just fairy tale about a legendary hero who was born to defend his people and land. That is why all the dramatic scenes in the film have a distinctive mythological character."[10] In an interview on October 18, 2005, Rustam Ibragimbekov, in response to a question as to why American actors had to play the main roles, says: "It was just that I, with my experience of communicating with foreign producers, understood that even if a good and expensive film was made, without American actors and producers, foreign audiences are not going to watch it. … If Forman produces a film about Kazakhs, it may seem interesting. Of course, there is the danger of stylization, but if you want that your film is watched in the world, you cannot do without the Americans."[11] The intention, therefore, was to make a film that would make the world take notice of Kazakhstan. The route to this was via Hollywood. Governments have done this before. The most successful attempt in this regard has been Ang Lee's *Crouching Tiger, Hidden Dragon* (2000), which is set in a mythical past and changed the rules of spectacle and action in Hollywood, while at the same time drawing attention to Taiwan, as a distinct country among the three Chinas. Ang Lee had studied cinema in the US and had made films that had been noticed prior to this; but, it was his use of Chinese martial arts for the creation of spectacle that made history. In this case, the makers of the film assumed that the nomad and his lifestyle would attract viewers. Ibragimbekov states that everybody knows what cowboys, gladiators, and samurai are. However, few people know who the nomads were, despite the fact that nomads rode horses like cowboys, fought like gladiators, and wielded the cold blade with as much virtuosity as the samurai. Spectacle, however, has to have an ideological component, which consists of the larger geopolitical positionings[12] as well as the cinematic framework in which there are bigger and greater returns of spectacle and action. *Nomad* was unable to serve up anything new on both counts. Beautiful panoramic scenes, with horses galloping gracefully across the large expanses of the steppes, are not enough to draw audiences internationally—intellectually, emotionally, or aesthetically.

The last scene in the film is a crucial one, relating this tale from the past to the present, creating a bridge in time frames. It also serves to posit this region as being scientifically advanced and forward-looking. Messengers come to the local king with a round object. "Is this someone's head?" asks the king. "No, an image of the earth which has been created by Ulugbek. This is called a globe," replies the messenger. "This is the city of Tienshan, and here are the Afghans and Hindus. And this is the land of the Ka-za-khs. A huge country," he continues. Ablai Khan has sent a message with the globe about the land of the Kazakhs: "Whoever thinks that that this land can be taken will … be drowned in his own blood. And our many neighbours whichever side they belong to, should know this. We are open to all who come to us with friendship, but we will be ruthless towards our enemies." As the king starts reading the message, images of Ablai Khan and his followers riding across the steppes appear, with the men and horses dissolving into light. When the film ends, a message from the President appears, marking the smooth transition from Ablai Khan to the present leader, drawing on Eurasianism as well as Mackinder's 'heartland' theory: "Between the East and West, there is the heart of the Eurasian continent, on the crossroads of world civilisations is the ancient land of the Kazakhs. For thousands of years we fought for our independence. … Independence is our blessed value that we must treasure. This has been handed down to us by our brave ancestors, *nomads* of the great steppe." The aim of the film is, thus, clearly to posit the identity of Kazakhs territorially, as well as politically.

Mustafa Chokai

Satybaldy Narymbetov's film focuses on a political leader, Mustafa Chokai (1890-1941) who was seen as a traitor during the Soviet period, and is now sought to be seen as a national hero. The scriptwriters Ermek Tursunov (writer and historian), Akim Tarazai (a Kazakh dramatist), and Sergei Bodrov (filmmaker) have tried to encapsulate 'the other history', a history that was not officially approved of during Soviet times. Chokai was not only a leader of Turkestan opposed to the Soviet Union, who believed in pan-Turkism, but was also a collaborator with Hitler, during World War II in the attempt to create a legion of Central Asian prisoners. The film is based on the memoirs of his wife Maria Gorina Chokai. "Generally, the film *Mustafa Chokai* reminds you a lot of *Admiral* by Alexander Kolchak. Possibly, more than anything else because in both films, the contradictory personality is shown from the point of view of women who love them. And as it happens, simultaneously painted the Bolsheviks in black."[13] The Nazis, in fact, appear in the film as more urbane and sophisticated; the Bolsheviks are coarse and manipulative. Pan-Turkism arose as a movement against russification and Russian expansionism and the pan-Slavic ideology in the late 19th and the early 20th century.[14] The Turkish-speaking people are the Soviet Union's most numerous ethnic group after the Slavs, forming nearly one-tenth of the population of the USSR. The Russian Revolution in 1917 and the dissolution of the Ottoman Empire in 1918 gave further impetus to this ideology.

Mustafa Chokai was born in the Turkestan Krai of the Russian Empire. He was an important player in the historical events at the time of the Revolution. He was member of the Muslim Council, *Shura-i-Islamiya*, the leader of the Provisional Government of Autonomous Turkestan (the Kokand Autonomous Government from November 27, 1917 to February 18, 1918) and delegate to the Orenburg Congress where Alash Orda the first Kazakh political party was created. At 26, Chokai had become a representative of the Muslim faction of the State Duma in the Czarist Russia. Kazan traders supported him on a Kazan seat, because he could not be elected as a Kazakh since Kazakhs and Kyrgyz were considered 'wild' *nomadic* peoples and had no representation in the Duma.

There were at least three main lines of debates in the first decades of the twentieth century in the region: the ideas of the Jadids, the Muslim Communists, the Europeanised secular intellectuals, and the Bolsheviks themselves. As Adeeb Khalid points out, "In choosing to wage his struggles in the sphere of politics rather than cultural reform, Chokai was of the secular intellectuals, whose activities went on in parallel with that of the Jadids. We find little evidence of interaction between the two groups before 1917. The Jadids represented the modernization of the Muslim cultural tradition of Central Asia; the secular intellectuals were fluent in the idiom of European thought. The Jadids spoke to Muslim society in order to achieve cultural change; the secular intellectuals spoke to the Russian state and Russian society in order to achieve political change."[15] These differences between the various positions on nationalism in the political arena are not charted out in the film. It posits Chokai as the leading figure of the time and creates a binary opposition between those who opposed Soviet rule and those who did not.

Chokai's writings give an indication of his very distinctive political positions at the time. Discussing, for instance, of the Regional Moslem Council after the fall of the Provisional Government that was held in Kokand, the industrial centre of Fergana region, Chokai says, "Additionally I considered, that power in Turkestan should be based not on soviets of workers' and soldiers' deputies, but on soviets of peasants' and workers' deputies. The exclusion of the of soldiers' (or Red Army) deputies was motivated by the fact that the soldiers in the Turkestan garrisons were not natives of the region and had no interest in civilian life in Turkestan; they could easily be swayed by propaganda inimical to the interests of the population. The experience of the preceding period had given us plenty of grounds for distrusting the 'revolutionary fraternity' of Russian soldiers. They had terrorized the Moslem population of the region to such an extent that many places sent in requests to 'restore the power of the former police officers and *volost* administrations.'"[16]

Mustafa Chokai hoped for a autonomous Turkestan under Soviet rule, but realized the impossibility of his position. Writing on the Constituent Assembly meeting convened by the Soviet Government on January 05, 1918, which the Turkestanis did not attend, he states:

> "At its only session the Constituent Assembly passed a law declaring Russia to be a federative republic, and early on the morning of 6 January it was dispersed by the Bolsheviks. Thus, the Constituent Assembly, on which the hopes of all the peoples of Russia had been pinned, perished. It perished, we must assume, forever. And with it, all our 'federative dreams' passed on to eternity. We set out on the road of struggle for

complete national liberation, for a free independent Turkestan, for the creation of a single Turkish State of Turkestan."[17]

There is, as we see, a development within his thinking in relation to historical circumstances, from being open to having workers and peasant representatives in the soviets to a rejection of it in favour of a State of Turkestan, evidenced in his writings, that in missing in the film. The protagonist of the film emerges as someone who is hostile to the Bolsheviks and is inflexible in his views. The film also picks up certain events to highlight, but the links are not clear. Michael Rouland, for instance, points out, "The conflation of two events, the fall of Kokand Autonomy movement to a Bolshevik military assault on Kokand and a Kazakh political movement that was divided over the question of alliance with the Bolsheviks, is never explained in the film."[18]

Chokai's collaboration with Hitler, too, is viewed uncritically. Narymbetov presents Chokai more as a man who wanted to 'save' the Central Asians who were taken as prisoners of war, rather than as a 'collaborator' with the Nazis. Of the approximately one to 1.5 million Soviet prisoners and émigrés who collaborated with the Third Reich, roughly one to three lakhs were Soviet Muslims. "Of these, between 70,000 and 1,80,000 are believed to have served in the Turkestan Legion or one of its spin-off units in the Wehrmacht. The Turkestan Legion grouped together not only Turkic soldiers from Central Asia but Tajiks as well. Some 8,000 Soviet Muslims also served in the Osttürkische Waffen-Verband and Neu-Türkistan, two Pan-Turkic SS units formed in late 1944."[19] The Turkestan Legion was formed after Chokai died by Veli Kayum[20]. According to Bruno de Cordier, "Contrary to what some propose, the Turkestan Legion was not an Islamist or a 'Jihadi' outfit. Its leadership and political wing did use Islamic symbols and had chaplain imams, but they were secular Turkic nationalists rather than religious zealots. The blueprint for a 'liberated Turkestan', for which the legion was to form the core of the armed forces after the USSR's dissolution, foresaw a republican and secular system, not a religious regime or emirate."[21]

Mustafa Chokai is neither a biopic nor a historical film. Historical films deal with an era and provide a panoramic and macro view on personages of import to the era as well. A biographical film on a historical personage focuses on the individual, inserting him into a larger historical context on the one hand, and providing an eye view into his interiority, and details of his personal life on the other. *Mustafa Chokai* fails to capture the protagonist's inner struggle, or the development of his ideas; it also fails to show the organic link between Chokai and his milieu, at home or abroad. This is not to imply that there are no spectacles to evoke the 'big events' of the time: the attack by the Bolsheviks on Kokand, the famine, the meeting of the Alash Orda.... The attempt at historical spectacle is there; what is lacking is the organic, live link between the person and the historical time of which he was an integral part. The script and direction create as it were two parallel lines of plot development, where Chokai and history move separately, and 'meet' at certain points. Needless to say, these 'meetings' between the man and history encapsulate the 'highpoints' chosen by the scriptwriters and director. The 'meetings' in which Chokai may be present (as in the Alash Orda meeting, or the meeting with Hitler and Ribbentrop) or in which Chokai is absent (as in the meeting Stalin has with his henchmen, in which he discusses with Yezhov the need to eliminate Chokai), do not further emotionally or intellectually saturate the image of Chokai for us. The scriptwriters and director fail to create a psychological portrait of a man, who is constantly referred to as a great leader of Turkestan, as a man whose word is heeded by the people, who seems to have no desire or power to negotiate the various turns of history. All postulates about Chokai are 'givens'—the viewer has to accept them. The man, whom Stalin is supposed to have feared and Hitler wanted to use to help in the fall of Soviet power in Central Asia, is never portrayed as being engaged in ideas or debating them. He has his view that he espouses in an almost historical way. The link between the people of whom he is said to be the leader is never shown. The film focuses on the relationship between Chokai and his wife in a maudlin way. Their troubles and persecution are more referred to than shown. Marina Gorina says in the course of the film that we are leading a vagabond life, but the images show us that they are pretty much grounded in Paris. As Michael Rouland puts it, "This is a big budget, professional film, supported by the Kazakh government. But the message is decidedly problematic. *Mustafa Chokai* is a mix of historical confusion and deliberate revisionism."[22]

Imagined Communities

How do the two films discussed above insert themselves into the discourses of the nation? Kazakhstan is going through its own kind of post-nationalism, as are other countries of the former Soviet Union. This post-nationalism is very different from the post-nationalism of globalization theorised by Arjun Appadorai and others. This is the post-nationalism of post-socialism which differs from the former in that the dominant construct here was the supranational Soviet identity. In the latter, the supranational identity only has a residual status. In the emergent identities, several discourses jostle for space: western, Soviet, ethnic, religious, Kazakh-nationalist. In the imaginary of different classes and communities—the working class, the cosmopolitan citizens, the traditionalists, the dissidents—there is an amalgamation of nostalgia and a forward-looking gaze. The immediate post-independence phase also saw the rise of the ideology of pan-Turkism; later, however, Eurasianism asserted itself as an equal if not dominant ideology. All these elements of what Alexander Motyl calls the 'identity repertoire' are further hierarchised according to the axis of urban/aul and official/people tendencies. The post-nationalism of postsocialism, thus has less to do with the deterritorialisation of the diaspora and its imaginings as it is in the case of the post-nationalism of globalisation. It has more to do with the reterritorialisation of the sense of the nation that has shrunk from the supranational Soviet space into that of the national. The dictum of socialist realism, 'National in form, socialist in content' does not hold any longer. What we witness in cultural production are hybrids in which global/local forms and content mingle.

An emerging particularist identity formation under Tsarist times, basing itself on ethnicity and religion, had been replaced by a specific kind of civic nationalism that privileged ethnic identity that had persevered through transformations in successive social formations. There is, since independence, a 'return' to particularist nationalist discourses. Of course, this return is not a simple one, since socialism has intervened in between. To borrow a phrase from Motyl once again, there is a strategic hierarchisation of identities. "There are only two ways of accounting for the hierarchy of the limited number of actions. First, it might be that some identities are more intensely held or felt or rooted than others, and it might then be the case that we act on just those more intensely held identities. Second, it might be that some identities are more prone to activation by the context or the interrogator. The result in both cases is a strategic heirarchisation of identities."[23] In both cases, Motyl adds there is a choice by the subject; discourses do not hierarchise on their own.

Both the films that have been discussed in this article raise the question of identity and the issue of the nation. *Nomad*, for instance, posits a 'secular ethnic' identity for the Kazakhs based on a way of life (that is nomadism), while giving it the spatial framework of the steppes (a geographical identity motif, woven together horses and tents as 'way-of-life' motifs). The 'Self' are the clans and tribes that have to be united; the 'Other', are the Dzungars. The land of the Kazakhs has belonged to them since time immemorial; it 'enters' history through the *nomads* and Ablai Khan; the baton of power is transferred to the present State and leadership. *Mustafa Chokai*, on the other hand, is aimed at a different audience, and proffers an identity that is ethnic, but in the hierarchy of which, the 'Turkic' identity is dominant, rather than religion. Both films are born of the urban, rather than the 'aul' impulse and both in different ways, look westwards. *Nomad*, in its ideological project of attracting a global audience, had foreign actors in main roles of the 'good guys' and the villains and secondary characters who looked Central Asian. This paradoxically, did not allow the local audiences to invest emotionally in the characters, or to identify with them; the global audiences found nothing new in terms of either spectacle, or action or theme or acting, which was barely passable. The makers of Chokai, too, did not place the finger on the pulse of the identity repertoire they could tap correctly. Chokai could not pass off easily as a tragic figure, and his martyrology could not be sustained. One of the main reasons could probably be that the Second World War, called the Great Patriotic War by the Soviet people is still a historical event whose signification has not passed into ambivalence as so many other historical events over the last century have. While the new imaginings of the Central Asian nations may reject the Bolshevik Revolution, they cannot easily square up Chokai's collaboration with Hitler and his men, to supposedly 'save' thousands of Central Asian Muslims. The official ideology of Eurasianism, too, does not dovetail easily with the Pan-Turkism that Chokai subscribed to. If cinema functions as a popular fund of geopolitical knowledge it has to create a forceful sense of 'us' and 'them', which has some resonance in the dominant political discourses of the day, which *Nomad* and *Chokai* do so with varying degrees of success. Both films, however, do testify to the ways in which Kazakhstan is trying to position itself distinctively in the Central Asian region as well as in the world.

Notes

1. *Natsiostroitelstvo v Kazakhstane i Drugikh Stranakh Tsentralnoi Azii*, Gulnara Abikeeva, Almaty, OF TSTSAK, 2006, p. 283.
2. '*Moi Prezident*', Interview with Akim Tarazi' in *Kazakhstanskaya Pravda*, December 22, 2009.
3. Marcus Power and Andrew Crompton (eds.), *Cinema and Popular Geopolitics*, (London: Routledge, 2007), p. 1.
4. Wikipedia entry on *Nomad*.
5. '*Kino v Tsentralnoi Azii Segodnya*', Asiya Baigozhina in the volume *Kino v Tsentralnoi Azii*, (Almaty: Goethe Institut).
6. Tagir, Comments in response to Stanislav Nikulin's review of *Nomad* on Kinomania.ru, September 20, 2006.
7. Status, Comments in reponse to Stanislav Nikulin's review of *Nomad* on Kinomania.ru, September 09, 2006.
8. Comments in response to Stanislav Nikulin's review of *Nomad* on Kinomania.ru, November 19, 2006.
9. Review of *Nomad* by Stanislav Nikulin on Kinomania.ru.
10. Gulnara Abikeeva, *Natsiostroitelstvo v Kazakhstane i Drugikh Stranakh Tsentralnoi Azii*, (Almaty, OF TSTSAK, 2006), p. 283.
11. From www.fergana.ru
12. This film, according to other reports, was brought by Nazarbayev for screening

during his visit to the US as part of the counterpropaganda to the film *Borat: Kulturnoe Izucheniye Ameriki na Polzu Slavnoi Natsii Kazakhstane* by the MTV comic Sasha Baron Cohen. Borat Sagdyev, the protagonist of this film goes to California in search of Pamela Anderson and this journey is an excuse to inform viewers about Kazakhstan: a land of peace and progress, where people drink horse's milk, and homosexuals only until recently had to wear blue caps and the prostitutes were the cleanest from Central Asia. *Nomad* was meant to 'set right' people's perception of Kazakhstan. *Nursultan Nazarbayev Skupaet Imidzh Kazakhstana na Americanskikh Telekanalakh*, 'Kommersant', September 27, 2006, p. 11. The article has been accessed from zona.kz on January 30, 2011.

13. Olga Khrabrykh, 'Zaklyaty Drug, Predanny Vrag', Express-K.KZ, No. 221 (16607), November 22, 2008.
14. Another movement was that of Pan-Turanism which preached the unity among Turkish, Mongol and Hungarian peoples in an anti-Slav collaboration.
15. Adeeb Khalid, *The Politics of Muslim Cultural Reform: Jadidism in Central Asia*, (Oxford: Oxford University Press, 2000), p. 106.
16. Source: S V Tyutkin et al, *Oktyabrskaya Revolyutsia – ot novykh istochnikov k novomu osmysleniyu*, Institut Rossiskoi Istorii, (Moscow, RAN, 1998), pp 429-435 (Accessed from the internet).
17. Source: S V Tyutkin et al, *Oktyabrskaya Revolyutsia – ot novykh istochnikov k novomu osmysleniyu*, Institut Rossiskoi Istorii, (Moscow, RAN, 1998), pp 429-435 (Accessed from the internet).
18. Michael Rouland, 'Satybaldy Narymbetov: Mustafa Shokai (2008)', *Kinokultura*, Issue 25, 2009, (Accessed from the internet).
19. 'The Shadow of the Legionaries', Bruno de Cordier, from www.caucacus.com, Conflict Research Group, Gent, July 16, 2009.
20. The aim of the Turkestan Legion was to bring together Turkmens, Uzbeks, Kazakhs, Kirgyz, Karakalpaks and Dagestanis. The Caucasus – Mohammedan Legion was to bring together Azeerbaijanis, Dagestanis, Ingush, Lezhins, Chechens. There were also the Georgian Legion, Armenian Legion, and North Caucasian Legion and Volga-Tatar Legion.
21. 'The Shadow of the Legionaries', Bruno de Cordier, from www.caucacus.com, Conflict Research Group, Gent, July 16, 2009.
22. Michael Rouland, 'Satybaldy Narymbetov: *Mustafa Chokai* (2008)'.
23. Alexander Motyl, 'The Social Construction of Social Construction: Implications for Theories of Nationalism and Identity Formation', *Nationalities Papers*, vol. 38, no. 1, January 2010, pp. 59-72.

17. State Initiatives and Activities of the Fund Forum in the Cultural Sphere

Dilorom Karomat

The disintegration of the Soviet Union, the importance of drifting away from 'sovietisation'[1] of culture, and the need to be a part of the globalisation process[2] placed before Uzbekistan a number of challenges and the search for priorities towards further development of culture. The state often plays a decisive role in the development of a culture. It is well known that culture is only one piece of the puzzle, which plays a hugely important role in state activities. Uzbekistan is a state that contains multiple cultures and subcultures, which are divided among five cultural zones—Bukhara-Samarkand, Ferghana-Tashkent, Khorezm, Surkhandarya-Kashkadarya and Republic of Karakalpakstan—with multinational population. Some of them are completely different from each other. In this case, culture plays an important role for uniting the nations and ethno groups, for better understanding among them. Thus, a symbiosis of national and universal values has been highlighted as a rough guide in cultural policy. The interaction of cultures promotes enrichment and mutual understanding between nations. The historical and archaeological *heritage* becomes the symbol for uniting the society in quest of new cultural and spiritual values. Based on century old *traditions* the culture of modern Uzbekistan has found new sides and directions. It has taken new directions for expanding cooperation on the international scene.[3] Uzbek musicologist Prof. Natalia Yanov-Yanovskaya said the following about affinity, but not identity of such categories as 'heritage' and 'tradition':

> "'Heritage' is something that already finished its own crystallization somewhere in the past, 'tradition' is the reality, which also has come

> from the past, but still continuing the development in the present. It is possible to tell, apparently: if 'heritage' is a result of certain creative process, the 'tradition' is [this] process itself, i.e. continuous updating of the initial beginning, the 'tradition' is always in a way… however we must point out that the verge between them is very mobile and flexible and sometime it is difficult to understand it [to discover it]…" [4]

The history of development of culture and art particularly, is always the process of constant development of tastes and purposes, which depend on the requirement of the time. Traditions can survived only in conditions of constant development and if it is open to innovation. It is necessary, that the present should have strong communication with the historical roots for preserving identity. Actually, for several reasons, the natural development of traditional culture has been interrupted in the first half of the 20th century. Therefore, the modern process of imitation of the old heritage with the purpose of restoration or 'return' to tradition is quite natural in independent Uzbekistan. The latter results in a problem like of 'tradition vs. innovation'. The well-known Uzbek researcher of applied arts Dr. Elmira Gyul emphasises the importance of both ways of development:

> "We are convinced that both ways of development are important. On the one hand for example, the strict imitation of initial drawings of Nurata's embroideries had an effect of a breath of fresh air. At last! We have seen the modern embroidery, which is made in purely classical style and with observance of all necessary technology and specificity of drawing! On the other hand a miniature painter N. Holmatov … categorically denies the imitation of a medieval miniature. He goes further by creating his own modern artistic language of expression based on structural principles and rules of space and form in the miniature. Therefore, both imitation and innovation based on fundamental traditional principles are equally important today, and should not be opposed to each other."[5]

The Activities of Funds and NGOs as an Important Component in Cultural Development

The international and domestic funds and organisations, which are supporting the development of traditions in modern Uzbekistan, are an important component of this process. However, there are cases when the commercial approach and/or the lack of knowledge assume dominance leading to prejudice against traditional ethno culture by 'promoting' something different. For example, under the pretext of 'revival of the heritage', various pseudo-oriental items are being produced on a commercial scale, which mainly address mainstream tourist tastes. In this case, the problem of the preservation of traditional art becomes most acute.

The specialised editions and several magazines carrying the popularisation and the scientific analysis of the country's cultural and artistic processes and events over the past 20 years are *Teatr*, *Moziydan sado*, *San'at* (edition of the Academy of Art), *Jannat Makon*, *Bella Terra*, and various independent online editions. Various seminars, meetings and colloquiums of experts[6] on cultural topics and numerous academic publications are aimed at achieving a number of important objectives—assessing prevailing tendencies and problems, looking into the quest for national identity and ways for their interaction with worldwide values, and to arrive at conclusions based on achievements of previous years and provide recommendations for future socio-cultural development. The basic directions of development of culture are defined in the Decrees of the President of Uzbekistan (for example, an establishments of the state National Agency *Uzbekkino*, the reorganisation of musical education, the activity of Institutes of Culture and Art), and in the Decisions of Cabinet of Ministers (like the measures on development of national dance and a choreography and other documents).

Various Funds and NGOs[7] play an important role in the process of revival of the heritage and traditional values along with the state organizations and the representations of foreign countries (Embassies, the cultural centres etc.).[8] *The Forum of Culture and Arts of Uzbekistan Foundation (the Fund)* is considered most influential among them.

It has been seven years since the establishment of the Fund Forum in February 2004[9]. A great deal has been achieved during this period; the organisation has been extending its activities far beyond the original concept of reviving Uzbekistan's traditional, cultural, and artistic heritage. The foundation projects and grants thoroughly promote and support the development of science and culture, education, and sport. The Fund also serves as a guide for the original culture of Uzbekistan globally and making the world aware of the modern achievements of the people of Uzbekistan. The activities of the Fund promote cultural dialogue and mutual understanding among nations. The grand projects of the Fund, among others, include:

Yangi Avlod Children's Creativity Festival (since 2004)
Uzbek Art Evenings in Moscow (since 2004)
Navqiron O'zbekiston Festival (once in two years) (since 2004)
Bazar-Art Exhibition-Fair (twice in a year, since 2005)
Kelajak ovozi Talented Youth Contest (since 2005)
M&TVA award ceremony of music, TV and video art (since 2006)
Art Week Style uz. (since 2006)
Bolajonlar-Shirintoylar Children's Fashion Festival (since 2007)
Kichkintoy (Baby) International Children's Tournament (since 2008)
Yil Ayoli (Woman of the Year) National Contest (since 2008)
Charity Ball *Vo imya detstva* (In the Name of Childhood; since 2008)
Asrlar Sadosi (Echo of Centuries) Festival of Traditional Culture (since 2008)
International Contemporary Choreography and Sporting Dance Contest (since 2009)
*Vo imya jizni (*In the Name of Life) Charitable Marathon (since 2010)
Theatre.UZ International Theatre Festival (since 2010)
Zolotoy Guepard (Golden Cheetah) Cinema Forum (since 2011)

The Projects of the Fund Forum for Young Generation

Most of the projects of the Fund addressed the needs of the youth. This choice is explained by the fact that over 62 per cent of the population of Uzbekistan is young under the age of 30. Harmonious, well-educated young generation is a powerful and stable foundation for the country's sustainable and progressive development in the future. Therefore, the upbringing of the educated youth and the preparation of Uzbekistan's new generation of professionals became a priority of state policy since the earliest days of independence. Most of the projects aimed to activate creativity and give to the youth a life full of various cultural activities and events. The purposeful state policy on supporting talented children and education of youth has been reflected in the activity of the Fund Forum. The grants for talented children, concerts and master classes, various thematic exhibitions of drawings of children and other events, most of them became the most cheerful events of the country. One of the first projects of the Fund Forum, which is dedicated to Children's Creativity named *Yangi Avlod*. This festival held in Uzbekistan since 2004, and later, received the status of state level event. From 2004 to 2011, more than 98 thousand children from all of Uzbekistan became participants of Festival. The Complex for Education, Healthcare, and Social Protection of Uzbekistan's Cabinet of Ministers, headed by Deputy Prime Minister Abdulla Oripov, honoured the Fund Forum with a Certificate 'For Discovering Young Talents' through its *Yangi Avlod* Project. Other grand projects for children are the Festival of a children's fashion named *Bolajonlar-shirintoylar*, the children's international tournament *Kichkintoy* ('Baby'), children's superiority on rhythmic gymnastics *Snezhinka* and charity ball *Vo imia detstva*.

The prize *Nihol* (prize of the President of the Republic of Uzbekistan) for gifted youth in the field of Art was founded in August 2000 and the award ceremony is conducted annually before Independence Day.[10] Since 2005, the Fund Forum has been conducting one of the most known Youth Contests named *Kelajak ovozi*, which obtained a state status in two years after the commencement. It is held annually under the auspices of the Ministry of Education of the Republic of Uzbekistan in all educational institutions over the country. From the beginning till now, the project has captured 3,09,000 participants from all parts of Uzbekistan. The project has been declared the best youth project in 2010 by the United Nations Information Centre in Uzbekistan (UNIC) and the Fund of the United Nations in the Field of the Population (UNFPA). In 2006, the Youth Initiatives Center (YIC) *Kelajak ovozi* was founded, which brings together all winners of various youth projects of the Fund Forum, including the Programme of educational grants, the Programme of grants for gifted students, and the Republican competition of gifted youth *Kelajak ovozi*. Nowadays, the Youth Initiatives Center is organising educational projects aimed to youth development in eight directions in all regions of the country.

The international conference on education in Tashkent was initiated by the President Islam Karimov in February 2012 named '*Fostering a Well Educated and Intellectually Advanced Generation as a Crucial Prerequisite for Sustainable Development and Modernization of the Country*'. The Fund Forum was among the main organisers and participants of the conference. Uzbek journalist Eldar Rakhmatullayev in his article *Investments into the Future* wrote:

> "It was impossible to achieve sustainable development in Uzbekistan without fundamental restructuring and reforming the educational system which existed for years. Two laws "On education" and "On the national program for training" were deeply though-out during drafting and adopted in 1997 became the platform for gradual reforming of our education system. In his speech at the international conference Fostering a Well Educated and Intellectually Advanced Generation as a Crucial Prerequisite for Sustainable Development and Modernization of the Country President of Uzbekistan Islam Karimov said: "The program, itself is a product of an in-depth research and study, summary of the practice hoarded by advanced nations, aims to completely eliminate stereotypes and dogmas of the communist ideology imposed in the past, consolidation of democratic values in the minds of people, first and foremost among the growing generation. In a word, the program is directed at nurturing a comprehensively advanced individual with independence in thinking and outlook, with its own preferences and firm civic position in life."[11]

Currently, Uzbekistan has 9,797 schools, about 6,000 pre-school and after-school educational institutions, 1,537 professional colleges and academic lyceums, 59 higher education institutions and 11 branches in regions along with 6 branches of the leading foreign universities, centres and institutes of training and retraining of specialists. Several grants were established by several Uzbek scholarships (for example, Fund Ulugbek, Umid, Kamolot), which help talented young people study in prestigious foreign education centers and universities. As was already mentioned the Fund Forum also has several grants, which are named the '*Educational Grants and Program of Scholarships for the Gifted Students*. If the aim of *Educational Grants*' is to fund their tuition expenses, then '*the Program of Scholarships for the Gifted Students*' is directed to encourage and support talented and active students of third and fourth courses.[12] Children with limited possibilities are also eligible for applying. In 2006, for example, the Fund Forum has started the socially significant project named *Inkliuzivnoe obrazovanie*, which has allowed getting the general education at ordinary schools to more then 600 disabled children. In addition, a number of training centers were created in various towns of Uzbekistan on traditional applied art in traditional system *Usto-shogird*. They provide quality leisure time for young people as well equip them with a useful skill they can benefit from in the future.

Traditional Art

Nowadays, traditional art occupies one of the most important places in the sociocultural space of the Republic. Therefore, the state gives particular attention to the support and development of the ethno cultural values, traditional crafts, and trade. All projects on support and revival of traditional art are part of government programs. Currently, this list includes the jewellery and metal art, sewing by gold, decorative embroidery, textile printing, silk weaving, carpet weaving, miniature lacquer painting [varnish miniature], work on a skin, ceramics (known by location as Gizhduvani and Rishton's schools), woodcarving and carving on *ganch*, the creation and decorative processing of musical instruments and many other things. In 1996 the International welfare fund *Oltin Meros*[13] was created. It has become one of the first organisations aimed at undertaking measures for restoration of the lost crafts and applied art and for preservation of unique items of historical and a cultural heritage. One of the main tasks has been an informational portal, which makes the world community acquainted with national culture and art of Independent Uzbekistan. A lot has been done for creating proper conditions for training young masters. The Research and Manufacturing Centre *Musavvir* was created in 1997 and the Republican Specialist Art Manufacturing Association *Usto*. Through the effort of these organisations, almost extinct crafts have been revived. The Decree of the President of the Republic named *On Measures of State Support to the Further Development of Traditional Crafts and Applied Arts* (March 31, 1997) one of the most important documents in a series of measures aimed at preserving the tradition. Based on the Decree, it was also decided to create an association of Uzbekistan's traditional craftsmen *Hunarmand* under the *Musavvir* RMC. These centres have established organisational networks in all provinces of the country. Valuable contribution to the revival of crafts has also been made by the Business Women's Association of Uzbekistan *Tadbirkor Oila.*[14] Since its establishment, the Fund Forum has been a leader in this area.

The measures taken by the government has raised the social status of artists and craftsmen working in traditional art, and created economic benefits to support their activities. For example, the republican contest *Tashabbus* gives an annual award *Yil Ustasi* (Craftsman of the Year). A number of other events and activities in field of applied arts shows the great interest of a government-level administration in relation to traditional arts. In the way of economic support, artisans were granted a 5-year exemption from income tax and customs duties on export sale of traditional crafts. To encourage the status of the artists, the government established an honorary title *Uzbekiston Respublikasi Khalq Ustasi.* Significant contribution to supporting traditional heritage is made by public organisations through their projects. The 11th anniversary of the Independence of the country was celebrated in the Central showroom of the Academy of Arts, where the first Republican youth exhibition named

Navkiron Uzbekiston[15] took place. One of the earlier projects of the Fund Forum since 2004 aimed to supporting young artists and masters of applied art was a festival of traditional and modern art *Navkiron Uzbekiston.* Once in two years, this festival has been organised jointly with the Academy of Arts of Uzbekistan. This festival gives a chance to young artists to discover themselves in all spheres of modern and traditional art and allows the wide public to be acquainted with young masters more closely. The motto of the *Navkiron O'zbekiston* is: "The modern view of traditional arts of Uzbekistan!" Therefore, over 700 artists and masters of applied art participated in the project during the period of 2006-10, and over 2,600 works were exhibited. As part of the festival, *Navkiron Uzbekiston,* various master classes of domestic artists, designers, critics of art and researchers take place. For instance, the master classes were conducted in 2010 by such reputable masters as Akmal Azlarov (the national master of Uzbekistan, the woodcarver) called 'Woodcarving' and Alisher and Akbar Rahimovs called 'Ceramics'.[16] Besides, the Fund Forum conducts exhibitions of traditional and modern art during the festivals *Art Week Style.uz*, *Bazar-Art*, *Ashlar Sadosi* and exhibition-fair the *Mehr Nur*, which are recognised as memorable events. Among them are the exhibition 'Travel to the miniature world' of Bahodyr and Behzod Hadzhimetovs' (2010),[17] the exhibition 'an eternity Tree' of Tashkent school of a carving by Ortiq Fayzullaev, the festival of the *khan-atlas* (2011), etc. Within the *Bazar-Art*, the Fund presented grants to craftsmen, who became laureates of the exhibition. The grants were aimed to further development of the handicrafts, revival of disappearing kinds of applied arts and traditional forms of arts in Uzbekistan.[18]

One of the grand projects of the Fund Forum is the *Asrlar Sadosi*. This is the Festival of Traditional Culture, which since 2008 annually presents all the diversity of the national traditions and customs, handicrafts and cuisine, unique oral and non-material heritage. *Ashlar Sadosi* is held in different regions of Uzbekistan in historical or cultural centres.[19] This year, the Festival was held in Republic of Karakalpakstan. One of the events, which took place was an opening of workshop for making traditional musical instruments. It has been inaugurated in Nukus, the capital of Karakalpakstan, under the auspices of the UNESCO Tashkent Office, Fund Forum, and the Korean Trust Fund.[20] The Practical seminar was led by Master Azat Otarbayev. He shared with the audience how clay, leather, and reeds can be used to create traditional musical instruments (part of Karakalpakstan's unique culture and crafts). He said:

> "I make traditional music instruments such as kobyz, dutar as well as wind instruments. I want to emphasize that the opening of this workshop is like a dream come true. I've had a passion for making the instruments since I was a boy and I learned the tricks of this trade from my grandfathers. I want to say a big thank you to the organizers who made this event possible as well as for the opportunity to teach skills to young people. At the seminar which will run till May 15 I will be talking about three national music instruments. And I will continue teaching skills to youngsters after the event. A true master must know not only how to make instruments but also how to play them. This will help him to make really good and high-quality instruments. I can't imagine living without music instruments and this is why the opening of this workshop is so important for me."[21]

The unique organisations like *Centre of National Arts* (2007)[22], *Meros* (Association of Antiques of Uzbekistan, established in 2008)[23] and *Ijod* (Associations of artists, critics and national masters of Uzbekistan, established in 2009)[24] are also associated with activity of the Fund Forum for preserving cultural heritage.

The cause of reviving traditional crafts still actively engages international foundations and organizations interested in developing tourism and supporting the economy of the post-soviet nations. One of the traditional forms of study '*Usto – shogird*' (from the master to the pupil) has been belittled in Soviet period, but not interrupted. Thanks to the support of the state and various domestic and international Funds, after independence the skill of the Uzbek handicraftsmen has got stronger and has found recognition abroad. For example, the Indian newspaper *The Indian Express* has published an article '*For Humayun's*

Sake, Samarkand Comes to Delhi with a Secret'. This article is dedicated to Uzbek masters, who are taking part in the reconstruction of a world famous monument, an architectural masterpiece of Baburid (Great Moguls) times—the tombs of Humayun. *The Indian Express* reports:

> "The tile-work is a complex, traditional art form in Uzbekistan, passed down from generations. So from the time they arrived in Delhi this February, architect Farkhod Bagirov and craftsmen Namandjon Mavlyanov, Kurbon Melikov and Bakhodurkhuja Rakhmatov have been working with the local conservation team to get those exact shades of green, lapis blue, turquoise blue, yellow and white on the tiles. "The artisans have picked up the skill from their forefathers and have over 40 years of experience in traditional tile-making. We have worked at the historic sites of Registan Square in Samarkand, Gur-e-Amir, Bibi Khanum Mosque. However, working here is a new challenge altogether. It is an overwhelming experience to recreate what the great rulers had originally made," Farkhod told The Sunday Express. As part of a larger urban renewal project in the greater Nizamuddin area, the Aga Khan Trust for Culture (AKTC) is undertaking conservation works on the World Heritage Site of Humayun's Tomb in partnership with the Archaeological Survey of India (ASI) and co-funding from the Sir Dorabji Tata Trust. Though craft traditions survive in India, AKTC discovered that the tile-making tradition of the Mughals had long been abandoned. A persistent research programme saw craftsmen being called from Uzbekistan and experimenting for six months."[25]

The workshops, which are engaged in process of the restoration works doing the hard work on restoration of historical monuments in Uzbekistan itself. Besides that, tourists have opportunity to buy the copies of tile-work in small souvenirs shops near historical places.

The first fair of the traditional crafts was held in 1995 in Tashkent. Since then a series of numerous fairs, festivals, contests, and sale exhibitions were held where contemporary masters exhibited their works. Fairs were organised with the support of the UN on its 50th anniversary. The motto of the fair *Usto – shogird* was symbolical in many ways. Subsequently, such UN-supported fairs become regular; they acquired regional scale. Nowadays, Uzbek masters have opportunity to participate in both, regional and foreign fairs and festivals. For example, in early 2012 Uzbek master had participated in the International Salon 'Collection Doll' and the International exhibition 'Handwork'[26] in Almaty (Kazakhstan) and the 'Surajkund Crafts Mela' in Haryana (India). The participation of the Uzbek representatives at the festival in Surajkund has been on the occasion of the 20th anniversary of an establishment of diplomatic relations between Uzbekistan and India.[27]

The Fund Forum established several projects, which develop the tradition of Fair and Festivals. One of them is exhibition-fair *Bazar-Art*, which is held twice a year (in spring and autumn) in metropolitan Centre of National Arts. The organisers of this bright and picturesque event are the Fund Forum and the Association of Artists, Critics and National Masters *IJOD*. The exhibition gathers the best masters of applied art from all parts of the country, among them are representatives of artists` families and young craftsmen. The project is aimed at discovering creative potential in modern applied arts, introducing the wider public with the most interesting trends in this field, supporting creative dynasties and talented craftsmen as well as preserving and enhancing of national heritage.[28]

Currently, *Bazar-Art* has become an international exhibition-fair due to participation of foreign craftsmen from neighbouring countries (like Kyrgyzstan etc.). The tenth exhibition-fair *Bazar-Art*-2012 took place on March 27-30 (in Tashkent). It was dedicated to celebration of national festival *Navruz*, and the 5th year of establishment of the Centre of National Arts. About 130 masters of traditional applied arts and crafts brought thousands of handiworks from all corners of the country. Most participants of this show, under the auspices of the association *Hunarmand*, are provided state support. Therefore, according to the Decree of the President, from December 30, 2011 members of *Hunarmand*, who make items of crafts and applied arts in their own houses, are subject to privileges. They are exempted from fixed tax[29] till January 2014. The

national artist of Uzbekistan, the chairman of the Academy of Arts of Uzbekistan Akmal Nur pointed out during an interview:

> "Bazar-Art is our common cause, therefore today's holiday of traditional culture and art is my holiday too. There is no East without a market, and Bazar-Art is not only a market, but also Art … Thanks to Bazar-Art; we have an opportunity to familiarize with works of masters from the different corners of Uzbekistan. Here we once again discover the rich history of our country. Our unique art is a face of our country. One of the main aims of Bazar-Art is supporting of our handicraftsmen. Talented and skilful people always need to be supported. So, we are always ready to support our masters."[30]

The tangible result of exhibitions organised by the Fund Forum is the award of special grants to the artisans offering high quality products to the market. Besides, the Fund published several books. One of them called '*Applied Art of Uzbekistan: Gradation of Values*'. This book presents systematised register of price characteristics of traditional art items in Uzbekistan, which makes it possible to give the art market in this area a civilised format. The activity of the Fund Forum is popularized by the first non-state satellite TV channel of Uzbekistan named *ForumTV*. This TV channel is created with the support of the Uzbek Communication Agency and Information within the limits of the government programme. It is kind of showcase of culture of Uzbekistan, which propagandised a rich cultural heritage, historical monuments and traditions to the world community (translation in Uzbek, Russian and English languages).[31]

TV Channels, Theatre and Cinematography

Television and cinema are powerful and significant forms of intellectual and ideological influence on the society. *Uzbekfilm* is the national cinematographic studio with 80-year history of development of national filmmaking[32] continues to create movies and programs broadcasted by the national television channels and the Forum TV as well as local cinema halls. Tashkent residents still remember the 'All-Union Tashkent's film festival of the countries of Asia, Africa and Latin America', which was first introduced in Tashkent in 1968. Its motto was '*The Peace, social progress and freedom of the people*'.[33] The Tashkent's film festival was an important event during the Soviet period. In the eve of opening the 9th International Film festival, the editor of the journal *Iskusstvo kino* requested well-known foreign cinematographers and film-makers to express their opinions on Tashkent's film festival the, who had participated in this forum before. Famous filmmaker Shyam Benegal commented:

> "In my opinion, the main attractive quality of the Tashkent international film festival is a unique grandiose film forum in the world, which is entirely devoted to cinematography of Asia, Africa, and Latin America. During the European film festivals, it is almost impossible to get acquainted with films of colleagues from such states, as, say, Indonesia, Senegal, Philippines or from the countries of the Arabian East. The Tashkent festival consistently supports and encourages them, gives stimulus to further work, opens the best films to all cinema worlds, and also gives a tribute to artists to state the sights, to share the valuable art experience. Here, in Tashkent, all of them are participants of the representative international film event, which are equal in rights. This is a very important factor."[34]

The Tashkent film festival became history after the collapse of the Soviet Union. Nowadays, it seems that Tashkent would like to bring back the grandeur of film festivals. In November 2008, two major events took place in Tashkent—Festival of the National Cinematography of Uzbekistan, and Central Asian Forum of Visual Anthropology *KinoVizA*, which included Film Forum, Video Forum, exhibitions, workshops and experimental multimedia project. These events, which aroused huge interest, were organised by the Swiss Cooperation Agency in Uzbekistan, the *Forum of Culture and Arts of Uzbekistan* with participation of the National Agency *Uzbekkino*.[35] In 2011, Festival of Traditional Culture *Asrlar sadosi* included a roundtable titled *Film festivals is a phenomenon of contemporary global culture*, which took place at Bukhara. The Tashkent International Film Forum *Zolotoy Gepard* (Golden Cheetah, since 2011) has been supported by the National Agency *Uzbekkino* and the Fund Forum. This festival continued Bukhara's roundtable event. The motto of the contemporary Tashkent film festival is '*The Civilizations of 21st centuries—dialogue of cultures*'. This idea is to express basic strategic target of the project—adjustment and development of intercultural dialogue between various countries of the world through the art of cinema. The general director of the film festival Dr. Akbar Khakimov compares new Tashkent festival to the former in these words:

> "All the former Tashkent festivals of the countries of Asia, Africa and Latin America passed very solemnly. They had a certain resonance ..., as a rule, they were extremely ideological. Tashkent, in Soviet film strategy of those years, played the role of the regulator of some processes on these continents, which were connected with so-called, movements for national independence. This ideological orientation of that festival is abundantly clear if we look through the period today. Therefore, when we made the concept, the idea and the strategy of the present festival, we had put in the foreground the quality and level of professionalism of those films which we will show on the big Tashkent screen and, naturally, their un-ideological orientation."[36]

The Tashkent's film festival '*Zolotoy Gepard*' has become one of the brightest events in the cultural life of Uzbekistan. First festival had demonstrated the high level of organisation of movie screening, wide geography of participating countries, recognised authority of members of the international jury and stellar status of honorary guests. Beside the main film contest for the best masterpieces of art cinema, which were sent to the film festival from all over the world, there were also out-of-contest screenings of Uzbek and foreign films. The film festival was accompanied by great premiers, workshops, round tables, and briefings, the press conferences with participation of international movie stars and prominent figures of cinema industry.

The creative processes, which are occurring today in the Uzbek theatres and cinematography, are complicated and ambiguous. Theatre and cinematography are the most effective factors contributing to the modernisation of public consciousness. All artists and intellectuals, who are working in the field of theatre and cinematography, feel the necessity of understanding the present situation and the nation's mainstream of ideas, notions and values based on which a new generation of audience is educated and raised. According to the Decree of the President of Republic of Uzbekistan 'About development of theatrical art of Uzbekistan' (March 26, 1998) enormous work has been done, including the updating the infrastructural base of theatres.[37] The capital successfully hosts such international theatrical festivals as *theatre, Uz*[38] and opera art festival *Toshkent bahori* (the Tashkent spring).[39] Both festivals are organised with the support of the Fund Forum. The main objective of festivals is an enrichment of theatrical life of the people of Uzbekistan by displaying the achievements of domestic and foreign theatres on the stage of Tashkent.

The Foreign Policy

After gaining sovereignty, Uzbekistan started to independently conduct its foreign policy. It is based on the standard principles, such as priority of international law, non-interference in internal affairs of other states, resolution of all disputes in peaceful manner etc. So far, Uzbekistan established diplomatic relations with more than 120 countries of the world, regional and international organisations, political, economical, and cultural centres, etc. The Fund Forum pays great attention to cooperation with diplomatic and public structures for adjustment of socially-humanitarian and universal communications between the countries and various national unifications. The Fund Forum was the first among the public organisations of Uzbekistan and CIS countries, which became the official partner of UNESCO. In March 2007, Memorandum of mutual understanding and cooperation was signed between the two organisations. For the past three years, some 20 projects have been carried out with the support of or jointly with UNESCO.[40]

The Fund Forum representative offices are opened in Russia, France, Germany, Switzerland, Austria, China, Japan, Republic of Korea, Italy, Spain, and the US. In 2010, the Fund Forum's *Mehr nuri* (charitable foundation) was granted Consultative Status with the UN ECOSOC.[41] Nowadays, the number of the projects, which are implemented by the Fund Forum in collaboration with partners in Uzbekistan and abroad, is more than 500 in 18 fields. One of them includes concert programmes of the Uzbek artists, the thematic exhibitions and also presentations of books such as '*Samples of eastern calligraphy and miniatures art 7th-21st century, Civilisations, states and cultures of the Central Asia, The Aroma of blooming roses, the Tanbur notation of Khorezm*', the book-photo album *Fund Forum presents: 'Uzbekistan*', and also '*The Fund Forum: an option of civil society a practical model*', etc.

The concert of the CIS Youth Symphonic Orchestra, under the direction of world famous prominent Russian conductor Vladimir Spivakov, has become a memorable event of the cultural life of Tashkent. The concert of the CIS Youth Symphonic Orchestra in Tashkent was organised by the Fund Forum, the Interstate Fund for Humanitarian Cooperation of CIS (IFESCCO)[42] and the Moscow State Academic Philharmonic organisation. The concert took place on the eve of Design and Fashion Week *Art Week Style.uz* (October 05, 2011) in Turkiston Palace. For young talented musicians the Fund Forum provided personalized invitations to the concert. The CIS Youth Symphonic Orchestra consists of 95 musicians and nine of them are representatives of Uzbekistan.[43] The prominent conductor V. Spivakov has constant collaboration with the Fund Forum. For example, Vladimir Spivakov conducted with the Youth musician's symphonic orchestra of Uzbekistan (the participants from 8 till 16 years old) at the concert on the occasion of the Uzbek culture in Moscow in 2007.

Throughout last year, public and cultural life of Uzbekistan has been stabilised. A special release of the journal *Diplomacia* (Spain, August 2011), which was dedicated to the 20th anniversary of independence of Republic of Uzbekistan, wrote:

> "We are convinced once again that in the modern world, along with the necessity of maintenance and development of bilateral interstate political dialogue and economical interactions, there is a growing factor of cooperation between countries in spheres of education and sciences, culture and tourism. We speak about key tools of 'soft power' as it is accepted to name them in the scientific environment. They are now one of the main sources for all subsequent processes of productive cooperation. Uzbekistan dynamically develops the international humanitarian communications throughout the world. The important role in the establishment and expansion of cultural-humanitarian communications is taken by various non-governmental organizations, among them the 'Forum of culture and arts of Uzbekistan' the largest public Foundation in the Republic ..."[44]

After gaining independency, traditional culture became the main component of 'soft power' of Uzbekistan. Moreover, culture oriented programmes assist to creating a favourable international image of the country. The Uzbek charitable foundation Fund Forum is the only one that, in a relatively short period, has succeeded in generating a notable degree of public activism. Various projects have been implemented to support artists, musicians, choreographers, designers, teachers, students etc. The Fund Forum's events are conducted at the best showrooms of Tashkent. For an outstanding contribution to cultural development, and rendering unstinting help and support to creative intellectuals as well as strengthening of the international cultural and educational relations, Gulnara Karimova, the Chairperson of the Board of Trustees of the Fund Forum was awarded by the Russian Gold Pushkin Medal in 2007. The activity of the Forum in the field of the fine arts of Uzbekistan and preservation of national traditions and support of talented youth was acknowledged by the Academy of Arts of Uzbekistan during the annual ceremony *TopArt-2011* in January 2012. The projects of the Fund Forum and their participants have been recognised as the best in various nominations. Currently, the Fund Forum is the most influential in the country. This organisation has real influence on many art processes, which are carried out in Uzbekistan today. A lot has been done so far, but new ideas and projects are still being born so the emblem of the Fund Forum decorates virtually all grand events in Uzbekistan.

Notes

1. Well-known, that in Soviet period the national values, traditions, and customs have been divided as progressive and reactionary. 20 years of Independence have allowed developing and propagandizing the art of Uzbekistan under ideological priorities of the nation.
2. "In the age of globalisation, the cultural originality and cultural consciousness have got the big importance, much more than ever earlier. Globalisation is conducts simultaneously to standardisation ("Macdonaldisation"), and to more obvious separation of local cultures ..." is writes Barno Turgunova in article "*Programma po kulture I iskusstvu Shveytcarskgo Agentstva po razvitiyu I sotrudnichectvu*", *Iskusstvo Uzbekistana na sovremennom etape sotcio-kulturnogo razvitia: materialy seminarov, dokladov kollokviuma ekspertov*, (Swiss Agency for Development and Cooperation, Tashkent, 2006), p. 4-5.
3. See: "*Kultura Uzbekistana – puti razvitiia v gody nezavisimosti*" at http://mcs.uz/ministry/press/pressculture/culturenews/206-kultura-uzbekistana-puti-razvitiya-v-gody-nezavisimosti.html
4. N. Yahov-Yanoskaya, "*Predislovie (O morfologii sovremennoi uzbekskoi muzyki*), in N. Yahov-Yanoskaya (ed.), *Uzbekskaia muzyka na styke stoletiy (20-21 veka): tendentcii, problemy*, (Tashkent, 2008), pp. 4-5.
5. E. Gyul, "*Traditcionnoe prikladnoe iskusstvo Uzbekistana:problemy I perspektivy razvitiia*", *Iskusstvo Uzbekistana na sovremennom etape sotcio-kulturnogo razvitia: materialy seminarov, dokladov kollokviuma ekspertov*, Swiss Agency for Development and Cooperation,(Tashkent, 2006), p. 243.
6. Remarkable book published by the Swiss Agency for Development and Cooperation, *Isskustvo Uzbekistana na sovremennom etape sotchio-kulyturnogo razvitiya*, (Tashkent, 2006), pp. 295.
7. The Law of Republic of Uzbekistan N 527-II about public funds and Decree of *Oliy Majlis* Republic of Uzbekistan dated 29.08.2003(N 528-II). First Funds were established in the beginning of 90s by resolution of President: Fund *Mahallia* (September, 1992; has branches over Republic) organised for maintenance of the state support of measures, which are directed to preservation and wide propagation of historically developed national and cultural wealth, for popularisation of the best folk customs and traditions and the expansion of cultural-educational work among *mahallias* so on; *Oltin Meros* (1996), the Academy of arts of Uzbekistan (January 1997) , Fund of the development of popular music (by the decision of the cabinet

of Republic of Uzbekistan on June 26, 2001), Literary-public Fund named after Muhammad Yusuf, The International welfare fund of Amir Temur, The International Fund of Bobur, Republican Fund of Ulugbek, the International Women's Fund *Sharq Ayoli,* etc.

8. One of them is The Swiss Agency for Development and Cooperation (SDC), which is supports artistic and cultural projects in Central Asia (CA) since 1998. B. Turgunova, article "*Programma po kulture I iskusstvu Shveytcarskgo Agentstva po razvitiyu I sotrudnichectvu*", *Iskusstvo Uzbekistana na sovremennom etape sotcio-kulturnogo razvitia: materialy seminarov, dokladov kollokviuma ekspertov*, (Tashkent: SADC, 2006).
9. The Forum of Culture and Arts of Uzbekistan Foundation (http://fundforum.uz/), is a voluntary self-controlled non-governmental association of citizens and public organisations.Fund is the umbrella organisation for *Mehr nuri* Charity Fund (www.mehrnuri.uz) , Women's Council Public Association (www.women.uz), Centre for Political Studies (CPS), Youth Initiatives Centre (YIC) *Kelajak ovozi* (http://uzbek.kelajakovozi.uz), Social Initiatives Support Fund (www.sisf.uz). The Chairperson of the Trustee Council of the Fund Forum is Gulnara Karimova, elder daughter of President of Uzbekistan, the permanent representative of Uzbekistan at UN, and other international organisations in Geneva.
10. More about Contests and Festivals see: Dilorom Karomat and Nigora Khasanova "Musical culture of Uzbekistan after Independence", in A. Sengupta, S. Chatterjee and S. Bhattacharya (ed.), *Eurasia Twenty Years After*, (New Delhi: Shipra, 2012), pp. 422-444.
11. Islam Karimov's Model is a scientific basis for reforms in education sphere. See: *Uzbekistan today*, February 24, 2012, at http://www.ut.uz/eng/opinion/investmen8ts_into_the_future.mgr;http://www.jahonnews.uz/rus/rubriki/sobitiya_i_dati/mejdunarodnaya_konfereniya_podgotovka_obrazovannogo
12. http://fundforum.uz/en/pages/fund-forum-grants/
13. *Oltin Meros* is created in 1996, in Tashkent. From the same year, several branches over the Uzbekistan are begun their work. The main aim of the Fund is restore the disappeared kinds of crafts and applied art, to care of masters and artists, to promote training of youth for revival and development of traditional art.
14. For more information see: E.Gyul, "*Traditcionnoe prikladnoe iskusstvo Uzbekistana:problemy I perspektivy razvitiia*", *Iskusstvo Uzbekistana na sovremennom etape sotcio-kulturnogo razvitia: materialy seminarov, dokladov kollokviuma ekspertov*, Swiss Agency for Development and Cooperation, (Tashkent 2006), pp. 237-248; "Traditional Arts of Uzbekistan of Independence Period", *San'at*, at http://www.sanat.orexca.com/eng/2-11/elmira_gyul.shtml
15. The main aim is revealing of the brightest creative works of young artists of the republic on the field of painting, graphic arts, a sculpture, applied arts and crafts,

design, a photography, computer graphics and textiles. The purpose is to raise professional level of young artists, to consolidate the most interesting, innovative initiatives of youth, to define creative potential of the modern art of Uzbekistan, to promote creation of new innovative projects of the Uzbek artists.

16. *Navkiron Uzbekiston-2010*: *Master-classes and Presentations*, at http://pr.uz/sobitiya/5436
17. The personal exhibition of Bahodyr and Behzod Hadzhimetovs "Travel to the miniature world" (from February 15), in the Center of national arts in Tashkent, the Art season-2012, organised by Fund Forum and *IJOD* , at http://news.olam.uz/culture/7647.html
18. http://fundforum.uz/en/pages/fund-forum-grants/
19. In 2008, the festival is took place near *Shakhrisabz* and in 2009 in Tashkent region. Since 2009, the Festival of Traditional Culture *Asrlar Sadosi* is organised in association with the UNESCO. In 2010, the Festival took place at *Ichan-Qala*, a historical architectural complex in the heart of city Khiva 2011-Bukhara 2012 - *Ellikqala* District in Karakalpakstan and *Tuproq Qala* ancient fortress at http://asrlarsadosi.com/
20. Head of the UNESCO Tashkent Office Jorge Ivan Espinal, the Ambassador of France to Uzbekistan Francois Gautier, the Ambassador of South Korea to Uzbekistan Chon Dewan, representatives of the Ministry of Culture and Sports of Uzbekistan, journalists as well as culture and art professionals are attend the opening ceremony. See at http://asrlarsadosi.com/en/news/workshop-for-karakalpaki-music-inaugurated-at-asrlar-sadosi-2012/
21. http://asrlarsadosi.com/en/news/workshop-for-karakalpaki-music-inaugurated-at-asrlar-sadosi-2012/
22. Under the single dome of the Centre of National Arts, one can discover various types of traditional and modern art of Uzbekistan, open unique sides of culture and traditions of the Uzbek people. The works by well-known national masters and young professionals on ceramics, stamping, woodcarving, jewellery, textiles, as well as musical instruments, including works by modern artists and antiquarian products are presented in the gift-shops of the Centre. at http://fundforum.uz/en/pages/established-fund-forum/
23. The full name of the *Meros* Association is "Multi Earned Rares of the Society" or "MEROS" which in translation from Uzbek means "heritage". at http://fondforum.uz/en/pages/meros-association-of-antiques-of-uzbekistan/
24. Currently, the Association *IJOD* is unites more then 300 masters and specialists of Art. at gulnarakarimova.com
25. Sweta Dutta, "For Humayun's sake, Samarkand comes to Delhi with a secret", *The Indian Express*, New Delhi, Sunday, June 26, 2011, at http://www.indianexpress.com/news/for-humayuns-sake-samarkand-comes-to-delhi-with-a-secret/808750/0;

"*Uzbekskiye mastera rekonstruiruyut grobnitcu Humayuna v Indii*", at http://news.olam.uz/society/3370.html

26. http://nepovtorim.ru/?page_id=15 ; http://www.timeout.kz/journal/feature/26327/ ;Addition information at www.collection-doll.com
27. "*Uzbekistan na mezhdunarodnom folklornom festivale v Indii*", IA "Jahon", February 23, 2012 , at http://www.uzapi.gov.uz/news/info/print/2109/ ; "*Uzbekistan – India: strategicheskoe partnerstvo – logicheskii rezultat shirokomashtabnoi raboty*", March 19, 2012, at http://www.jahonnews.uz/rus/rubriki/politika/uzbekistan_indiya_strategicheskoe_partnerstvo1_1logicheskiy_rezultat_shirokomasshtabnoy_raboti.mgr
28. *Bazar-Art* Exhibition-Fair; at http://fundforum.uz/en/pages/fund-forum-projects/
29. http://gazeta.norma.uz/publish/doc/text80017_prazdnik_masterstva
30. http://fundforum.uz/ru/news/net-vostoka-bez-bazara/
31. Forum –tv.uz is different kind of programmes, which are including the news telecasts, tele-projects on culture art and history of Uzbekistan related with the activity of Fund Forum; Forum –tv.uz are used the new digital technologies. Its programs are orienting to wide multi-purpose audience in Europe, the Central and Western Asia. at http://www.forum-tv .uz ; http://vefire.ru/channel/ForumTV/
32. Nigora Karimova, "Modern Cinema of Uzbekistan: Social Functions and Poetics", *San'at,* at http://www.sanat.orexca.com/eng/1-09/nigora_karimova.shtml
33. http://www.rudata.ru/wiki/%D0%9C%D0%9A%D0%A4_%D0%B2_%D0%A2%D0%B0%D1%88%D0%BA%D0%B5%D0%BD%D1%82%D0%B5
34. "*Navstrechu Tashkentskomu kinofestivaliu* 1986 goda", at http://raveena2.narod.ru/Text/3/tashkent.html
35. Press-release, *KinoVizA(Festival natcionalnogo kino Uzbekistana; Tcentralno-Aziatskii forum vizualnoi antropologii),* Swiss Agency for Development and Cooperation, Tashkent 2008, p. 2.
36. http://podrobno.uz/friends/Gost-Podrobnouz-Akbar-Hakimov/
37. "*Prazdnik na teatralnoi ulitce Uzbekistana*", at http://www.12.uz/ru/news/show/culture/9155/
38. The Youth theatre of Uzbekstan is became of initiator of this festival within the Fund Forum's grand festival ART WEEK. at http://mtu.uz/index.php/festival/160-festival
39. The festival has been organised by the Ministry of Culture and Sport Affairs of Uzbekistan in collaboration of the Fund Forum, *Uzbekteatr* Creative Association, and Alisher Navoi Theatre with support of the Embassies of Italy, Belarus, Ukraine, Russia, Bulgaria, and Azerbaijan.
40. http://gulnarakarimova.com/en/pages/gulnara-karimova-biography/
41. http://fundforum.uz/ru/pressa/diplomacia-fond-forum-kultury-i-iskusstva-uzbekistana/
42. The interstate fund of humanitarian cooperation of the states-participants CIS

(IFESCCO) is created in 2006 by the governments of the states-participants of the Commonwealth of Independent States. In IFESCCO have entered Armenia, Belarus, Kazakhstan, Kyrgyzstan, Russia, Tajikistan, Uzbekistan, and since 2008-Azerbaijan. The mission of IFESCCO is to promote development of the general humanitarian space of Commonwealth, a development and intercultural dialogue through education, a science, culture, the information and communications, archive work, sports, tourism and work with youth.IFESCCO works in close collaboration with Council of the humanitarian cooperation of the states the participants of CIS.

43. http://fondforum.uz/ru/news/molodejniy-simf-orkestr-sng-sygraet-v-tashkente/; http://santamara.livejournal.com/

44. http://fondforum.u2/ru/pressa/diplomacia-fon-forum-kultury-i-iskusstva-uzbekistana/